ONE-POT WONDERS

Cooking in One Pot, One Wok,

One Casserole, or One Skillet with

250 All-in-One Recipes

Clifford A. Wright

WILEY

JOHN WILEY & SONS, INC.

3 1257 02420 5683

This book is printed on acid-free paper.

Published by John Wiley & Sons, Inc., Hoboken, New Jersey.
Published simultaneously in Canada.

For general information on our other products and services, or technical support, please contact our Customer Care Department within the United States at 800-762-2974, outside the United States at 317-572-3993 or fax 317-572-4002.

Wiley publishes in a variety of print and electronic formats and by print-on-demand. Some material included with standard print versions of this book may not be included in e-books or in print-on-demand. If this book refers to media such as a CD or DVD that is not included in the version you purchased, you may download this material at http://booksupport.wiley.com. For more information about Wiley products, visit www.wiley.com.

Book design and composition by Ralph Fowler/RLF Design
Cover photography by Jason Wyche
Cover design by Suzanne Sunwoo
Illustrations by Rashell Smith

Visit the author at www.CliffordAWright.com

Library of Congress Cataloging-in-Publication Data

Wright, Clifford A.
One-pot wonders : cooking in one pot, one wok, one casserole, or one skillet with 250 all-in-one recipes / Clifford A. Wright.
        page   cm
Includes biographical references and index.
ISBN 978-0-470-61536-2 (pbk.)   ISBN 978-1-118-39483-0 (ebk.)
ISBN 978-1-118-39482-3 (ebk.)   ISBN 978-1-118-39484-7 (ebk.)
1. One-dish meals   I. Title.
TX840.O53W75   2013
641.82—dc23

Printed in the United States of America

10 9 8 7 6 5 4 3 2 1

ONE-POT WONDERS

Also by Clifford A. Wright

Hot & Cheesy

The Best Soups in the World

Bake Until Bubbly

Some Like It Hot

Real Stew

Mediterranean Vegetables

Little Foods of the Mediterranean

A Mediterranean Feast

Grill Italian

Lasagne

Italian Pure & Simple

Cucina Rapida

Cucina Paradiso

For my children
Ali, Dyala, and Seri

Contents

Acknowledgments

Cookbook authors are always grateful to the people who actually eat all the food we cook in our seemingly endless recipe tests. I would like to thank my children, Ali, Dyala, and Seri, and those enthusiastic good-eaters Michelle van Vliet and Madeline Sitterly for sharing all this food and enjoying the writing of this book because they only had to clean one pot. I would also like to thank my agent, Angela Miller; my editor at John Wiley, Justin Schwartz; copy editor Valerie Cimino, and proofreader Leah Stewart for their typically excellent editing, suggestions, and production.

Introduction

While explaining the idea behind this book to a friend, I said that at the end of the meal you only have to wash one pot. My friend asked me to explain further. I said, you've probably seen one-pot cookbooks before, but if you read them closely you will realize that there is often some preparation involved that might require sautéing something else first, or boiling something first, so that even though it all goes into one pot, actually you've used several. The recipe is really a little more complicated than you were led to believe, although the end result is served from the one pot.

Everyone wants a way to cook quickly and easily, yet they also demand the best-tasting food. The central idea in this book is that no recipe utilizes more than one pot to be cleaned later. Now, that "pot" really should be called a "cooking vessel" because the idea here is that your entire meal, whatever it is—the meat, the starch, and the vegetable—all gets cooked in that one vessel, whether the vessel is a saucepan, a stewpot, a casserole, a wok, a sauté pan, a barbecue grill, or a cast-iron skillet. This book provides 250 recipes, guidance on various cooking methods, and an explanation of how one-pot cookery melds complementary flavors so the whole becomes greater than the sum of its parts. The recipes emphasize healthy and natural foods, although that will ultimately depend on how you shop.

Everyone loves a fancy meal, the kind of supper you might fuss about on a cold winter Sunday, but for everyday cooking we want a quick, delicious, easy, and, if possible, one-pot meal that makes everyone happy, including the person washing the dishes. What is a one-pot meal? Well, let me say it again: It's a meal where everything goes into one cooking vessel and gets cooked together to provide an all-in-one dining experience with protein, starch, and vegetable in every bite. The idea that ties it all together is that there is no advance cooking or use of more than one cooking implement.

One-pot meals, whether stews, casseroles, soups, or stir-fries, are a perennial favorite in my family and many others. They are easy to make and usually don't require endless tasks and constant stirring. The idea of everything going into one pot—not two or three—is mighty appealing to all home cooks. Over several decades while writing other books, about Italian food or Mediterranean food or Asian, Mexican, or American food, I've come across hundreds of such dishes that for one reason or another didn't quite fit into the concept of the book I was writing at the time. But when you have three kids, now in their twenties, with big appetites and who visit home often, then an easy one-pot meal is the name of the game.

It's fun, too, because these days our supermarkets have a greater variety of foods than they did thirty years ago, and the Internet has so many great food resources, starting with the Grocery & Gourmet Foods section of www.amazon.com. This availability of ingredients means that one's recipe repertoire can easily grow as well.

Many of the recipes in this book rest on the notion of flavor layering, whereby the whole pot becomes greater than its parts by way of a melding of different complementary flavors. Sometimes flavor layering is literal, as when you lay down a foundation such as potatoes, then a layer of herbs and spices, then a layer of meat, a layer of vegetables, and a layer of condiment (maybe cheese sauce or sour cream). Other times flavor layering comes about by cooking different foods at different temperatures, such as a pork and bok choy stir-fry, where pork tenderloin is seared over very hot heat until crispy and golden, then bok

About Slow Cookers

I don't cook with slow cookers mostly because I'm a hands-on cook who likes to stir, likes to fiddle, likes to taste, likes to add, and I would miss the wonderful smells of properly cooked foods. However, if you have a slow cooker and would like to use it for some of the recipes in this book—such as the stews and braises—they can be adapted with a little forethought. Keep in mind some of the following tips.

The low heat on most slow cooker models is 200°F, so adjust accordingly. Always use fully thawed meats. Don't use whole chickens or meat roasts: Cut them into smaller chunks or pieces so they cook evenly and thoroughly. Fill the slow cooker one-half to two-thirds full, not more or less. Do not open the lid during the cooking process. Do not stir. The ceramic insert of a slow cooker can crack with rapid temperature changes. Slow cookers often require some preparation to the food before it goes in so that you will have better-tasting food, such as the browning of meat or the sautéing of vegetables. Add dairy products to the slow cooker in the last 15 minutes of cooking so they don't break down. When adapting a recipe, remember that the liquid called for will not evaporate, so reduce it by 25 percent. Use half the amount of spices and herbs called for.

choy, bell peppers, and Chinese condiments are added to cook at a reduced temperature. Other flavor layering results from how distinct foods interact with each other; for example, how a neutral-tasting potato is enhanced by piquant chiles.

There's an unintentional—and delightful—consequence of one-pot cookery: Most recipes are healthy and low in calories. Don't get me wrong: This is not a health or diet book, but rather a book where healthy, fine-tasting food won't start "layering" on the pounds. A heavy emphasis on vegetables flavored with meat as opposed to meat flavored with vegetables means a wide range of healthy meals for the family that do not compromise on taste while monitoring calorie intake. This is not magic-bullet cooking but complementary cooking to a healthful and active lifestyle.

Typical Cooking Vessels for One-Pot Cookery

Stewpot

We start with the vessels uppermost in our minds: a pot and a pan. The first pot that comes to mind when we think of one-pot cookery is the stewpot, naturally enough. The stewpot is what we cook stews in, but another similar vessel used for the same purpose is the flameproof baking casserole (as opposed to the baking casserole, which may or may not be cooktop-safe as well), such as the enameled cast-iron ones made by Le Creuset and Staub,

or the Dutch oven. Stews are many families' favorites, as they usually get made on the weekend when cooks have the time to cook and enjoy the wafting aromas all day long.

A one-pot stew in a stewpot might be a lamb and mushroom stew where, literally, everything is put in, the heat is turned on, and with just a couple of hours of simmering you've got a memorable meal. I love all-in-one mixed meat stews because the flavors are so complex and enticing. One recipe in the book is an American interpretation of the classic French Pot-au-Feu (page 252), with a combination of beef ribs, sausage, lamb shoulder, onion, beans, carrots, celery, and tomatoes all put into the pot and stewed for a long time. It just may be your new Super Bowl dinner. A one-pot book cannot be without an old-fashioned New England Beef Stew (page 133) rich with potatoes, carrots, parsnips, and turnips all melting together for a few hours. The stewpot also gives the cook the opportunity to play around with some new ideas and spicy tastes such as Veal, Cabbage, and Pumpkin Ragoût (page 152), with its piquant flavors of turmeric, ground chile, and the North African chile paste condiment harīsa.

Skillet, Frying Pan, Sauté Pan

Our next vessels, skillet, frying pan, and sauté pan, allow the cook to pan-roast, a method that produces skillet dinners that provide wonderful seared flavor for our one-pot concept. First, let me describe the main difference between these three. The skillet and the frying pan are the same thing; this is a flat pan with sloping sides. The word *skillet* is usually used when referring to cast-iron skillets, but many people, including me, also use the word to refer to a sauté pan, which technically is not correct. A sauté pan is a frying pan with straight sides. For this book, the ideal skillet is a 12- to 14-inch cast-iron skillet. A huge variety of meals can be made in such a pan. Pan-Roasted Kielbasa, Brussels Sprouts, and Potatoes (page 186) delivers tastes and textures that you may not have expected from such humble ingredients. The ingredients are each seared in a hot skillet to create a crispy golden brown surface before being finished at a low temperature. A Pan-Seared Rib-Eye Steak with Scallion Pancakes (page 96) is also cooked in a skillet, but the method and result are a bit different yet just as lip-smackingly good. The scallion pancakes with jalapeño chiles are cooked first, and then the thin rib-eye steaks are cooked next, and they're eaten together. You can cook fish in a sauté pan, and a flavorful and quite easy recipe is the Albacore Tuna with Baby Carrots, Fresh Peas, and Dill (page 368), which will make you think of Greek taverna food enjoyed while overlooking the Aegean.

Baking Casseroles, Flameproof Baking Casseroles, and Roasting Pans

Baking casseroles are an all-American favorite kitchen tool, and nearly every family already has a rectangular and a square low-sided baking casserole. The one basic characteristic of a baking casserole is that it is made of ceramic, earthenware, or Pyrex. Generally it is not flameproof (although some earthenware and

stoneware ones are, and one of those would be very handy for this book). The baked casserole is a versatile preparation because it's easy to put together, often utilizing leftovers, and has something for everyone. An appealing attribute of the casserole is its versatility: as a family dinner at home, an elegant dish for company, a popular dish to bring to a potluck, a surprising leftover, a brunch dish, or a next-day appetizer. A one-pot casserole needs to be a little more than macaroni and cheese or tuna-noodle casserole, as we would want it to provide us everything from the starch to the vegetable to the protein. But there is no paucity of such recipes in this book.

A Yam, Pecan, and Beef Casserole (page 138) is a rich Southern-inspired casserole that is both delicious and pretty. A layered cabbage casserole is a marvelous lasagna-like layering of ground beef, cabbage leaves, potatoes, and apples that is easy to assemble hours ahead of time and can be baked when you need dinner on the table.

A flameproof baking casserole—or even a roasting pan—is a terrific "one-pot" concept for the oven. What is a flameproof baking casserole? It is a heavy, high-sided round or oval vessel made of cast iron, cast aluminum, enameled cast iron, or earthenware that can be used both over a cooktop burner and in the oven. The Le Creuset company has made enameled cast-iron casseroles that fill the bill for generations. Again, everything goes into the flameproof baking casserole while it's over the burner for some initial sautéing and then it can all go into the oven and you let dinner bake while you attend to other things, letting the wafting aromas entice you all the while. A great example is Southwest Turkey Bake (page 353). The oven is cranked up high and into the casserole goes all those typical southwestern flavors of chiles, onions, tomatoes, Colby cheese, and cumin. The leftovers make a pretty good taco too.

For a longer, slow-roasted recipe ideal for a leisurely and cold weekend, Garlic-Stuffed Nine-Hour Roast Leg of Lamb (page 212) is pretty amazing. This is where your large two-handled roasting pan, sometimes only pulled out for the Thanksgiving turkey, comes into play. The lamb is studded with garlic and mint, coated with a spice mix and drizzled with olive oil, and slow-roasted until the rich and succulent meat falls off the bone. About halfway through the cooking, some potatoes are added to the roasting pan. When the roast comes out of the oven it is a sight to behold, and how surprised people will be when you don't reach for the carving knife: It's so tender you can eat it with a spoon.

You can always wow your guests and family with the richly flavored, easily cooked Sea and Mountain Rice Casserole (page 292). The combination of sausage and seafood is enticing and the rice is flavored not only with the juices from the meats but also with full-flavored bold spicing and aromatics. Another easy dinner I enjoy is Spanish Sausage with Chickpeas and Tomatoes (page 179), an easily prepared cooktop casserole because one uses canned cooked chickpeas. It's all flavored with sausage and tomatoes and makes for great leftovers as well.

The flameproof baking casserole is excellent for braises. All braises are, essentially, stews without much liquid or only the liquid emitted by the ingredients themselves. Braises are cooked very slowly and result in very tender meat and flavorful syrupy sauces. Braised Chicken, Leeks, and Yogurt (page 323) is a nice and easy family dinner. Another favorite braise I like very much is the French daube (page 122). I once had a Daube Languedocienne, a famous braise in the region of the Languedoc, that is slowly simmered for many hours, making it a perfect Saturday afternoon project. Although easy to make, it has a good number of ingredients (the secret to great stews and braises) that flavor the pieces of stew beef. The recipe calls for carrots, onions, leeks, garlic, tomatoes, dried mushrooms, spices, juniper berries, orange zest, red wine, grappa, and olives. This is died-and-gone-to-heaven food.

Soup Pot

Soups are obviously made in one pot, and although not all soups are main courses some fish soups certainly fit the bill, and especially soups that are minestrone-like. The substantial Pasta and Cod Soup (page 28), with its flaky cod, soup pasta, and flavor of fennel, is not only a soup, but also a soul- and stomach-satisfying supper. In fact, many Italian-derived soups include pasta and are substantial enough to be dinner in a pot. There is more than one minestrone, and they can become very complex with upwards of thirty ingredients. But I've got a very nice five-ingredient recipe (not including olive oil and the garnish) that will make you feel wonderful. Kale, pork, carrots, garlic, and macaroni all go into the pot with some water and presto: a minestrone in an hour to serve sprinkled with some Parmesan cheese and fresh parsley.

Wok

One of the great one-pot styles is wok cookery. A good wok is made of steel and reaches a very hot surface temperature quickly, making stir-frying a cinch. In this book you'll discover that wok cooking is not just Chinese cooking. You can cook anything in a wok as long as a few principles are followed, and those principles are clearly explained in the appropriate recipe headnotes, methods, and sidebars. A quick stir-fry is popular in my house, such as a fragrant Diced Chicken with Peppers and Cashews (page 332), where chicken is tossed with bell peppers, eggplant, and cashews for a satisfying dinner in less than fifteen minutes of cooking time. Of course, who would want to ignore Chinese cooking, because a dish such as Stir-Fried Shrimp with Bell Peppers and Bok Choy (page 402) is easy and too wonderful to pass up, flavored as it is with sesame oil, leeks, zucchini, scallions, pork belly, and cashews. You'll think you've just gone to a Chinese restaurant, and I'm sure you'll also think, "I can't believe I just cooked that."

Grill

Don't forget to think about your grill as a "cooking vessel." There are plenty of meals that get cooked right on the grill, especially meats and large vegetables. The so-called recipe Steak, Corn on the Cob, and Peppers on the Grill (page 106) is too easy to even call it cooking. I say "so-called" because all you're doing is placing the food on the grill. And remember, there's no need to scrub a grill grate: simply use the fire of the coals to burn off the food particles from the previous grilling and scrape the ash off once it carbonizes.

I haven't mentioned all the cooking vessels used in the book; there are many other cooking vessels that are used in one-pot cookery, and they'll be introduced when you get to the appropriate recipes. You can immediately tell what you'll need when you go to a recipe: Next to the recipe name will be an icon/drawing of the cooking implement needed. Here is a full review of all the cooking vessels used in one-pot cooking:

Cooking Implements Used in One-Pot Cooking

Baking Casserole

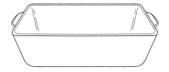

Flameproof Baking Casserole

Cast-Iron Skillet

Fryer Pot

Deep Fryer

Griddle

Earthenware Casserole

Grill

Fish Poacher

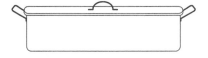

Large Pot

Microwave

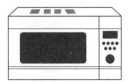

Nonstick Skillet

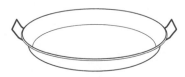

Paella Pan

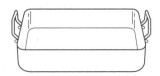

Roasting Pan

Salad Bowl

Saucepan

Sauté Pan

Soup Pot

Stewpot

Tagine

Wok

Salads for Dinner

||||||||||||||||||||||||||||||||||||||||||||||||||||||||||||||||||||||||||||||||||||||||||||||||||||||||||||

Salad for dinner is often an option in my house when it's either too hot to cook or we're all wanting something light with minimal cooking. You'll find in this chapter truly substantial salads that are all-in-one dinner options. You're not going to feel the need to have more food—and that's the idea! The Heirloom Tomato, Sweet Pepper, and Bean Salad (page 5) is perfect on a summer day, and the variety of heirloom tomatoes you can use will provide a platter as pretty as a picture. In the late fall and winter, you might want to make the Spelt and Shrimp Salad (page 8), which is a bit more substantial and healthy too. The Mâche and Baby Greens Dinner Salad with Smoked Salmon (page 24) uses the leafy green known as mâche, pronounced "mosh," a wonderful, nutty-flavored underused green with delicate rosette leaves found in farmers' markets and better supermarkets. The combination of greens is extraordinary with the smoked salmon.

Bean, Pea, and Tuna Salad with Preserved Lemon

In the summer, I sometimes want dinner to be satisfying, easy, and cool, and this dish fits the bill. This is a simple and very satisfying dinner salad that takes as long to make as the beans do to cook. If you are serving four, you can double the recipe.

⅓ cup (about 2 ounces) dried white beans
⅓ cup (about 2 ounces) dried black beans
Salt, to taste
⅓ cup (about 2 ounces) frozen peas
One 3½-ounce can tuna in olive oil with its oil
1 small garlic clove, finely chopped
½ small white onion, cut in half and thinly sliced
2 tablespoons capers
¼ Preserved Lemon (see box page 3), chopped
2 tablespoons extra-virgin olive oil
Freshly ground black pepper, to taste

1. Place the white and black beans in a large saucepan and cover with water by several inches. Bring to a boil over high heat, salt the water, and cook until tender, replenishing the water if necessary, 1 to 1¼ hours.

2. Add the peas to the beans and cook for 3 minutes. Drain and cool.

3. Meanwhile, in a bowl, toss the tuna and its oil, garlic, white onion, capers, preserved lemon, olive oil, and pepper. Add the beans and peas and toss again. Taste for salt, then serve.

Preserved Lemons

In Morocco, preserving lemons is a favorite way of conserving the bounty of the land's abundant lemon trees, and you can do the same. Preserved lemons are easy to prepare, and once they're in your refrigerator you'll find yourself using them as a condiment far beyond the recipes in this book. You can add cinnamon sticks, whole cloves, and coriander seeds to the marinade if you like. It's important to use the thin-skinned Meyer lemons because the excessive white pith of the more common Eureka lemons is much too bitter.

2 Meyer lemons, washed well, dried well, and cut into 8 wedges each
⅓ cup salt
½ cup fresh lemon juice
Extra-virgin olive oil to cover

1. In a bowl, toss the lemon wedges with the salt, then place in a half-pint jar. Cover the lemons with the lemon juice, screw on the lid, and leave at room temperature for 1 week, shaking it occasionally.

2. Pour in olive oil to cover, and then refrigerate for up to 1 year.

Makes ½ pint

Red and White Bean Salad with Tomatoes

This simple dinner salad is a wonderful way to fill your belly on a hot summer day. There may be a desire to start adding more ingredients, but you don't really need to if you're using some juicy and beautiful homegrown or farmers' market heirloom tomatoes.

½ cup (about ¼ pound) dried white beans
½ cup (about ¼ pound) dried red beans
Salt, to taste
6 tablespoons extra-virgin olive oil
2 tablespoons balsamic vinegar
1 teaspoon Dijon mustard
2 large garlic cloves, very finely chopped
4 heirloom tomatoes (about 2 pounds; preferably
    of different colors), cut irregularly
4 scallions, chopped
Freshly ground black pepper, to taste
15 large fresh basil leaves

1. Place the beans in a large saucepan of water to cover. Bring to a boil, salt lightly, and cook until tender, replenishing the water if necessary, about 1 hour. Drain and let cool.

2. In a bowl, whisk together the olive oil, balsamic vinegar, mustard, and garlic. Add the beans, tomatoes, scallions, salt, and pepper and toss well. Lay the basil leaves on top of each other and roll up. Snip the rolled-up basil leaves with kitchen scissors into the salad. Toss again and serve at room temperature.

Heirloom Tomato, Sweet Pepper, and Bean Salad

This is a wonderful late summer, hot day dinner salad for which you could use fresh fava beans in the place of the white beans. I also make this dish in the fall with dried yellow fava beans, which is an excellent variation. Serve with crusty bread to soak up the juices.

One 14-ounce can white beans, rinsed
1¾ pounds multicolor heirloom tomatoes, cut into chunks
1¾ pounds multicolor bell peppers, seeded and cut into chunks
1 fresh jalapeño chile, seeded and sliced
One 6-ounce can tuna in olive oil, with its oil
2 sliced red scallions or ½ cup sliced red onion
12 black olives, pitted and halved
¼ cup extra-virgin olive oil
1½ tablespoons fresh lemon juice
3 salted anchovy fillets, rinsed and very finely chopped
1 garlic clove, very finely chopped
½ teaspoon dried oregano
Salt and freshly ground black pepper, to taste

1. Put the beans, tomatoes, peppers, chile, tuna, scallions, and olives in a bowl and toss well.

2. Stir the olive oil, lemon juice, anchovies, garlic, and oregano together, pour onto the salad, and toss well. Season with salt and pepper and toss again, then serve.

Red Kidney Bean, Walnut, and Pomegranate Salad

I first encountered the alluring tastes of the Caucasus when I tasted Armenian food. The food of that region encompasses Armenia, northeastern Turkey, Georgia, and Azerbaijan. It often combines beans and legumes with fruit, nuts, and fresh herbs. This is a very satisfying and delicious autumn dinner salad, which I adapted from Darra Goldstein's *The Georgian Table*.

1½ cups (about ¾ pound) dried red kidney beans
Salt, to taste
1½ cups finely chopped onion
¾ cup shelled walnuts, crushed slightly
¾ cup pomegranate seeds
2 garlic cloves, very finely chopped
2 small fresh green serrano chiles, seeded and chopped
2½ tablespoons finely chopped fresh cilantro (coriander leaf)
1½ tablespoons finely chopped fresh flat-leaf parsley
¼ cup extra-virgin olive oil
¼ cup pomegranate juice
¼ teaspoon ground cinnamon
⅛ teaspoon ground cloves

1. Place the beans in a large saucepan and cover with water by several inches. Bring to a boil over high heat, salt lightly, and cook until tender, 1 to 1¼ hours.

2. Drain and toss with the onion. Toss again with the walnuts, pomegranate seeds, garlic, chiles, cilantro, parsley, olive oil, and pomegranate juice.

3. In a small bowl, mix the cinnamon, cloves, and salt, then toss with the beans. Let cool for 1 hour before serving.

Eggplant, Bell Pepper, and Tomato Salad

This is a salad I once had in the Mediterranean, and I often felt I never needed to eat anything else because it was so satisfying. The only thing that gets cooked is the eggplant, and the salad is eaten at room temperature with pita chips or warm pita bread.

4 pounds eggplant, sliced ½ inch thick
¾ to 1 cup extra-virgin olive oil, or as needed
2 large ripe tomatoes, peeled if desired, seeded, and chopped
2 large red bell peppers, seeded and chopped
One 15-ounce can chickpeas, rinsed and drained
3 tablespoons finely chopped fresh mint leaves
Salt and freshly ground black pepper, to taste

1. Preheat a ridged cast-iron skillet or cast-iron griddle over high heat, or prepare a hot charcoal fire, or preheat a gas grill on high for 15 minutes.

2. Brush the eggplant slices with olive oil on both sides and cook until streaked with black grid marks and beginning to turn light golden, about 8 minutes in all. You might use up to ¾ cup of olive oil doing this, and you will have to cook in batches. Remove from the griddle or grill, let cool, and dice a little smaller than bite-size.

3. In a large serving bowl, toss the eggplant together with the tomatoes, bell peppers, chickpeas, mint, and remaining olive oil, if desired or necessary. Season with salt and pepper, toss again, and serve.

Spelt and Shrimp Salad

There's some confusion as to what farro is; this recipe will help clarify at the same time as providing a wonderful-tasting whole-grain salad. This salad, called *insalata di farro* in Italian, is a typical summer salad in the regions of Tuscany and Abruzzo made with spelt wheat (*Triticum aestivum* subsp. *spelta*). In the Italian vernacular *farro* is also used to refer to two other ancient wheat species known as emmer (*Triticum turgidum* subsp. *diococcum*) and einkorn (*Triticum monococcum* L. subsp. *monococcum*). The salad is often made with summer vegetables such as fava beans, peas, or zucchini and with shrimp or tuna in oil.

Salt, to taste
1 pound large shrimp
1½ cups (about ¾ pound) spelt wheat berries (farro)
10 ounces sweet grape tomatoes, halved, or cherry tomatoes, quartered
½ pound arugula (preferably wild), coarsely chopped
1 small red onion, chopped
½ cup extra-virgin olive oil
3 tablespoons fresh lemon juice
Freshly ground black pepper, to taste

1. Bring a large saucepan of water to a boil over high heat, salt the water, cook the shrimp for 1½ minutes, then remove with a skimmer and cool. Leave the water in the saucepan to cook the spelt. Shell the shrimp and cut it into thirds.

2. Bring the water in the saucepan back to a boil if it isn't boiling already, add a little salt to the saucepan along with the spelt, and cook until tender, replenishing the water if necessary, 1½ to 2 hours. Drain well and place in a bowl. Toss the spelt with the shrimp, tomatoes, arugula, and onion.

3. In a bowl, stir together the olive oil and lemon juice and season with salt and pepper. Toss the salad again with the dressing, arrange on a serving plate, and serve at room temperature.

Mango and Cucumber Salad

This deliciously refreshing salad can be served either as an accompaniment to other dishes such as Coconut Mung Bean Dal (page 76) or as a main course dinner salad. If you are making it as a dinner salad use the tofu, otherwise leave it out.

For the salad

8 Persian cucumbers or 2 to 3 regular cucumbers, peeled or unpeeled,
    split lengthwise and sliced
6 scallions, trimmed and cut into 1½-inch lengths
4 small ripe tomatoes, quartered and then sliced
2 fresh green serrano chiles, seeded or not, chopped
2 shallots, cut in half and then sliced
2 large garlic cloves, finely chopped
2 celery stalks, sliced
2 slightly ripe mangoes, peeled, flesh cut off and sliced
One 1-inch piece fresh ginger, peeled and finely chopped
½ pound extra-firm tofu, diced (use only if making as a dinner salad)
½ cup unsalted whole cashews

For the dressing

6 tablespoons vegetable oil
3 tablespoons rice vinegar
2 tablespoons palm sugar (preferably) or brown sugar
1½ tablespoons soy sauce
1 tablespoon sesame oil
Salt, to taste

1. In a large bowl, toss all the salad ingredients together.

2. In a small bowl or cup, blend the dressing ingredients. Toss with the salad until blended well. Refrigerate for at least 2 hours before serving.

3. Remove from the refrigerator 1 hour before serving time and serve cool but not cold.

Potato and Papaya Salad

This interesting salad came about when I had a request to make an "Indian salad." Indians don't eat salads, their raitas and chutneys generally filling that role. However, I was inspired to assemble this flavorful salad when I found a ripe papaya at my market (so often they're sold not quite ripe). It's important to have piquant chiles, which, sadly, are sometimes difficult to find as more and more supermarkets sell chiles whose heat has been toned down or eliminated. This recipe is adapted from Julie Sahni's *Indian Regional Classics*.

14 small Yukon gold potatoes (about 2 pounds)
Salt, to taste
1 pound medium shrimp
½ cup fresh lemon juice
2 tablespoons honey
4 teaspoons ground cumin seeds
2 ripe papayas, peeled, pitted, and diced
8 fresh green serrano chiles, seeded and sliced
½ cup finely chopped fresh mint leaves
1 cup finely chopped fresh cilantro (coriander leaf)
2 teaspoons peeled and very finely chopped fresh ginger
Lettuce leaves, any type

1. Place the potatoes in a large saucepan, cover with water, bring to a boil over medium heat, and cook the potatoes until tender, 45 to 50 minutes. Remove with a skimmer and let cool.

2. Bring the water to a rolling boil again over high heat, salt the water, and cook the shrimp until orange-red, 1 to 2 minutes. Drain the shrimp and shell them. Slice the potatoes ¼ inch thick.

3. In a bowl, stir the lemon juice, honey, cumin, and salt together. Gently toss the lemon juice and honey mixture with the potato, shrimp, papayas, chiles, mint, cilantro, and ginger. Place the lettuce leaves on a platter, spoon the potato salad on top, and serve.

Potato, Ham, and Egg Dinner Salad

This one-pot dinner salad is eaten cold. I don't think you need anything else, but it can also serve as a side dish for grilled foods. I actually prefer the salad the next day as a leftover dinner, but you don't need to wait. I like the greater amount of mayonnaise, though you can use the lesser amount and it will taste great.

2 pounds Yukon gold potatoes, peeled or unpeeled
4 large eggs
1 cup (about 5 ounces) frozen peas
½ cup mayonnaise, or as needed
2 tablespoons extra-virgin olive oil
1 tablespoon sherry vinegar
1 teaspoon sweet paprika
1 teaspoon salt, plus more to taste
½ teaspoon freshly ground black pepper, to taste
½ pound cooked ham, diced
3 tablespoons finely chopped fresh flat-leaf parsley
Iceberg lettuce leaves or Bibb lettuce leaves

1. Place the potatoes in a large saucepan and cover with cold water. Turn the heat to high and when the water starts to boil, carefully lower the eggs into the boiling water with the potatoes. Remove the eggs exactly 9 minutes after you put them in and immediately cool them in a bowl of ice water. Continue cooking the potatoes until a skewer slides easily into them, about 30 minutes in all. Add the peas to the pot with the potatoes and cook for 3 minutes.

2. Drain all the potatoes and peas and cool. Cut the potatoes into ¾-inch cubes. Shell the eggs and cut into quarters or sixths.

3. In a large bowl, whisk together the mayonnaise, olive oil, vinegar, paprika, salt, and pepper. Add the potatoes, peas, ham, and parsley, toss gently but well, and serve on top of lettuce leaves.

Napa Cabbage and Ham Dinner Salad

This dinner salad is eaten cold. As simple as it sounds, it's very satisfying and is perfect as a summer dinner salad or, if you're so inclined, as an accompaniment to a chicken dinner. Napa cabbage is not actually a cabbage but rather a vegetable that belongs to the mustard family.

>One 2¼-pound napa cabbage
>½ pound cooked ham, cut into thin strips
>2 avocados, cut in half, pitted, and flesh scooped out and sliced
>2 medium tomatoes, chopped
>½ fresh red or green serrano chile, seeded or not, finely chopped

For the dressing
>3 tablespoons soy sauce
>4 teaspoons sesame oil
>3 teaspoons sugar
>½ teaspoon salt

1. Bring a large pot of water to a boil, then cook the whole cabbage for 2 minutes. Drain and cool completely. Dry with paper towels. Slice into thin strips and place in a strainer to drain some more, patting drier with paper towels. Transfer to a bowl and toss with the ham, avocado slices, tomatoes, and chile.

2. Blend the dressing ingredients together in a cup. Pour the dressing over the salad, toss well, and serve.

Makes 4 servings

Cabbage and Duck Salad

This is an ideal preparation for leftover duck, or turkey for that matter. I like to use the duck breast, searing it golden crispy on both sides and then thinly slicing it to be tossed in the salad. Duck legs are cheaper, and I use those, too. If you don't have leftover duck, follow step 1. Savoy cabbage is a tender, crinkly-skinned cabbage; you can use regular green head cabbage if you can't find savoy.

2 duck breast halves (about ¾ pound)
¼ cup mayonnaise
3 tablespoons sour cream
2 teaspoons Dijon mustard
1 tablespoon extra-virgin olive oil
1 teaspoon white wine vinegar
1¼ pounds savoy cabbage, cored and shredded
6 scallions, trimmed and chopped
1 small white onion, quartered and then sliced
¼ cup finely chopped fresh cilantro (coriander leaf)
Salt and freshly ground black pepper, to taste

1. Preheat a cast-iron skillet over medium heat, then cook the duck breast halves, skin side down first, until golden brown, about 6 minutes. Turn and cook until rare, another 4 to 5 minutes. Cover if the duck fat is splattering too much. Remove and let rest until needed.

2. In a large bowl, whisk together the mayonnaise, sour cream, mustard, olive oil, and vinegar. Toss with the cabbage, scallions, onion, duck, and cilantro. Season with salt and pepper and toss again. Serve cold or at room temperature.

Summer Rice Salad

The only thing that gets cooked in this potpourri of flavors is the rice. This dish is quite satisfying when you want a light dinner on a hot midsummer's night, but it could also be served as an antipasto or side dish for any kind of summer barbecue. The mixed marinated seafood is sold in a variety of ways in a variety of places. It usually consists of baby octopus or squid, mussels, clams, cuttlefish pieces, scallop pieces, and so forth. Usually a supermarket will sell it as part of their take-out salad bar. Sometimes it's sold in cans or jars.

1 tablespoon unsalted butter

1 cup medium-grain rice such as Calrose or short-grain rice such as
    Arborio, soaked in water for 30 minutes, drained

2 cups water

1 carrot, scraped and diced small (⅔ cup)

½ cup (about 2½ ounces) frozen or fresh peas

1 teaspoon salt, plus more as needed

¼ pound mixed marinated seafood, freshly made (see box page 15) or
    from a jar, can, or supermarket salad bar

4 marinated baby artichoke hearts (about 2½ ounces), quartered

12 green olives (preferably Castelvetrano), pitted and coarsely chopped

3 tablespoons extra-virgin olive oil

1 teaspoon orange zest

1 large garlic clove, very finely chopped

1 tablespoon finely chopped fresh flat-leaf parsley

Freshly ground black pepper, to taste

1. In a heavy saucepan, melt the butter over medium-high heat. Add the rice and cook, stirring, for 1 to 2 minutes. Add the water, carrot, peas, and 1 teaspoon salt and bring to a boil. Cover, reduce the heat to low, and cook without uncovering or stirring until the water is completely absorbed and the rice is tender, about 15 minutes.

2. Pour the rice out onto a platter and let cool completely. Add the marinated seafood, artichokes, olives, olive oil, orange zest, garlic, and parsley and toss well. Season with salt and pepper and toss again. Serve at room temperature.

Marinated Seafood

This recipe is a simple way to make freshly made marinated seafood for the Summer Rice Salad on page 14. Steam ½ pound of littleneck clams and ½ pound of mussels in a covered pot with a few tablespoons of water until they open, 5 to 8 minutes. Remove the meats and discard the shells. Place the meats in a bowl. In a frying pan, heat 1 teaspoon olive oil over medium heat and cook 2 small cleaned squid cut into rings and tentacles and 2 ounces bay scallops until they turn color, about 4 minutes. Transfer them to the bowl with the clams and mussels. Toss with 3 tablespoons extra-virgin olive oil, 1 tablespoon white wine vinegar, a little salt, and a little pepper. Let marinate in a bowl or a jar for 24 hours before using.

Russian Salad Dinner

This much-maligned salad is often served poorly prepared with too much mayonnaise in countless tourist restaurants in the Mediterranean. It is said that the original version was invented in the 1860s by Lucien Olivier, the chef of the Hermitage restaurant in Moscow, and its name was Salad Olivier. It was a very popular preparation that originally contained rare and expensive ingredients such as grouse, veal tongue, caviar, and crayfish tails. Its popularity spread widely, too, and it eventually took on the name "Russian salad." It became very popular as *insalata russe* in Italy during the 1950s. I happen to love a properly prepared Russian salad, and this recipe is a simple, delicate version that can be served as an all-vegetable dinner salad.

3 pounds Yukon gold potatoes, peeled and cut into ⅜-inch cubes

4 carrots, scraped and cut into ⅜-inch cubes

½ pound (about 2 cups) fresh or frozen peas

6 large butter lettuce leaves

2 cups teardrop or sweet grape tomatoes or halved cherry tomatoes

1 cup chopped sweet gherkins

Salt and freshly ground black pepper, to taste

¾ cup mayonnaise

¼ cup extra-virgin olive oil

¼ cup white wine vinegar

4 large hard-boiled eggs, shelled and quartered

1. Bring a large saucepan of water to a boil over high heat, then add the potatoes and carrots and cook, stirring occasionally, until almost tender, about 7 minutes. Add the peas to the potatoes and carrots and cook for 4 minutes more. Drain all and cool completely.

2. Arrange the butter lettuce leaves on a large platter. In a large bowl, toss the potatoes, carrots, and peas with the tomatoes and gherkins. Season with salt and pepper and toss again.

3. In a bowl, whisk together the mayonnaise, olive oil, and vinegar. Pour the dressing into the salad bowl and toss gently until well mixed. In the center of each lettuce leaf, mound the salad and then garnish the edges and top with the eggs. Refrigerate for 1 hour before serving; serve cold.

Barley Salad with Baby Lima Beans, Red Bell Pepper, and Mint

The rustic taste of whole barley grains makes this a satisfying dinner salad. I'm usually too full to want anything else, but a simple green salad is a nice accompaniment.

3 cups water
1 cup pearl barley
1 cup (about ¼ pound) frozen baby lima beans
1 red bell pepper, seeded and chopped
1 celery stalk, finely chopped
6 tablespoons extra-virgin olive oil
3 tablespoons white wine vinegar
3 tablespoons finely chopped fresh mint
Salt and freshly ground black pepper, to taste

1. Bring the water to a boil in a saucepan over high heat, then cook the barley, covered and without stirring, until the liquid is mostly absorbed, about 35 minutes. Add the lima beans to the pan with the barley and cook, without stirring, until there is no liquid left, making sure it doesn't burn, another 10 minutes. Transfer to a bowl and let cool.

2. Once the barley is cool, toss with the red bell pepper, celery, olive oil, vinegar, mint, salt, and pepper. Serve at room temperature.

Pinto Bean Salad with Feta Cheese

In the summer I love bean salads not only because they can be prepared ahead of time to let their flavors mingle but also because they are satisfying as a dinner. In this recipe, make sure you don't buy crumbled feta cheese; you'll want the distinct large pieces for both appearance and texture. The roasted red bell peppers are sometimes labeled as "pimientos" when they come in jars.

Salt, to taste
1 cup (about ½ pound) dried pinto beans
1¼ cups chopped red onion
1 roasted red bell pepper, from a can or jar, chopped
1 scallion, trimmed and chopped
½ celery stalk, chopped
1 tablespoon finely chopped fresh mint
1 large garlic clove, finely chopped
3 tablespoons extra-virgin olive oil
Freshly ground black pepper, to taste
One ¼-pound piece feta cheese (preferably Greek or Bulgarian), cut into 8 cubes

1. Bring a large saucepan of water to a boil over high heat, then salt the water and add the pinto beans. Cook until tender, 40 to 60 minutes, replenishing the water if necessary. Drain and cool.

2. In a bowl, toss the pinto beans with the onion, bell pepper, scallion, celery, mint, garlic, and olive oil. Toss again with salt and pepper and arrange on a serving platter. Arrange the feta cheese on top in an attractive fashion and serve at room temperature.

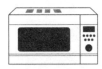

Japanese Dinner Salad

In Japanese cooking there are two basic salads, *aemono* (mixed things) and *sunomono* (vinegared things). The *aemono* salads usually are a mixture of raw or cooked ingredients tossed with a salad dressing made of a blend of miso (fermented soybean paste) and very soft tofu and sesame seeds. Some supermarkets sell "Japanese miso salad dressing" in bottles that you could use and then skip making the dressing, but I can't recommend it as the taste of the bottled product is inferior.

For the dressing
¼ pound very soft tofu
3 tablespoons finely chopped onion
2 tablespoons white miso
1 tablespoon rice vinegar
1 tablespoon finely chopped fresh flat-leaf parsley

For the salad
1 ear corn on the cob (unhusked)
One 9-ounce package spinach leaves
½ pound daikon, peeled and shredded
½ pound sashimi-quality fresh boneless, skinless salmon fillet,
    cut into ¼-inch slices, or 1 cup canned salmon, drained
Sesame seeds, for sprinkling

1. Prepare the dressing by vigorously blending the tofu, onion, miso, vinegar, and parsley in a bowl with a fork or whisk.

2. For the salad, wrap the ear of corn with its husk in a damp paper towel and place in the microwave. Microwave for 1½ minutes at full power. (Microwave oven strengths vary, so use common sense and your experience based on your own microwave oven.) Remove, and when cool enough to handle remove the husk and scrape off the kernels.

3. Arrange the spinach on a large platter. Sprinkle the corn kernels around, then the daikon, and arrange the salmon attractively. Sprinkle with sesame seeds. Drizzle a little of the salad dressing over everything (you won't need to use it all) and serve.

Shrimp Salad

The Thai eat a lot of salads served at room temperature, which are quite unlike European salads with their copious lettuces and vinaigrettes. The balance of flavors is critical in making Thai salads or, for that matter, any Thai dish because any one of these strongly flavored ingredients could easily tip the entire dish out of balance. In this well-known and popular shrimp salad called *yam gung* the shrimp are highly seasoned—this is a very piquant dish—but light tasting.

Salt, to taste
1 pound large shrimp, shelled
3 tablespoons Thai fish sauce
3 tablespoons fresh lime juice
1 tablespoon cayenne pepper
12 fresh red Thai chiles or 4 red jalapeño chiles, seeded and finely chopped
3 large garlic cloves, finely chopped
2 lemongrass stalks, tough inedible outer portion removed,
    tender inner portion finely chopped
2 scallions, trimmed and finely chopped
1 large shallot, thinly sliced
1 tablespoon finely chopped fresh cilantro (coriander leaf)
1 small head Bibb lettuce, leaves separated
½ cup loosely packed fresh mint leaves

1. Bring a saucepan of water to a boil and salt the water abundantly, then plunge the shrimp in and cook until they turn color, about 2 minutes. Drain and place in a bowl.

2. In a small bowl, stir together the fish sauce, lime juice, and cayenne. Pour this over the shrimp and toss well. Add the chiles, garlic, lemongrass, scallions, shallot, and cilantro and toss again. Refrigerate at least 2 hours.

3. When ready to serve, arrange the lettuce leaves on a platter and sprinkle some of the mint leaves in the center. Mound the shrimp on top of the mint and garnish with additional mint leaves. Serve cool or at room temperature.

‖‖‖

Stuffed Lettuce Bundles

This dish is just one thing after another stuffed into something else and then all wrapped up in lettuce leaves. You'll dress it with a little olive oil and vinegar and that's all there is to it. Make sure you use a lettuce with soft, pliable leaves so that they can roll without ripping, and dry them before using.

12 small round tomatoes (about 1½ pounds, 1½ inches in diameter)
¼ pound mascarpone cheese
¼ pound prosciutto
2 tablespoons finely chopped fresh basil
Salt and freshly ground black pepper, to taste
1 to 2 heads Boston head lettuce, butter lettuce, or green leaf lettuce leaves
    separated, washed well, and dried well
1 Belgian endive, leaves separated
2 ounces fresh mozzarella cheese, cut into 12 pieces
3 large canned artichoke hearts (foundations), cut into 12 slivers
2 scallions, trimmed and chopped
3 tablespoons extra-virgin olive oil
1½ teaspoons red wine vinegar

1. Hollow out all the tomatoes with a paring knife and spoon or a serrated grapefruit spoon and then stuff them with the mascarpone and a piece of prosciutto (tear up the prosciutto as needed). Season with the basil, salt, and pepper.

2. Arrange a lettuce leaf on the work surface in front of you and place an endive leaf on top. Place a stuffed tomato on the endive leaf along with a sliver of cheese and artichoke. Wrap the ensemble up and arrange attractively on a serving platter and continue making the rest. Sprinkle the top with whatever food remains and then with the scallions. Drizzle with the olive oil and vinegar and serve at room temperature.

Mâche and Baby Greens Dinner Salad with Smoked Salmon

Mâche, pronounced "mosh," is a wonderful, nutty-flavored, and underused green with delicate rosette leaves. I usually find it at Whole Foods or similar supermarkets and local farmers' markets. If you can't find it, then just use a greater amount of baby greens in its stead.

For the vinaigrette

¼ cup extra-virgin olive oil

1 tablespoon sour cream

1 tablespoon mayonnaise

2 teaspoons tarragon vinegar

½ teaspoon truffle honey (optional)

½ teaspoon Dijon mustard

½ teaspoon herbes de Provence

For the salad

One 4-ounce bag mixed baby greens

2 ounces mâche or other fancy greens such as baby spinach leaves or frisée

1 yellow bell pepper, seeded, cut in half widthwise, and then cut into strips

1 small red onion, cut in half and then sliced

1 avocado, cut in half, pitted, flesh scooped out and cut into thin wedges

2 marinated artichoke hearts (foundations), quartered

1 cup walnut halves

1 ripe tomato, cut into wedges

Salt and freshly ground black pepper, to taste

½ pound smoked salmon, cut into strips

1. In a small container, vigorously blend the olive oil, sour cream, mayonnaise, tarragon vinegar, truffle honey, if using, Dijon mustard, and herbes de Provence with a fork.

2. For the salad, arrange the greens on a large serving platter and attractively place the bell pepper, red onion, avocado, artichokes, walnuts, and tomato over the greens. Season lightly with salt and pepper. Lay the strips of smoked salmon on top. Drizzle the vinaigrette over the salad and serve.

Soups for Dinner

||||||||||||||||||||||||||||||||||||||||||||||||||||||||||||||||||||||||||||||||||||||||||||||||||||||||||

Normally, one serves soups as a first course, but in this chapter the soups have been chosen for their appropriateness in providing a one-pot dinner. These are thick soups with lots of flavor, lots of nutrition, and lots of wonderful tastes. The Shrimp and Lemongrass Noodle Soup (page 32) is not only substantial in terms of its ingredients providing all you need for a one-pot meal but is also packed with many good things, such as vitamin C derived from the citrus and chiles, that complement the spinach and bean thread noodles. You're probably already familiar with minestrone, but you might not have known that minestrone is a category of hearty soups and not just one soup. So when you try one of the several minestrone recipes in this chapter, such as Minestrone of Beans and Squash (page 42), remember that there are others you will equally enjoy, all with different ingredients and flavors. The Meatball and Yogurt Chowder (page 49) might sound unusual, but once you taste this melodious blend of spinach, lentils, dill, and meatballs in a rich yogurt-based broth, I'm sure it will become an oft-made soup.

Pasta and Cod Soup

Many kinds of special pasta that are used only for soup are sold in Italian markets. Supermarkets carry some, too, but usually not as wide a variety. *Acini di pepe*, which means "peppercorns" in Italian, is a dry soup pasta the size of peppercorns (hence the name) that is perfect for this soup. Many fishmongers sell pieces of cod, haddock, or other fish scraps as "chowder fish," and this is what you want when you make this soup. Use whatever local fish is available and freshest (and usually cheapest), and use whatever tiny pasta your market sells.

3 tablespoons extra-virgin olive oil
½ fennel bulb, finely chopped
½ small onion, finely chopped
1 garlic clove, finely chopped
¼ cup finely chopped fresh flat-leaf parsley
1 small plum tomato, peeled, seeded, and finely chopped (see box page 47)
4 cups cold water
10 ounces boneless cod or similar fish, cut into small pieces
½ cup dried soup pasta such as acini di pepe or stelline
1 dried red chile
4 salted anchovy fillets, rinsed (optional)
1 teaspoon salt
Freshly ground black pepper, to taste

1. In a soup pot, heat the olive oil over high heat, then add the fennel, onion, and garlic and cook, stirring constantly so the garlic doesn't burn, until softened, about 2 minutes. Add the parsley and cook, stirring, for 1 minute. Add the tomato and continue cooking for 1 minute.

2. Pour in the water, bring to a boil over high heat, then add the fish, pasta, chile, anchovies, if using, salt, and pepper and reduce the heat to medium. Cook for 10 minutes. Taste and correct the seasoning and serve.

Fish and Bell Pepper Soup

Although there are a number of steps in this recipe, it's worth it, as this rich soup makes a ful-filling one-pot meal. It has a kind of potato sauce as its base. The ideal fish for the soup is grouper; however, I provide alternatives depending on where you live. Although you will cook everything in one pot, you can serve it as two courses: first the soup, and then the fish.

2 large red bell peppers

4½ cups cold water

1 tablespoon salt

1 Yukon gold or white potato (about ½ pound), peeled and cubed

½ pound grouper, halibut, sea bass, Chilean sea bass, redfish (ocean perch), or mahimahi

1 teaspoon cumin seeds

2 garlic cloves, peeled

Pinch of saffron, crumbled

2 teaspoons hot or sweet paprika

1 ripe tomato, peeled, seeded, and chopped (see box page 47)

1 cup beef broth or water

6 tablespoons extra-virgin olive oil

1. Place the bell peppers on a wire rack set over a burner on high heat and roast until their skins blister black on all sides, turning occasionally with tongs. Remove the peppers and place in a paper or heavy plastic bag to steam for 20 minutes, which will make peeling them easier. When cool enough to handle, rub off as much blackened peel as you can and remove the seeds by rubbing with a paper towel (to avoid washing away flavorful juices) or by rinsing under running water (to remove more easily). Slice or chop and set aside.

2. Put the water in a soup pot with the salt and bring to a boil. Add the potato and boil for 12 minutes. Remove the potato with a slotted spoon and reserve. Add the fish and boil for 2 minutes. Remove the fish with a slotted spoon and set aside. Reserve the cooking broth.

3. In a mortar, pound the cumin seeds, garlic, saffron, and paprika into a paste. Add the tomato and a few cubes of reserved potato and transfer to a food processor or blender to blend (or continue pounding with a pestle) until smooth; while the processor or blender is running, or if you are continuing to pound in the mortar, add the beef broth in a slow stream until the sauce is homogenous. Whisk in the olive oil in a slow stream, as if you were making mayonnaise.

4. Return the remaining potato cubes to the cooking broth and bring to a boil. Add the bell peppers and cook for 10 minutes over medium-high heat. Strain the broth through a fine-mesh strainer and pass the vegetables through a food mill or push through a strainer back into the broth. Add the reserved fish to the broth, along with the spice mixture from Step 3, and heat gently. Serve hot.

Shrimp and Lemongrass Noodle Soup

This spicy hot soupy dish requires preparing lemongrass first. Trim the lemongrass by cutting away the grassy tops of the stalks and then cutting away any hard parts of the root. Remove the tough outer leaves and then bruise the lemongrass to release its flavor by crushing it with the side of a cleaver. Lime leaves can be found at Thai markets; otherwise you may substitute lime zest. Roasted chile paste can be found in Thai markets and some supermarkets, in the Asian/international aisle.

2 quarts chicken broth

6 large lemongrass stalks, tough outer portion removed (see headnote)

20 fresh lime or lemon leaves or 2 tablespoons grated lime zest

12 fresh Thai chiles or 8 fresh serrano chiles, split lengthwise and crushed

7 tablespoons fresh lime juice

7 scallions, trimmed and cut into 1-inch lengths

¾ pound bean thread noodles, soaked in hot water for 15 minutes

Four 3.25-ounce cans (drained weight) canned straw mushrooms (about 2 cups), drained

3 tablespoons Thai roasted red chile paste (see headnote)

2 pounds medium shrimp, shelled

1¼ pounds baby spinach leaves

¼ cup Thai fish sauce

1. In a large soup pot, bring the chicken broth to a boil over medium heat. Add the prepared lemongrass stalks and half the lime leaves (or half the zest), reduce the heat to low, and simmer for 5 minutes. Remove and discard the lemongrass and lime leaves (or zest) with a fine mesh skimmer.

2. Put the crushed chiles, lime juice, scallions, and remaining lime leaves (or remaining zest) in a large soup tureen or pot that you can use as a tureen.

3. Increase the heat to high and add the noodles, mushrooms, and Thai chile paste to the chicken broth. When it begins to boil, about 5 minutes, cook for 2 minutes more and then add the shrimp, spinach, and fish sauce. Cook until the shrimp are orange-red, about 3 minutes. Pick up the noodles with a fork and cut them into smaller pieces with kitchen scissors. Pour or ladle the soup over the ingredients in the soup tureen, stir quickly, and serve, making sure you ladle broth into the individual bowls.

Thai Chicken and Spinach Soup

This is a beautiful-looking soup, as the bright green spinach leaves are quite appetizing. The soup is slightly piquant, which I think you will find very appealing. I will always remember this soup because I once was about to serve it to latecomers to the table and the spinach had by then lost its luster and was dull in color—but I was saved by a power outage, and they ate by candlelight and couldn't tell. This soup is delicious even in the dark.

¾ pound boneless, skinless chicken breasts

6 cups water

Salt, to taste

2 tablespoons Thai fish sauce

⅓ cup medium-grain rice such as Calrose or short-grain rice such as Arborio

3 dried red chiles, crumbled slightly, or 2 teaspoons dried bird's eye chiles, bruised in a mortar

2 lemongrass stalks, tough outer portion removed, finely chopped or thinly sliced

1 tablespoon peeled and finely chopped fresh ginger

Grated zest of 1 small lime

5 ounces spinach leaves

¼ cup coarsely chopped fresh cilantro (coriander leaf)

3 tablespoons fresh lime juice

One 3.25-ounce can (drained weight) straw mushrooms (about ½ cup), drained and rinsed

1. Place the chicken in a large saucepan, cover with the water, and bring to just below a boil over high heat, about 7 minutes. Immediately reduce the heat to low, salt the water lightly, and simmer until the chicken can be pulled apart with a fork, 1 to 2 minutes. Remove the chicken and shred into smaller pieces. Set aside.

2. Season the soup with 1 tablespoon of the fish sauce. Add the rice, chiles, lemongrass, ginger, and lime zest. Stir and simmer until the rice is almost cooked through, about 12 minutes. Add the spinach and simmer, stirring occasionally, for 4 minutes. Add the reserved chicken.

3. Stir in the remaining 1 tablespoon fish sauce, the cilantro, and lime juice. Add the straw mushrooms, stir, and let sit for 2 minutes. Serve hot immediately, making sure to ladle out the rice, which will have sunk to the bottom of the pot.

Udon Noodles with Scallops

The thick noodles known as udon are popular in Japanese soups and available in supermarkets. They are usually sold fresh, but dried are available, too. This soup is light but filling and is more than a one-pot meal: It's a bowl filled with delicious and nutritious ingredients. All the Asian ingredients called for are usually found in the international aisle of your supermarket.

½ ounce (8) dried shiitake mushrooms
3 cups warm water
Salt, to taste
2 tablespoons soy sauce
1½ tablespoons rice vinegar
1½ tablespoons sugar
1½ tablespoons bonito powder (dashi powder)
1½ teaspoons rice wine (mirin)
1 pound fresh udon or soba noodles
2 bunches (14 ounces) baby bok choy, trimmed and sliced
1 carrot, scraped and cut into matchsticks
8 sea scallops
4 scallions, trimmed and chopped
2 teaspoons toasted sesame seeds
¼ ounce sliced dried seaweed (nori)

1. Soak the dried shiitake mushrooms in the warm water for 30 minutes. Remove the mushrooms, cut off their stems and discard, and slice the caps. Reserve the soaking liquid.

2. Pour the mushroom soaking liquid into a saucepan and bring to a boil over high heat. Salt lightly and add the sliced mushrooms, soy sauce, rice vinegar, sugar, bonito powder, and rice wine and stir well. Add the noodles, bok choy, and carrot and cook for 4 minutes. Add the scallops and cook until the noodles are soft and the scallops are barely cooked through, about 3 minutes more.

3. Divide the noodle mixture among four bowls and top with the scallions, sesame seeds, and seaweed. Ladle some broth into each bowl and serve.

Shrimp Chowder Diablo

If you can find manzano chiles, extremely hot chiles native to South America, they will provide an eye-opening experience when eating this dinner soup. It is the intense floral and piquant taste of chiles like manzano, cherry chiles, or habanero that enliven dishes like this chowder. There are two methods you can use to finish the soup: In the first, you add the shrimp with the chowder not quite near bubbling and cook them for about 5 minutes. Or you can add the shrimp to the saucepan and leave it to simmer over very low heat, perhaps with the use of a heat diffuser.

> 3 ounces salt pork, diced
> 1 medium onion, chopped
> 1 pound medium shrimp
> 6 cups water
> 1 pound Yukon gold potatoes, peeled and diced
> 2 ears corn on the cob, kernels scraped off (about 2 cups kernels)
> 1 manzano, cherry, or habanero chile, seeded and sliced
> ½ teaspoon ground coriander
> ¼ teaspoon ground cardamom
> Salt and freshly ground black pepper, to taste
> ¾ cup whole milk
> ¾ cup heavy cream
> Chopped scallions, for garnish
> Chopped fresh cilantro (coriander leaf), for garnish

1. In a large saucepan over low heat, add the salt pork and cook, stirring, until nearly crispy, about 15 minutes. Add the onion and cook, stirring occasionally to deglaze the pan, until golden and very soft, about 20 minutes. Remove the onion and salt pork from the saucepan and set aside.

2. Shell the shrimp and place the shells in the same saucepan you cooked the salt pork. Cover with the water, bring to a boil over high heat, then reduce the heat to low and simmer for 30 minutes. Remove the shrimp shells with a skimmer and discard the shells. You should have about 5 cups of broth; if you don't, add water until you do. Bring to a boil, reduce the heat to low, add the potatoes, corn kernels, and chile, and cook until almost tender, 30 minutes.

3. Return the reserved onion and salt pork to the saucepan and stir. Stir in the coriander and cardamom and season with salt and pepper. Add the shrimp, milk, and cream and simmer over very low heat until the shrimp are orange-pink, about 30 minutes, or cook over medium heat, without letting the broth bubble or the milk will curdle, for 10 minutes. Serve hot, garnished with the scallions and cilantro.

Cabbage Soup

It may be called cabbage soup, but this Italian soup is a lot more than that. It is delicious, rich, and complex. It is a minestrone in every sense of the word (*minestrone* meaning "big soup") that everyone will find satisfying in an elemental way, yet it began as nothing more than cabbage cooked in water. I know that Whole Foods Markets sell prosciutto fat because that's where I buy it, but any Italian market should, too.

½ cup extra-virgin olive oil, plus more for drizzling (optional)
1 medium onion, finely chopped
1 carrot, scraped and finely chopped
1 celery stalk, finely chopped
½ cup finely chopped fresh flat-leaf parsley
3 tablespoons finely chopped fresh basil leaves
2 ounces pancetta, finely chopped
1 ounce prosciutto fat, finely chopped
1 pound green cabbage, damaged outer leaves removed, cored, and coarsely chopped
½ pound red cabbage, damaged outer leaves removed, cored, and coarsely chopped
6 cups water
½ pound (about 1 cup) dried cannellini or other white beans, soaked in cold water to cover for 2 hours and then drained
1 pound Yukon gold or white potatoes, peeled and coarsely diced
Salt and freshly ground black pepper, to taste
¼ pound small tubular macaroni such as pennine or elbow macaroni
¼ cup freshly grated Parmigiano-Reggiano cheese

1. In a soup pot, heat the olive oil over medium heat, then add the onion, carrot, celery, parsley, basil leaves, pancetta, and prosciutto fat and cook, stirring occasionally, until the onion is softened and some fat has rendered, about 10 minutes.

2. Add both cabbages and toss until all the leaves are coated. Add the water and beans. Cover, reduce the heat to medium-low, and cook with the soup bubbling gently until the beans are slightly softened, about 1 hour. Add the potatoes and cook just until tender, 25 to 30 minutes more.

3. Season the soup with salt and pepper and add the pasta. Cook uncovered, until the pasta is al dente, 12 to 15 minutes. Serve with the cheese and more olive oil, if desired.

Minestrone of Beans and Squash

This is a wonderful fall dinner in a bowl. To make a vegetarian version, just leave out the prosciutto and pancetta. If you're using them, you can get prosciutto skin at any store that sells prosciutto; just ask the deli person when they're trimming the prosciutto for slicing to save you the skin. *Minestrone* means "big soup" in Italian, and this soup certainly qualifies as one to satisfy your cravings.

5 tablespoons extra-virgin olive oil

1 medium onion, chopped

3 large garlic cloves, finely chopped

1 ounce pancetta, cut into strips (optional)

6 cups water

½ pound (about 1 cup) dried red kidney beans

One 3-ounce piece prosciutto skin (optional)

Bouquet garni, tied in cheesecloth, consisting of flat-leaf parsley,
    thyme, bay leaf, basil, and rosemary

2 teaspoons salt

¾ pound winter squash flesh, diced

¾ pound green cabbage, cored and sliced

½ pound zucchini, diced

¼ pound carrots, scraped and diced

1 cup canned chickpeas, rinsed and drained

Freshly ground black pepper, to taste

Freshly grated Parmesan cheese, for garnish (optional)

1. In a soup pot, heat the olive oil over medium-high heat, then add the onion, garlic, and pancetta, if using and cook, stirring, until softened, about 3 minutes. Add the water, beans, prosciutto skin, if using, bouquet garni, and salt and bring to a boil. Reduce the heat to medium and cook, stirring occasionally, for 45 minutes.

2. Add the winter squash, cabbage, zucchini, carrots, and chickpeas and cook, covered and stirring occasionally, until softened, about 1 hour. Remove and discard the bouquet garni. Sprinkle with the freshly ground black pepper. Serve hot in bowls with cheese, if desired.

Bean and Pasta Soup

This hearty and delicious soup of pasta and beans is so full-bodied that you need only a green salad to accompany it. If you decide to use the pork or prosciutto skin, which are used for flavoring, they can easily be bought from the deli counter of an Italian market or supermarket. Often they will give it to you for free. If you want to eat the prosciutto skin once it is cooked, cut it into strips before adding it to the soup; otherwise leave it in one or two pieces that can be discarded after the soup is cooked.

3 tablespoons extra-virgin olive oil

1 pound boneless pork shoulder or butt, diced

¼ pound pancetta, cut into strips

¼ pound prosciutto skin or skin from salt pork, whole or
    cut into strips (optional)

1 large onion, chopped

6 garlic cloves, chopped

1 fennel bulb (about ¾ pound), chopped

1 celery stalk, chopped

8 to 10 cups chicken broth

1½ cups (about ¾ pound) dried white beans

1 cup cooked chickpeas, rinsed and drained

1 cinnamon stick

1 bay leaf

1 fresh rosemary sprig

¼ pound Parmigiano-Reggiano cheese rind (optional)

Salt and freshly ground black pepper, to taste

¼ pound short tubular macaroni such as tubetti, ditali, ditalini, or
    elbow macaroni

Extra-virgin olive oil, for drizzling

Freshly grated Parmesan cheese (preferably Parmigiano-Reggiano),
    for sprinkling

1. In a large soup pot, heat the olive oil over medium-high heat, then add the pork, pancetta, and prosciutto skin, if using, and cook, stirring, until they turn color, about 5 minutes. Add the onion, garlic, fennel, and celery and cook, stirring occasionally, until softened, 12 to 15 minutes.

2. Add the chicken broth, white beans, and chickpeas along with the cinnamon stick, bay leaf, rosemary, and Parmesan rind, if using. Season with salt and pepper. Bring to a boil, about 10 minutes, then reduce the heat to medium-low and cook until the white beans are softened, about 1½ hours.

3. Add the pasta and cook uncovered, stirring, until al dente, 12 to 15 minutes. Remove and discard the cinnamon stick, bay leaf, and rosemary sprig. Both the prosciutto skin and Parmesan rind can be eaten, if desired. Serve with a drizzle of olive oil and cheese.

Potato and Chickpea Soup

Here's another substantial vegetable soup based on chickpeas and potatoes, but in this case spiced with saffron and paprika. With the addition of fresh spinach, it's not only healthy but also a very pretty soup.

6 tablespoons extra-virgin olive oil
¼ pound French or Italian bread, cut into 4 slices
3 tablespoons sherry vinegar
1 medium onion, chopped
2 tomatoes, peeled, seeded, and chopped (see box page 47)
2 teaspoons sweet or hot paprika
2 cups canned chickpeas, rinsed and drained
1 pound spinach, trimmed of stems and torn into smaller pieces
3 potatoes (about 1 pound), peeled and cut into small pieces
½ cup dry white wine
2 teaspoons salt
1 teaspoon freshly ground black pepper
4 cups water
3 large garlic cloves, finely chopped
3 tablespoons pine nuts
¼ cup finely chopped fresh flat-leaf parsley
Pinch of saffron
1 large hard-boiled egg, shelled and chopped

1. In a soup pot or flameproof baking casserole, heat 4 tablespoons of the olive oil over medium heat, then cook the bread until golden brown and crispy, 4 to 5 minutes. Remove the bread, tear into smaller pieces, place in 6 soup bowls, and douse with the vinegar.

2. In the same pot, add the remaining 2 tablespoons olive oil, then add the onion, tomatoes, and paprika and cook, stirring occasionally, until a thick sauce has formed, 10 to 12 minutes.

3. Add the chickpeas, spinach, potatoes, wine, salt, pepper, and water. Turn the heat to high, and once the spinach wilts and the broth is beginning to boil, reduce the heat to low and cook until the potatoes are very nearly tender, about 45 minutes.

4. Add the garlic, pine nuts, parsley, saffron, and hard-boiled egg. Turn the heat off, let rest for 10 minutes, then serve by ladling the soup over the bread in the bowls.

Peeling Tomatoes

The way to peel a tomato is to drop it into boiling water for about a minute. The skin will loosen and it can be pinched off.

Potato, Cabbage, and Chard Soup

This all-purpose minestrone-like soup is a perfect and filling dinner soup for a cold day when you need to feed lots of people or you want leftovers for the next cold day. It's satisfying, healthy, and hearty, and it could also contain carrots, celery, leeks, and dandelion greens, depending on seasonality.

¼ pound pork fat, chopped (preferably), or ½ cup extra-virgin olive oil
2 pounds Yukon gold potatoes, peeled and diced
1 small green cabbage (about 1½ pounds), cored and chopped
¾ pound Swiss chard leaves (no stems), chopped
1 medium onion, chopped
2 large garlic cloves, finely chopped
6 cups water
1 cup (about ½ pound) dried red kidney beans
1 ham hock or smoked bacon chunk (about ½ pound)
1 large tomato, peeled, seeded, and chopped (see box page 47)
6 slices day-old French country bread (6 ounces) or ¼ pound lasagne sheets
1 tablespoon salt
Freshly ground black pepper, to taste
Extra-virgin olive oil, for drizzling

1. In a large soup pot or flameproof baking casserole over medium-high heat, add the pork fat and cook, stirring, until some fat has rendered in the bottom of the pot, about 5 minutes. Add the potatoes, cabbage, chard, onion, and garlic and cook, stirring, until the greens are wilted, about 5 minutes. Pour in the water, bring to a boil, then reduce the heat to low, add the beans, ham hock, and tomato, and cook, stirring every now and then, until the beans are tender, 2 to 3 hours.

2. Add the slices of bread or lasagne sheets and continue to cook until a spoon can stand straight up in the center of the soup or, if using lasagne, until the pasta is tender, about 15 minutes. Season with the salt and pepper, drizzle with olive oil, and serve.

Meatball and Yogurt Chowder

This exceedingly simple preparation can be whipped up in about 30 minutes. It will surprise you because you'll think you're tasting far more spices and ingredients than are actually in the chowder. At the end you need to be careful that the yogurt doesn't cook too much, as it will curdle, so only keep it on the stovetop long enough to heat it, then serve immediately.

5 cups water
One 15-ounce can chickpeas, rinsed and drained
¼ cup brown lentils
2½ teaspoons salt, or more as needed
1 teaspoon freshly ground black pepper, or more as needed
1 pound ground beef
1 medium onion, finely chopped
10 ounces baby spinach leaves
⅓ cup chopped fresh dill
3 cups whole-milk plain yogurt, whipped with a fork

1. In a large saucepan, bring the water to a boil over high heat with the chickpeas. Add the lentils, 2 teaspoons of the salt, and the pepper and boil, stirring occasionally, for 15 minutes.

2. Meanwhile, in a bowl, mix together the beef, onion, and remaining ½ teaspoon salt and form into walnut-size meatballs.

3. Reduce the heat to medium-low. Place the meatballs in the soup and stir to coat them. Cook the meatballs, turning occasionally, for 15 minutes.

4. Reduce the heat to low. Add the spinach and dill and cook, stirring and folding gently to immerse the leaves without breaking the meatballs, for another 5 minutes. Stir in the yogurt and cook only until it is heated through, about 2 minutes. Toss and correct the seasoning if necessary, then serve.

Barley Soup

This long-simmering thick soup is typical of a class of Persian soups that are really more like a medieval pottage. They are loaded with legumes and herbs and include only a little meat. It's a nice dinner soup for a cold evening.

¼ cup extra-virgin olive oil
1 large onion, finely chopped
2 large garlic cloves, crushed
½ teaspoon dried mint, rubbed in the palm of your hand to make it powdery
½ pound boneless leg of lamb or shoulder, diced
1 teaspoon salt
½ teaspoon ground turmeric
5 cups water
2 tablespoons dried red kidney beans
2 tablespoons brown lentils
2 tablespoons dried chickpeas
½ cup pearl barley
2 tablespoons long-grain rice
½ cup chopped spinach leaves
¼ cup chopped fresh flat-leaf parsley
¼ cup chopped fresh cilantro (coriander leaf)
¼ cup chopped fresh dill
½ cup whole-milk plain yogurt
Freshly ground black pepper, to taste

1. In a flameproof baking casserole, heat 1 tablespoon of the olive oil over medium-high heat, then add one-third of the onion and the garlic and cook, stirring almost constantly, until golden brown, 4 to 5 minutes. Remove from the casserole, add the mint to the onion-garlic mixture, and set aside.

2. Add the remaining 3 tablespoons olive oil to the casserole and heat over medium heat, then add the remaining onion and the lamb and cook, stirring, until the lamb loses its pinkness, about 6 minutes. Add the salt and turmeric. Pour in the water and add the kidney beans, lentils, and chickpeas. Bring to a boil over high heat, then reduce the heat to low, cover, and simmer, stirring occasionally, for 50 minutes.

3. Add the barley and rice and cook, stirring occasionally, for another 50 minutes. Add the spinach, parsley, cilantro, and dill and cook for another 50 minutes.

4. Stir a few tablespoons of soup broth into the yogurt and then stir the yogurt mixture into the soup along with pepper. Serve immediately with the onion-garlic mixture alongside for garnish.

Beggar's Soup

The Persian tradition behind this dish called "Beggar's Soup" is that long ago someone in need would leave an empty soup pot by the road, into which travelers would toss some coins so that the beggar could buy the ingredients for the soup. Today, visitors to a dinner bring an ingredient to throw into the soup pot. As with all Persian soups, called *ash*, they are thick pottage-like bowls rich in herbs and legumes.

6 teaspoons extra-virgin olive oil
3 large garlic cloves, crushed
¼ pound boneless beef chuck, diced
1 large onion, chopped
½ teaspoon ground turmeric
1 teaspoon salt
Freshly ground black pepper, to taste
6 cups water
¼ cup brown lentils
3 tablespoons dried red kidney beans
2 tablespoons dried chickpeas
2 tablespoons dried mung beans
2 tablespoons long-grain rice
¼ cup chopped spinach leaves
2 tablespoons finely chopped fresh flat-leaf parsley
2 tablespoons finely chopped fresh dill
2 tablespoons chopped scallions

1. In a flameproof baking casserole, heat 2 teaspoons of the oil over medium-high heat, then add the garlic and cook, stirring, until light golden, about 1½ minutes. Remove and set the garlic aside.

2. Add the remaining 4 teaspoons oil, then add the beef and onion and cook, stirring, until the beef loses its pinkness, about 6 minutes. Add the turmeric, salt, and pepper and stir, then add the water, lentils, red kidney beans, chickpeas, and mung beans. Cover and simmer over low heat for 1 hour.

3. Add the rice and cook for 20 minutes more. Add the spinach, parsley, dill, and 1 tablespoon of the scallions and cook, stirring occasionally, for 40 minutes. Taste to make sure everything is cooked through, and serve with the reserved crushed garlic and the remaining 1 tablespoon scallions.

Meatball and Spinach Soup

These delicious little balls of ground lamb and beef are poached in a chicken broth with spinach and cream, making for a very satisfying and rich soup.

¾ pound ground lamb
¾ pound ground beef
Salt and freshly ground black pepper, to taste
2 tablespoons extra-virgin olive oil
½ cup finely chopped onions
1 garlic clove, finely chopped
4 cups chicken broth
One 5-ounce bag baby spinach leaves, chopped
2 tablespoons pine nuts
1 cup heavy cream

1. In a bowl, knead the lamb, beef, salt, and pepper together with both hands and quickly form into walnut-size balls, keeping your hands wet with cold water so the meat doesn't stick. Set the meatballs aside.

2. In a large flameproof baking casserole, heat the olive oil over medium-high heat, then add the onions and cook, stirring occasionally, until translucent, about 6 minutes.

3. Add the meatballs to the casserole along with the garlic and shake the pan vigorously to keep the meatballs from sticking. Once the meatballs are browned on all sides, about 5 minutes, cook them for another 3 to 4 minutes, and then remove the meatballs and reserve. Discard all the accumulated fat with a spoon or ladle.

4. Add the chicken broth, chopped spinach, and pine nuts. Taste and correct the seasoning if necessary. Reduce the heat to medium and cook for 3 minutes. Return the meatballs to the casserole, add the cream, and cook until velvety, about 5 minutes. Serve immediately.

Vegetarian Dinners

||||||||||||||||||||||||||||||||||||||||||||||||||||||||||||||||||||||||||||||||||||||||||||||||||||||||||||||||||||||||||

In this chapter are meatless vegetarian dinner recipes chosen to satisfy all the omnivores as well. The first recipe, Jardinière Printanière (page 56), translates from the French as "the gardener's springtime vegetables," and it is a varied potpourri of deliciously fresh spring vegetables. Personally, I'm pretty wild about Vegetarian Dinner Pancakes (page 88), not only because they've got great flavor but also because I find the concept of savory pancakes so appealing; I'm sure you will, too. And if you're a meat eater who thinks vegetarian food isn't substantial enough, I'm sure you'll think differently when you sink your teeth into a Black Bean and Spinach Burrito (page 90) with all its rib-sticking goodness.

Jardinière Printanière

The French name of this dish tells you all you need to know about how and when to cook it. *Jardinière* means a gardener's style of mixed vegetables cut in sticks, while *printanière* means "springlike," meaning the vegetables are harvested tender and young in the spring. This is a perfect recipe for a farmers' market cornucopia. For the fullest flavor it's best to cook all the vegetables at the same time, although the green vegetables will not look as vibrant as they would should you add the peas and green beans after 20 minutes. It's up to you.

4 tablespoons (½ stick) unsalted butter
1 cup fresh peas
½ pound thin green beans, trimmed
½ pound baby carrots, scraped
½ pound new potatoes such as fingerling, white, Finn, or Yukon gold, peeled or unpeeled
½ pound baby turnips (preferably), scraped, or more mature turnips cut into 1-inch pieces
1 head butter or Bibb lettuce, shredded
2 cups water
2 tablespoons finely chopped fresh flat-leaf parsley
2 fresh thyme sprigs
Salt and freshly ground black pepper, to taste
2 tablespoons heavy cream

1. In a large sauté pan, melt the butter over medium-low heat. Add the peas, green beans, carrots, potatoes, and turnips and stir until coated with the butter. Add the lettuce, water, parsley, thyme, and salt and pepper and cook, stirring occasionally, until the lettuce looks melted and the root vegetables are tender, 50 to 55 minutes, adding a little water, if necessary, to keep the sauté pan from drying out. There should be almost no water left.

2. Remove from the heat, add the cream and incorporate, and transfer to a hot platter for serving.

Provençal Vegetable Dinner

Root vegetables are surprisingly filling, so this vegetable platter with its Provençal seasoning will be all you'll need for dinner. It's best served at room temperature.

For the dressing

¼ cup extra-virgin olive oil

2 tablespoons mayonnaise

1 tablespoon tarragon vinegar

1 garlic clove, finely chopped

1 teaspoon heavy cream

1 teaspoon herbes de Provence

½ teaspoon Dijon mustard

¼ teaspoon Worcestershire sauce

Salt and freshly ground black pepper, to taste

For the vegetables

Salt, to taste

Six 2½-inch diameter orange beets (1 pound)

1 pound carrots, scraped and cut into 2-inch chunks

One 2-pound cauliflower, trimmed

1 pound green beans, trimmed and cut into 2-inch lengths

¼ pound goat cheese

1. In a bowl, stir the dressing ingredients together.

2. For the vegetables, bring a large pot of water to a boil over high heat, lightly salt the water, and cook the beets for 25 minutes. Add the carrots and cook for 5 minutes, add the cauliflower and cook for 4 minutes, and then add the green beans and cook for 6 minutes. Test the beets by pushing a skewer into them; it should slide in easily. Drain the vegetables and set aside until cool enough to handle, then peel the beets and quarter them, and break the cauliflower up into florets.

3. Arrange all the vegetables attractively on a platter. Scatter the goat cheese around, drizzle the dressing over, and serve at room temperature.

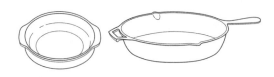

Potato and Vegetable Phyllo Skillet Pie

I like to make this dish in a round flameproof earthenware baking casserole, but a cast-iron skillet will work well, too. If you use a skillet the cooking times will be shorter. The entire dish can be prepared ahead of time and kept in the refrigerator until its final baking (just remember to take the earthenware out 30 minutes before baking). This recipe can also be made with any leftover vegetables, in which case they only need to be tossed in the casserole for 5 minutes to absorb all the spices. This recipe is based on a Moroccan dish and uses a typical Moroccan spice called *ras el hanout,* which in Morocco is a blend of up to twenty-seven different spices. The recipe in the box on page 60 is equally authentic, but less involved. You may also purchase ras el hanout blends. The dried rosebuds called for can be ordered by searching in the grocery and gourmet foods section of amazon.com.

½ cup extra-virgin olive oil

¾ pound small new potatoes such as fingerling, white, Finn, or Yukon gold, each about 1 inch in diameter, halved

¼ pound orange beets, peeled and diced

1 large carrot (about ¼ pound), scraped and diced

¾ cup cauliflower florets (2 ounces)

¾ cup green beans (2 ounces), diced

1 small onion, chopped

½ cup water

1 tablespoon honey

¾ cup sliced almonds (2 ounces)

1 tablespoon finely chopped fresh cilantro (coriander leaf)

1½ teaspoons ground rosebuds (about 4) or ½ teaspoon rose water (optional)

1 teaspoon ras el hanout (see box page 60)

1 teaspoon salt

½ teaspoon ground cinnamon

½ teaspoon ground ginger

Freshly ground black pepper, to taste

8 sheets phyllo pastry

1. Preheat the oven to 350°F.

2. In a 9- to 10-inch round flameproof earthenware baking casserole or a 10-inch cast-iron skillet, heat 2 tablespoons of the olive oil over medium heat, then add the potatoes, beets, carrots, cauliflower, and green beans and cook, stirring, until al dente and golden, about 20 minutes. (If using earthenware, you may need to use a heat diffuser. Earthenware heats up slower but retains its heat longer than other casseroles. When using earthenware, food may cook slower when first heating up and then cook very quickly and retain its heat longer.) Add 2 tablespoons of the oil to the skillet, then add the onion and cook, stirring, until translucent, about 5 minutes. Add the water and honey and cook until the water evaporates, about 5 minutes.

3. Add the almonds, cilantro, rosebuds, if using, ras el hanout, salt, cinnamon, ginger, and pepper and stir. Turn the heat off. Lay each sheet of phyllo over the vegetables, covering the vegetables completely and brushing each sheet with the remaining ¼ cup olive oil. As the phyllo leaves will be larger than the casserole or skillet, fold and tuck the excess overhang into the sides of the casserole. Place the casserole or skillet in the oven and bake until golden brown on top, 25 to 30 minutes. Serve hot.

Ras el Hanout

This complex spice blend used in Moroccan cooking (the name translates as "head of the shop") sometimes contains up to twenty-seven different spices. This is a simple version you can mix up, preferably using spices that you've ground yourself.

2 teaspoons ground cinnamon
1 teaspoon ground turmeric
½ teaspoon freshly ground black pepper
¼ teaspoon ground nutmeg
¼ teaspoon ground cardamom
¼ teaspoon ground cloves

Mix all the ingredients together and store in a spice jar. It will keep indefinitely but lose its pungency over time.

Makes about 4½ teaspoons

Tourlu

Tourlu is a Greek vegetable stew sometimes called *youvetsi* or *briami*. The stew is easy to prepare: Simply toss it all together and stick it in the oven. This dish is often eaten at room temperature.

1 pound tomatoes

1 red bell pepper

1 yellow bell pepper

1 green bell pepper

2 cups extra-virgin olive oil

1 large parsnip, peeled and cut into chunks

3 medium zucchini or 2 zucchini and 1 yellow summer squash, cut into thick rounds

1 medium red onion, cut into eighths

1 leek, white and light green parts only, split lengthwise, washed well, and coarsely chopped

½ fennel bulb, including leaves, coarsely chopped

2 large garlic cloves, finely chopped

3 tablespoons finely chopped fresh cilantro (coriander leaf)

⅛ teaspoon ground cinnamon

Salt and freshly ground black pepper, to taste

1. Preheat the oven to 425°F.

2. Place the tomatoes and bell peppers in a large earthenware casserole (preferably) or other baking casserole with a little water and roast until the skin blisters black on the peppers, 35 to 40 minutes. Remove the peppers and tomatoes and, when cool enough to handle, remove the seeds and peel off the skin of the peppers, and peel the skin from the tomatoes.

3. Reduce the oven temperature to 375°F.

4. In the same casserole, toss the bell peppers and tomatoes with the olive oil, parsnip, zucchini, red onion, leek, fennel, garlic, cilantro, and cinnamon, and season with salt and pepper. Place the casserole in the oven and bake until the parsnips are tender and portions of whatever vegetables on top are beginning to show black spots, 1¼ to 1¾ hours. Serve hot or let come to room temperature before serving.

Couscous with Vegetables

This simple Algerian couscous is made only with vegetables, although another version from the eastern Algerian town of Setif adds lamb shoulder and chicken legs to the mix. This recipe calls for instant or precooked couscous, which is what the box label will say.

¼ cup extra-virgin olive oil
1 medium onion, grated
2 large garlic cloves, very finely chopped
2 tablespoons tomato paste
1 teaspoon harīsa (page 140), plus more for garnish
½ teaspoon cayenne pepper
¼ teaspoon ground cumin
¼ teaspoon ground cinnamon
1 teaspoon salt
Freshly ground black pepper, to taste
5 to 6 quarts water
1 cup canned chickpeas, rinsed and drained
1 large turnip (1 pound), peeled and cut into 1-inch cubes
½ pound pumpkin or winter squash, peeled and cut into 1-inch cubes
2 cups instant or precooked couscous (from a package)
4 tablespoons (½ stick) unsalted butter, at room temperature
6 thin carrots (¾ pound), scraped and cut in half
4 small zucchini (¾ pound), quartered

1. In the bottom portion of a *couscousière* or in a large pot that can fit a colander on top, heat the olive oil over medium-high heat, then add the onion and garlic and cook, stirring frequently, until softened and golden, 2 to 3 minutes. Add the tomato paste, harīsa, cayenne pepper, cumin, cinnamon, salt, and pepper and cook, stirring, for 1 minute. Pour in 2 quarts of the water and the chickpeas, bring to a boil over high heat, and add the turnip and pumpkin. Reduce the heat to medium-high.

2. Put the couscous into the top part of the couscousière or a colander lined with cheesecloth. Place on top of the bottom part of a couscousière or the large pot, if using a colander, and cover with the lid. If using a colander and there is a space between the colander and the pot, wrap with a wet kitchen towel to seal the space. Steam the couscous for 20 minutes. Once you see steam rising from the couscous, add 1 tablespoon of the butter and 1 teaspoon salt, stir and fluff with a fork, and continue cooking, covered.

3. Add the carrots to the broth in the bottom portion, replenish it with some of the remaining water, and bring back to a boil, leaving the top part off. Add the zucchini to the broth, place the top part back on top, and cook until all the vegetables are softened, about 20 minutes. Remove the top part with the couscous, fluff the couscous with a fork, then carefully (so they don't break apart too much) remove the vegetables with a slotted spoon and place in a bowl. Add some more water to the broth, replace the top part or colander, and continue steaming the couscous, covered, until soft and fluffy, 50 to 60 minutes more. Add the reserved vegetables to the broth 10 minutes before the couscous is finished.

4. Transfer the couscous to a serving bowl and fold the remaining 3 tablespoons butter into the couscous. Once the butter is melted, stir with a fork until all the grains are glistening. Mound the couscous attractively in a large serving bowl or platter. Transfer the vegetables and broth to a tureen for serving. When diners serve themselves, have each person place 3 large spoonfuls of couscous into a bowl. Top with vegetables and two or three ladlefuls of broth. Add a dab of harīsa if desired and let the bowl sit to let the couscous and vegetables absorb some broth before eating.

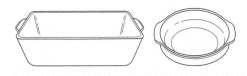

Baked Rice with Green Beans and Peas

This baked rice dish is made in an earthenware casserole, although you can use whatever baking casserole you have. Although completely satisfying as is, you could add shrimp to the rice. This recipe calls for canned or frozen artichoke hearts, but fresh is preferable; however, if that's too labor-intensive for you then skip the fresh ones.

¾ pound tomatoes, peeled, seeded, and chopped (see box page 47)
1½ cups medium-grain rice such as Calrose or short-grain rice such as Arborio
1 medium onion, chopped
½ pound fresh or frozen peas
½ pound green beans, trimmed and cut into 1-inch lengths
4 canned, frozen, or fresh artichoke hearts (foundations)
6 tablespoons extra-virgin olive oil
2 large garlic cloves, finely chopped
1½ teaspoons salt
Freshly ground black pepper, to taste
Pinch of saffron, crumbled
2 cups water
Allioli (see box page 388), for garnish

1. Preheat the oven to 350°F.

2. To a large baking casserole (preferably a round 12-inch earthenware casserole), add the tomatoes, rice, onion, peas, green beans, artichoke hearts, oil, garlic, salt, pepper, and saffron. Pour in the water, stir once, and bake until the water is absorbed and the rice is tender, without ever stirring, 45 to 60 minutes; the rice and the green beans should be tender. Serve hot with the allioli.

Eggplant Parmesan

There are many recipes for eggplant Parmesan, which is both a traditional Neapolitan dish and an old Italian-American favorite. This is my "simple" recipe in which the eggplants are not fried first. It's easy to assemble and although not as rich as the full-fledged version, it's quite satisfying.

One 32-ounce can tomato purée
1 medium onion, finely chopped
2 large garlic cloves, finely chopped
1 cup chopped fresh basil (from about 1 large bunch)
Salt and freshly ground black pepper, to taste
¼ cup extra-virgin olive oil
4 large eggplants (about 4 pounds), sliced ¼ inch thick
1 pound fresh mozzarella cheese, very thinly sliced or chopped
¼ pound freshly grated Parmesan cheese (preferably Parmigiano-Reggiano)
4 large eggs, beaten one at a time as needed

1. Preheat the oven to 350°F.

2. In a bowl, stir together the tomato purée, onion, garlic, and ¼ cup of the basil. Season with salt and pepper. Stir in 2 tablespoons of the olive oil.

3. Cover the bottom of a 13 × 9 × 2-inch baking casserole (or similar) with a few tablespoons of the tomato purée mixture and the remaining olive oil. Cover it with one layer of eggplant slices. Sprinkle on some mozzarella, Parmesan, basil, 1 beaten egg, salt, pepper, and tomato purée. Continue layering in this order until the eggplants are used up, finishing the last layer with a sprinkling of Parmesan cheese. Bake until bubbling and the Parmesan top is beginning to brown slightly, about 45 minutes. Serve hot or at room temperature.

Oven-Baked Vegetable Platter

This is a preparation from southern Italy called *gianfottere* for which there are many variations depending on seasonality. The secret to this dish is absolutely fresh vegetables, and if you can also use young heirloom-type vegetables, all the better. Although I provide some examples in the list of ingredients, you can make do with whatever is locally available. The slow baking process causes the vegetables to emit their natural sugars, and the whole dish is quite heavenly. Serve with warm crusty bread.

½ cup extra-virgin olive oil, plus more for oiling the caserole
8 young carrots (about ½ pound), scraped and trimmed slightly, leaving on
   a bit of their stem
4 new fingerling or new Yukon gold potatoes, about the size of a golf ball
   (about ¾ pound), halved
3 small red onions (about 1 pound), trimmed and cut in half lengthwise
5 small summer squash (about 1 pound), split in half lengthwise
2 large garlic cloves, crushed
3 tablespoons finely chopped fresh basil leaves
2 tablespoons finely chopped fresh oregano leaves
Pinch of saffron, crumbled in a mortar usaing a pestle with ½ teaspoon salt
½ teaspoon sugar
Salt and freshly ground black pepper, to taste
2 fresh rosemary sprigs
One ¾-pound ripe tomato, sliced

1. Preheat the oven to 350°F.

2. Lightly oil a 13 × 9 × 2-inch baking casserole. Arrange the carrots, potatoes, onions, and squash in the pan. Season with the garlic, basil, oregano, saffron, sugar, salt, and pepper. Stuff the rosemary sprigs in between the vegetables. Lay the tomato slices on top and season again with salt and pepper. Pour the remaining olive oil over the vegetables. Bake until the tomatoes look like they have melted and the potato and carrot can be pierced easily by a skewer but are not breaking apart, 1¼ to 1½ hours. Serve hot.

Roasted Root Vegetable Dinner

This slightly sweet vegetarian dinner is very satisfying and filling and would benefit from a simple green salad dressed with oil and vinegar on the side. The bulk and substance for the dish come from the squash; the red kabocha is not only pretty but also luscious and meaty and a nice contrast to the yams and parsnips.

½ cup extra-virgin olive oil

2 tablespoons honey

1 teaspoon chopped fresh marjoram or oregano

¼ teaspoon ground star anise or aniseed

One 3¾-pound red kabocha, butternut, or pumpkin squash, cut in half, seeded, peeled, and cut into 1½-inch pieces

1¼ pound yams, peeled and cut into 1½-inch pieces

1 pound parsnips, peeled and cut into 1½-inch pieces

½ pound young carrots, scraped

¼ pound walnuts

Salt and freshly ground black pepper, to taste

2 tablespoons finely chopped fresh flat-leaf parsley

2 teaspoons grated orange zest

1. Preheat the oven to 425°F.

2. In a small bowl, stir together the olive oil, honey, marjoram, and star anise. In a large bowl, toss the root vegetables and walnuts with the olive oil mixture, salt, and pepper. Transfer to a large roasting pan (use two pans if necessary to avoid crowding) or baking sheet and roast until tender, about 45 minutes. Sprinkle with the parsley and orange zest and serve hot.

"Hooded" Rice

This recipe from north of Barcelona in the Empordà along the Costa Brava is called *arròs caputxí* in Catalan, which means "hooded" rice; "hooded" the way a Capuchin monk's habit covers his head. I've adapted the recipe from one by the well-known Catalan writer Eliane Thibaud-Comelade. So, what is the "hood"? It's the peas and hard-boiled eggs and red bell pepper that reveal the rice underneath. This recipe serves a lot of people and it's perfect for a casual party.

3 medium onions, finely chopped

¼ cup water

½ cup extra-virgin olive oil

3 tomatoes, halved, seeds squeezed out, and grated against the largest holes of a grater into a bowl

4 roasted red bell peppers, peeled and seeded; 2 finely chopped and 2 cut into strips

6 large garlic cloves, finely chopped

6 tablespoons finely chopped fresh flat-leaf parsley

1 teaspoon saffron threads, crumbled in a mortar using a pestle with 3 teaspoons salt

1 tablespoon sweet paprika

Salt and freshly ground black pepper, to taste

3 cups medium-grain rice such as Calrose or short-grain rice such as Arborio

6 cups boiling water

3 cups fresh peas, cooked until almost soft, or defrosted frozen peas cooked in boiling water for 3 minutes and drained

6 large hard-boiled eggs, shelled and sliced into rounds

1. Preheat the oven to 375°F.

2. To a large earthenware casserole (preferably) or any large flameproof baking casserole, add the onions and the ¼ cup water, turn the heat to high, and cook, stirring, until the water has nearly evaporated and the onions have softened, about 12 minutes. (If using earthenware and it is not cooktop-safe, you will need to use a heat diffuser. Earthenware heats up slower but retains its heat longer than other casseroles. When using earthenware, food may cook slower at first and then cook very quickly and retain its heat longer.) Add the olive oil and cook, stirring, until the onions are translucent, about 5 minutes. Add the tomatoes, chopped bell peppers, garlic, parsley, and saffron mixture, and season with the paprika, salt, and pepper. Cook until the liquid has evaporated and the mixture looks mushy but is not sticking to the casserole, about 25 minutes.

3. Add the rice to the casserole, mix well, and add the boiling water. Bake until about three-quarters cooked (when the rice is pushed aside with a fork in the center, you will see that it is still quite moist), about 30 minutes, without stirring the rice. Cover the top of the rice completely with the peas, so the rice is hidden, and continue cooking until there is no liquid left and the rice is tender, about another 10 minutes. Remove from the oven and garnish the top with the slices of hard-boiled egg and the strips of red bell pepper placed in spoke fashion. Serve hot, although it will remain warm for a long time.

Quinoa Stew

This spicy-hot stew from Peru is a nice way to introduce eaters to the famous South American grain quinoa (pronounced KEEN-wa). This version is an all-vegetable one, but many cooks will add small amounts of beef or lamb and even fish. You can make this in a stewpot, a large flame-proof baking casserole, or any large pot.

3 large garlic cloves
1 teaspoon salt
½ teaspoon freshly ground black pepper
1 cup quinoa
4 cups very hot water
2 tablespoons unsalted butter
1 medium onion, finely chopped
1 teaspoon ground red chile or cayenne pepper
½ teaspoon ground cumin
½ teaspoon hot paprika
1 pound Yukon gold, red, or white potatoes, peeled and cut into ½-inch cubes
1 cup whole milk
1 cup fresh corn kernels (from about 1 ear of corn)
½ cup fresh or frozen peas
¼ pound cheddar cheese, shredded
2 large eggs, lightly beaten
2 tablespoons finely chopped fresh mint
2 tablespoons finely chopped fresh cilantro (coriander leaf)
1 ripe avocado, cut in half, pitted, flesh scooped out and cut into ¼-inch dice

1. Using a mortar and pestle, pound the garlic with the salt and pepper.

2. To a large saucepan, add the quinoa, cover with 3½ cups of the hot water, and bring to a boil over high heat. Cover, reduce the heat to low, and simmer until the quinoa has absorbed all the water, about 12 minutes. Remove all the quinoa from the saucepan with a rubber spatula and reserve.

3. Place the butter in the saucepan and melt over low heat. Add the onion and cook, stirring occasionally, until translucent, about 8 minutes. Stir in the garlic paste, ground chile, cumin, and paprika and cook, stirring, for 1 minute. Add the remaining ½ cup hot water, reserved quinoa, and potatoes and simmer, partially covered, until the potatoes are tender, about 20 minutes. Add the milk, corn kernels, and peas and simmer for 5 minutes. Add the cheese and eggs and cook, stirring constantly but very gently (you don't want to scramble the eggs, you want to whirl them), until the cheese has melted and the eggs have set. Serve hot with the mint, cilantro, and avocado alongside for sprinkling on top.

Sardinian Vegetable Stew

Sardinian food is simple, local, and emphasizes fresh vegetables and, to a lesser extent, fish. This earthy vegetable stew has rich aromatic flavors and is all you need for a wonderful dinner. The secret behind this stew is the pesto used in the initial frying. Serve with crusty French or Italian bread.

½ bunch fresh flat-leaf parsley, leaves only (a good-size handful)
1 large garlic clove
½ cup extra-virgin olive oil
1 pound small white onions
1 ripe tomato (about ½ pound), peeled, seeded, and chopped (see box page 47)
6 fresh basil leaves
Salt, to taste
1 pound small new potatoes (any kind), peeled
1 pound green beans, trimmed

1. In a mortar, pound the parsley and garlic with the pestle until the pesto mixture is mushy.

2. In a large flameproof baking casserole, heat the olive oil over medium-high heat, then add the whole onions and cook, stirring, until yellow, about 4 minutes. Reduce the heat to low. Quickly stir in the garlic and parsley pesto so it doesn't burn from the hot casserole. Let it sizzle for 1 minute, and then stir in the tomato and basil. Cook for 30 minutes, covered, over low heat.

3. Season the stew with salt and add the potatoes and green beans. Cover and simmer until the potatoes are easily pierced with the tip of a skewer, about 1 hour. Serve from the casserole.

Lentils with Spinach, Ginger, and Tamarind

This Indian-influenced dish is a meal in itself, but leftovers make for a nice side dish. Although an easy dish to make, some of the timing is exact, so pay attention. One goal you should set for yourself is to watch the cooking of the spinach so that it stays a bright, appetizing green and doesn't overcook into an olive drab color. Tamarind pods and paste are found in Indian markets or on the Internet at www.friedas.com.

1½ cups green or brown lentils, rinsed and drained
2¾ cups water
1 teaspoon salt
6 tablespoons vegetable oil
2 or 3 fresh green serrano chiles (seeded or not), thinly sliced
One ¾-inch piece fresh ginger, peeled and finely chopped
2 ounces (about 1 bunch) fresh cilantro (coriander leaf), chopped
1½ pounds spinach, trimmed of heavy stems and coarsely chopped
Seeds from 2 dried tamarind pods, soaked in ¼ cup hot water for 15 minutes, tamarind flesh rubbed off seeds, seed cores discarded; or 1-inch cube tamarind paste, soaked in ¼ cup hot water for 15 minutes
3 tablespoons fresh lemon juice
Freshly ground black pepper, to taste

1. Put the lentils in a saucepan large enough to hold all the raw spinach, too and cover with the water. Bring to a boil over high heat, add the salt, cover, reduce the heat to low, and simmer until tender, about 25 minutes. There should be no water left. If there is, drain the lentils and return them to the saucepan. If the water evaporated before the lentils are tender, add ½ cup hot water and finish cooking.

2. Add the vegetable oil, increase the heat to medium, and let it heat through. Add the chiles and ginger and cook, stirring, until sizzling vigorously, about 20 seconds. Add the cilantro, spinach, and tamarind, stir, cover, and simmer until the spinach has wilted, turning occasionally, about 10 minutes. Add the lemon juice and pepper, stir, and cook, uncovered, for 5 minutes. Serve hot.

Lenten Vegetable Stew

There are so many fast days in the Greek Orthodox Church that it sometimes seems like every dish is tied to a religious holiday. In every region of Greece there is a variety of Lenten stews made without meat, of course. The variations are based on local produce, and always fresh vegetables. Typically, a lot of olive oil is used in a vegetable stew. Cumin, pepper, coriander, allspice, and dried herbs are used in winter stews, while fresh dill, parsley, savory, thyme, and mint are used in the summer. It's typical to serve Greek-style vegetable stews at room temperature with crusty bread.

2 tablespoons unsalted butter

½ cup extra-virgin olive oil

1 large onion, chopped

2 Yukon gold, red, or white potatoes, peeled and coarsely diced

3 zucchini, cut into 2-inch-thick pieces

½ pound green beans, trimmed and cut in half

4 large ripe tomatoes (about 1½ pounds), quartered

8 scallions, trimmed and cut into 1-inch pieces, including the dark green part

1 cup chopped fresh flat-leaf parsley

2 tablespoons finely chopped fresh mint

1 teaspoon dried oregano

1 teaspoon salt

Freshly ground black pepper, to taste

1 bay leaf

2 cups water

1 pound spinach, trimmed of heavy stems

1. In a large flameproof baking casserole, melt the butter with the olive oil over medium heat, then add the onion and cook, stirring, until softened, 5 to 6 minutes. Add the potatoes, zucchini, green beans, tomatoes, scallions, parsley, mint, oregano, salt, pepper, and bay leaf and toss so they are coated with butter and oil.

2. Add the water, bring to a boil, then reduce the heat to low, cover, and cook, stirring occasionally, until the potatoes are tender, about 45 minutes. Add the spinach, cover again, and once it wilts, about 5 minutes, remove the casserole from the burner. Remove and discard the bay leaf. Serve hot or at room temperature.

Coconut Mung Bean Dal

This vegetarian dinner is simple and easy to cook. Meat lovers might look at it and think "no thanks," but they would be too quick to judge because dals are very satisfying food. Whenever I eat legumes I feel just as full and content as when I eat a steak, especially when they are seasoned in such a flavorful way as this dish from the Indian state of Goa. If you can't find dried mung beans, you may use black lentils. I like to serve this preparation along with Mango and Cucumber Salad (page 9).

¼ cup vegetable oil

4 small onions, 2 thinly sliced and 2 grated

2½ cups dried mung beans (about 1¼ pounds), soaked in water for 1 hour (soaking optional) and then drained

2 quarts boiling water

¾ cup unsweetened grated coconut

4 large fresh serrano chiles, finely chopped

2 bay leaves, crumbled

2¼ teaspoons salt

½ teaspoon ground cumin

½ teaspoon ground turmeric

1. In a large flameproof baking casserole, heat the vegetable oil over medium heat, then add the sliced onions and cook, stirring frequently and making sure they don't burn, for 8 to 9 minutes. Remove the onions and set aside on a paper towel–lined platter.

2. Add the mung beans to the casserole and cover with the water. Bring to a boil over high heat, then reduce the heat to medium and cook, stirring occasionally, until the beans are tender and very little water remains, 1 to 1¼ hours. Attend to the beans more closely as the water is nearly evaporated and absorbed so that they don't stick and burn.

3. Stir in the coconut, chiles, grated onions, bay leaves, salt, cumin, and turmeric. Stir well and simmer, covered, over very low heat for 5 minutes. Stir the reserved onions into the saucepan and serve.

Bavarian Vegetable Stew

From the mid-1950s as a child to the late 1960s as an unaccompanied teenager and throughout the 1970s as a university student, I traveled extensively in Germany, both as a traveler and when I lived in Basel, Switzerland, and later Salzburg, Austria. This kind of vegetable stew I loved to have with sausages or really any kind of meat, but especially pork. It all sounds so simple, and in fact sounds like it doesn't have a lot of flavor, but it does because the mix of vegetables is a good one, and the heavy lid traps all the flavors. In Bavaria they call this preparation *Gemüse-Pichelsteiner*. I almost never see parsley root in the market, but should you find it, it's a very nice and authentic addition to this stew.

6 tablespoons (¾ stick) unsalted butter
4 carrots, scraped and sliced into ⅜-inch-thick slices
¼ cup finely chopped fresh flat-leaf parsley
Salt and freshly ground black pepper, to taste
1 large celery root, peeled and sliced into ¼-inch-thick slices
1 parsley root, peeled and sliced into ¼-inch-thick slices (optional)
4 leeks, split lengthwise, washed well, and sliced
1 small cauliflower, trimmed, cored, and broken into florets
½ pound snap peas
½ pound green beans, trimmed and cut into 1-inch pieces
½ head savoy or green cabbage, cored and thinly sliced
1 pound potatoes (any kind), peeled and sliced into ¼-inch-thick slices
1½ cups water

1. In a large flameproof baking casserole, melt 3 tablespoons of the butter over medium-high heat, then turn the heat off and layer the carrots on the bottom. Season with a little of the parsley, salt, and pepper. Continue layering with the vegetables in the order in which they are listed in the ingredient list, sprinkling each layer with parsley, salt, and pepper. The last layer should be of potatoes followed by a sprinkle of parsley. Dot the top of the potatoes with the remaining 3 tablespoons butter.

2. Pour the water over, cover tightly, bring to a boil, then reduce the heat to low and cook until all the vegetables are tender, about 1 hour.

Hindu Vegetarian Stew

This is the classic Hindu vegetarian stew called *avial* from the Indian state of Kerala, on the south-western tip of the subcontinent, which is known for its spicy foods. This recipe is spicy; however, the counterpoint to the heat is found in the sweetness of the mango. Do not add the yogurt to the stew until the end and then only to heat it; otherwise it will separate if it cooks. Serve with griddled naan.

1 tablespoon coconut oil (preferably), grapeseed oil, safflower oil, or vegetable oil

1 small eggplant (about ½ pound), peeled and cut into 1-inch cubes

1 small sweet potato (about ½ pound), peeled and cut into 1-inch cubes

1 cup green beans, trimmed and cut into 1-inch lengths

½ cup fresh or frozen peas

1 carrot, scraped and sliced

1 small onion, sliced

½ cup seeded and chopped green bell pepper

2 fresh jalapeño chiles, seeded or not, finely chopped

¾ teaspoon ground turmeric

¼ teaspoon ground cumin

1 cup water

1 teaspoon salt

1 medium tomato, peeled and diced

Pulp of ½ mango, diced

⅓ cup unsweetened grated coconut

1 cup whole-milk plain yogurt

1 tablespoon unsalted butter, at room temperature

1. In a stewpot, combine the oil with the eggplant, sweet potato, green beans, peas, carrot, onion, bell pepper, chiles, turmeric, and cumin. Add the water and salt, bring to a boil, reduce the heat to low, and simmer until the vegetables are softened and very little water remains, 1 to 1¼ hours.

2. Add the tomato, mango, and coconut, stir, and simmer until they blend into the stew, about 15 minutes. Remove from the heat, stir in the yogurt and butter, taste and correct the seasoning, and serve.

Summer Vegetable Stew

This summer vegetable stew is a meal in itself and can be eaten at room temperature if you like. The key to the dish (besides very fresh vegetables) is using very ripe tomatoes filled with juice. These will not be available in your supermarket, so if you don't grow your own or buy them at the farmers' market you'll need to use canned whole tomatoes.

½ cup extra-virgin olive oil

1 medium onion, thinly sliced

2 pounds large very ripe tomatoes, peeled, seeded, and chopped,
    with all their juice

4 long fresh mild green chiles (peperoncini or New Mexico/Anaheim),
    cored, seeded, and coarsely chopped

1 fresh red chile, seeded and very finely chopped

3 large garlic cloves, pounded using a mortar and pestle with 1 teaspoon salt

1 Yukon gold potato (about ½ pound), peeled, halved, and then
    sliced into ¼-inch pieces

2 medium zucchini, peeled in zebra stripes and cut into 1-inch chunks

2 cucumbers, peeled, seeded, and cut into 1-inch chunks

Salt and freshly ground black pepper, to taste

1 cup fresh green peas

¾ pound spinach, trimmed of heavy stems, if desired

1. In an earthenware casserole (preferably) or any flameproof baking casserole, heat the olive oil over medium-high heat, then add the onion and cook, stirring, until translucent, about 5 minutes. (If using earthenware and it is not flameproof, you will need to use a heat diffuser. Earthenware heats up slower but retains its heat longer than other casseroles. When using earthenware, food may cook slower at first and then cook very quickly and retain its heat longer.) Add the tomatoes, all the chiles, and the garlic and continue to cook, stirring, until the chiles begin to soften, about 12 minutes.

2. Add the potato and cook until it starts to soften, about 5 minutes. Reduce the heat to low, add the zucchini and cucumbers, season with salt and pepper, and cook, covered, until the potatoes are softened, about 40 minutes. Add the peas and continue to cook until tender, about 10 minutes. Add the spinach and cook until it wilts, 4 to 5 minutes. Let the stew rest in the casserole for 15 minutes before serving.

Mixed Vegetable Stew

The sheer variety of vegetables and spicing makes this vegetable stew a winner. Buy the freshest vegetables you can and you won't be sorry. Notice that the olive oil called for is not the more expensive and finer quality extra-virgin olive oil, because in this preparation it is not necessary, although if you have access to an inexpensive extra-virgin olive oil, by all means use it.

2 cups olive oil

2 zucchini (about 9 ounces), trimmed, split lengthwise, and cut into 2-inch slices

2 green bell peppers, seeded and cut into 1½-inch squares

1 cup okra, trimmed

1 cup green beans trimmed and cut into 1-inch pieces

2 medium onions, cut into ⅜-inch slices

1 large eggplant (about 1 pound), peeled and cut into ½-inch slices

2 teaspoons salt, or more as needed

½ teaspoon freshly ground black pepper

½ teaspoon ground cinnamon

4 large garlic cloves, finely chopped

½ cup finely chopped fresh cilantro (coriander leaf)

3 tomatoes (about 1½ pounds), peeled and cut into ¾-inch slices

1. In a large earthenware casserole (preferably) or any flameproof baking casserole, heat the olive oil over medium-high heat, then cook each vegetable in turn until lightly golden (be sure to fry the eggplant last). The zucchini will take 2 to 3 minutes, the bell peppers 4 to 5 minutes, the okra 2 to 3 minutes, the green beans 2 minutes, the onions 4 to 5 minutes, and the eggplant about 6 minutes. Remove each vegetable to a platter, being sure to drain thoroughly with a skimmer, and set aside as you continue cooking. (If using earthenware and it is not flameproof, you will need to use a heat diffuser. Earthenware heats up slower but retains its heat longer than other casseroles. When using earthenware, food may cook slower at first and then cook very quickly while retaining its heat.)

2. Preheat the oven to 350°F.

3. Layer the eggplant back in the casserole, then layer in the cooked zucchini, onions, and okra. Season with some of the salt and pepper and half the cinnamon. Layer the bell peppers and beans in the casserole and season with the remaining salt, pepper, and cinnamon. Sprinkle with the garlic and cilantro and cover with the tomato slices. Sprinkle some water on top. Cover and bake until the tomatoes have collapsed and the liquid is boiling furiously, about 1¼ hours.

4. Remove from the oven and cool in the casserole until it reaches room temperature. If you like, you can remove some of the liquid in the casserole. In any case, serve warm or at room temperature.

Spanish Ratatouille

This famous vegetable stew from La Mancha is called *pisto* and always contains tomatoes, bell peppers, and zucchini. There are versions of *pisto* all around Spain, and its similarity to ratatouille is self-evident. Some cooks like to add previously fried bacon chunks to turn the dish into a light supper. Alternatively, it is also very good with a couple of fried eggs on top. Another way to serve this one-pot meal is at room temperature as a tapa with small pieces of toasted bread. My favorite way of eating it is warm—neither hot nor cool.

½ cup extra-virgin olive oil
1 large onion, finely chopped
2 large garlic cloves, finely chopped
4 green bell peppers, seeded and cut into small pieces
1 pound zucchini, cut into small pieces
1 pound ripe tomatoes, peeled, seeded, and chopped (see box page 47)
2 tablespoons finely chopped fresh flat-leaf parsley
¼ teaspoon sugar
1 teaspoon salt

1. In a large flameproof baking casserole or large sauté pan, heat the olive oil over medium-high heat, then add the onion and garlic and cook, stirring frequently so the garlic doesn't burn, until translucent, about 5 minutes. Add the bell peppers and cook until softer but still firm, about 10 minutes. Add the zucchini and cook until the pieces are also softer but still firm, about 15 minutes.

2. Add the tomatoes, reduce the heat to low, and simmer, stirring occasionally, until the juice of the tomatoes has evaporated, about 30 minutes. Stir in the parsley and sugar and season with the salt. Cook for another 5 minutes and serve.

Stew of Potatoes, White Beans, and Rice

This stew is as thick and rib-sticking as a stew without meat can get. It's rustic, simple, filling, and hearty. This stew should be somewhat soupy by the end of the cooking time, so if it isn't pour in a little water. For a meat version, add slices of cooked sausage or cooked ham.

1 cup (½ pound) dried white beans
4 cups water, or as needed
1 medium-large onion (10 ounces), chopped
6 large garlic cloves, finely chopped
3 tablespoons extra-virgin olive oil
1 bay leaf
¾ pound potatoes (any kind), peeled and diced
2¼ teaspoons salt
½ cup medium-grain rice such as Calrose or short-grain rice such as Arborio
1 teaspoon hot or sweet paprika

1. Place the beans in a large saucepan or stewpot and pour in 3 cups of the water. Add the onion, garlic, olive oil, and bay leaf. Bring to a boil, then reduce the heat to low, cover, and simmer for 1 hour.

2. Add the potatoes and salt, then cook until almost tender, 20 minutes. Add the rice and paprika, bring to a boil, reduce the heat to low, cover, and cook until the rice is tender, about 15 minutes. Check the soup's consistency and if it is thick, dilute it with the remaining 1 cup water to make the stew soupy. Remove from the heat, remove and discard the bay leaf, and let stand, uncovered, for 5 minutes before serving.

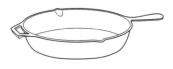

Vegetarian Dinner Pancakes

At first it will seem like this recipe can't work, that you won't have enough batter, but trust me: It will. This is a great dish. The secret to the dish is twofold: First, slice the chiles and bell peppers thinly, and second, once you put the vegetables and batter into the skillet and spread it to the sides evenly, don't touch it until instructed to. If you can't find red jalapeños, use green ones and change the green bell peppers to red ones. If you double the recipe, make sure you cook four pancakes and not two big ones. Keep the pancakes warm in a low oven as you cook them all.

1 cup all-purpose flour

2 large eggs

¾ cup water

¼ pound scallions, trimmed and cut into 3-inch pieces (about 2 cups)

2 large fresh red jalapeño chiles, seeded and thinly sliced lengthwise

2 green bell peppers, seeded and thinly sliced lengthwise

½ teaspoon salt

3 tablespoons vegetable oil

Soy sauce, for garnish

1. Preheat a large cast-iron skillet over medium heat.

2. In a bowl, stir together the flour, eggs, and water until they have the consistency of a crêpe batter, stirring all the time until smooth. Add the scallions, chiles, bell peppers, and salt, and blend well with the batter.

3. Add 1½ tablespoons of the oil to the skillet, let it heat for a minute, then pour in half the batter and vegetables (mixing before doing so), spreading it thin in the skillet. Cook on one side without stirring, flipping, lifting, or looking until golden brown on the bottom, about 7 minutes. Turn with a spatula in one flip and continue cooking until golden on the other side, 6 to 7 minutes. Remove and keep warm. Add the remaining oil to the skillet, let it heat, add the remaining vegetables and batter, and cook. The second pancake will not need as much time as the first because the skillet will have become hotter, so figure about 5 minutes for the first side and 4 minutes for the second. Cut each pancake into quarters and serve with soy sauce.

Black Bean and Spinach Burritos

This vegetarian burrito is full of spicy, satisfying flavor. You can replace the mildly hot Anaheim chiles with a red bell pepper if you want, and the cream cheese may be replaced with shredded Colby cheese. Served with sliced avocado and sour cream, it's a meal in itself.

3 fresh Anaheim/New Mexico chiles

Four 12-inch flour tortillas

2 tablespoons extra-virgin olive oil

1 small onion, chopped

1 large garlic clove, finely chopped

1 fresh serrano chile, seeded and sliced

1 pound spinach leaves, coarsely chopped

One 15-ounce can black beans, rinsed and drained

¾ teaspoon ground cumin

½ teaspoon salt

¼ teaspoon sweet paprika

Freshly ground black pepper, to taste

3 ounces cream cheese

3 tablespoons chopped fresh cilantro (coriander leaf)

1 cup sour cream

1 avocado, cut in half, pitted, flesh scooped out and sliced or cubed

1. Preheat the oven to 350°F.

2. Place the Anaheim chiles on a rack set over a burner on high heat and roast until their skins blister black on all sides, turning occasionally with tongs. Remove the chiles and place in a paper or heavy plastic bag to steam for 20 minutes, which will make peeling them easier. When cool enough to handle, rub off as much blackened peel as you can and remove the seeds by rubbing with a paper towel (to avoid washing away flavorful juices) or by rinsing under running water (to remove more easily). Chop the chiles.

3. Wrap the burritos in aluminum foil and heat in the oven for 15 minutes.

4. In a large sauté pan, heat the oil over medium heat, then add the onion, roasted Anaheim chiles, garlic, and serrano chile and cook, stirring, until softened, about 3 minutes. Add the spinach in handfuls and the black beans and cook, stirring, until the spinach is wilted, about 7 minutes. Season with the cumin, salt, paprika, and pepper. Add the cream cheese and cook, stirring occasionally, until the cheese softens, about 2 minutes. Stir in the cilantro.

5. Spoon the mixture in the middle of each of the tortillas. Fold the tortillas over the filling once, then fold the two sides over into the middle and continue rolling. Serve immediately with the sour cream and avocado.

Scrambled Egg and Black Bean Burritos

When I mentioned this burrito to my son, he wanted to know if it was for breakfast. Although you could make it for breakfast, it's really a supper burrito. It's filling yet not overly so, very satisfying, and surprisingly easy to make.

2 tablespoons unsalted butter

6 large eggs

2 tablespoons extra-virgin olive oil

½ pound potato (any kind), peeled and diced

1 small onion, chopped

1 pound Swiss chard, leaves removed from stems and coarsely chopped

1 fresh green serrano chile, seeded or not, sliced

One 29-ounce can black beans, rinsed and drained

1 teaspoon ground cumin

¼ pound Monterey Jack cheese, shredded

¼ cup chopped fresh cilantro (coriander leaf)

Salt and freshly ground black pepper, to taste

Four 12-inch flour tortillas

Sour cream, for garnish

Sliced avocado, for garnish

1. In a large nonstick pan, melt the butter over medium-high heat. Add the eggs and cook, constantly folding the eggs over on themselves with a silicone spatula, until scrambled but moist and not dry. Remove and reserve.

2. Add the olive oil to the pan and heat. Add the potato and onion and cook, stirring occasionally, until crispy golden brown, about 10 minutes. Add the Swiss chard in handfuls and the serrano chile and cook until the chard wilts. Stir in the black beans and cumin and cook until heated through. Remove from the heat, and fold in the eggs, cheese, and cilantro. Season with salt and pepper. Let the heat of the vegetables melt the cheese.

3. Heat the tortillas over a burner for 30 seconds, then lay a tortilla in front of you and spoon some filling on the bottom third. Fold over once away from you, tightly, then fold the left and right sides into the middle and continue rolling up tightly. Continue with the remaining tortillas. Serve hot with sour cream and avocado.

Beef

Beef is ideally suited for one-vessel cookery because if it is stew beef it goes into a stewpot and if it's a steak it goes into a skillet. A stunning example of the first is the Daube Languedocienne (page 122), a classic French slowly braised beef stew with tomatoes, garlic, and wild mushrooms. One of my favorite examples of the second is the first recipe in this chapter, Pan-Seared Rib-Eye Steak with Scallion Pancakes (page 96), which will change your ideas about your cast-iron skillet, about steaks, and about pancakes and their uses. Another ideal cooking vessel for one-pot cookery is the wok, in which you can make more than Chinese stir-fries. For example, the He-Man Beef and Chile Stir-Fry (page 102) is so-named because it's all about beef and chile, an explosive combo and a delicious dish that'll put hair on your chest. Another favorite certainly will be the Korean Braised Short Ribs and Kimchi Sandwich with Wasabi Mayonnaise (page 108), which, although it only involves braising the beef, ends up being one of the most spectacularly good sandwiches you'll ever have and substantial enough to be called dinner. Have fun in this chapter!

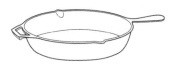

Pan-Seared Rib-Eye Steak with Scallion Pancakes

In this recipe, everything is cooked in a cast-iron skillet. It's pancakes first and steak second, cooked in batches. Chives and scallions are both quite common in Korean cooking and much loved in a variety of dishes. One of my favorite dishes is scallion pancakes, which I ordered in the first Korean restaurant I had ever been to, and I still love them. Here they're the perfect foundation for juicy rib-eye steaks.

1 cup all-purpose flour
2 large eggs
¾ cup water
16 scallions, white and green parts, sliced 2 inches long (about 2 cups)
2 fresh red jalapeño chiles, seeded and thinly sliced lengthwise
½ teaspoon salt, plus more as needed
3 tablespoons vegetable oil
2 rib-eye steaks (about 2 pounds), pounded until ¾ inch thick
Freshly ground black pepper, to taste
Soy sauce, for garnish

1. Preheat a 12-inch cast-iron skillet over medium heat for 10 minutes.

2. Meanwhile, in a bowl, stir together the flour, eggs, and water until they are the consistency of a crêpe batter. Add the scallions, jalapeño chiles, and the salt and blend well with the batter.

3. Pour 1½ tablespoons of the oil into the skillet and let it heat for 5 minutes. Pour in half the batter, spread it thin in the skillet, and cook on one side without stirring, flipping, lifting, or looking until golden brown on the bottom, about 7 minutes. Turn with a spatula in one flip and continue cooking until golden on the other side, 6 to 7 minutes. Remove and keep warm. Add the remaining oil to the skillet, let it heat for a minute or two, and cook the remaining pancake.

4. Increase the heat to high and let it heat for 2 minutes. Cook the steaks, individually if necessary, until crispy and blackened on both sides, turning once, about 10 minutes in all. Remove and season with salt and pepper. Cut each pancake into quarters and each steak in half and serve with the soy sauce on the side.

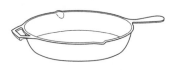

Skillet Steak with Peppers and Mushrooms

This is one of the simplest recipes in this book, and you'll notice how few ingredients there are. Don't be tempted to start adding things—it just doesn't need it, as these particular ingredients will provide the entire flavor you need. I usually serve this with a simple side salad of butter lettuce, endive, and dill with an oil-and-vinegar dressing. However, you could also serve the final dish with warm tortillas for wrapping or a thick slice of toasted French or Italian country bread to act as a kind of trencher.

¼ cup extra-virgin olive oil
1 pound brown mushrooms, sliced
2 large fleshy red bell peppers (1 pound), seeded and cut into strips
2 large fleshy green bell peppers (1 pound), seeded and cut into strips
2 large garlic cloves, finely chopped
Salt and freshly ground black pepper, to taste
One 1¼-pound flank steak

1. Preheat a 12-inch cast-iron skillet over medium-high heat.

2. Add the olive oil and then the mushrooms, bell peppers, and garlic to the skillet. Reduce the heat to medium-low and cook, stirring, until softened, about 45 minutes. Season with salt and pepper. Remove all the vegetables and set aside, making sure there are no bits left in the skillet.

3. Increase the heat to high. Season the flank steak with salt and pepper, place in the skillet, and press down with a spatula as it cooks or place a smaller cast-iron skillet on top of it. Cook until crispy golden brown on both sides, 8 minutes in all for rare. Cook for a minute or two longer for medium-rare. Turn the heat off. Transfer the steak to a cutting board and let rest for 2 minutes.

4. Return the vegetables to the skillet to heat while you thinly slice the steak. Arrange the steak strips on a platter or individual plate and either top with the vegetables or place them on the side and serve.

Sirloin Tips with Peppers and Cheese

You can use either a skillet or a wok for this very simple dish that's perfect for a harried midweek dinner when you don't want to put in too much effort. It all cooks quickly, and, more important, is very satisfying. All the cooked ingredients are wrapped in warm tortillas, served two per person.

3 tablespoons extra-virgin olive oil
5 green bell peppers, seeded and cut into thin strips
1¾ pounds sirloin tip, cut into thin strips
1 teaspoon ground cumin
Salt and freshly ground black pepper, to taste
Eight 12-inch flour tortillas, warmed
2 cups shredded Monterey Jack cheese (about 6 ounces)

1. In a large sauté pan or wok, heat the olive oil over high heat. Add the bell peppers and cook, tossing and stirring, until softened, about 8 minutes. Add the sirloin tip, cumin, salt, and pepper and cook, tossing or stirring, until browned, about 6 minutes.

2. Meanwhile, have the tortillas warming in the oven. Sprinkle each warm tortilla with some cheese and spoon the beef and pepper mixture on top. Roll up the tortillas and serve two per person.

Beef Rags on a Raft

The "raft" is a piece of pan-fried bread that acts as the foundation for the ingredients, which get cooked in succession, one after the other, and then piled on top of one another, the beef on top so the juices drip down on all the vegetables. The "rags" are the slices of beef. For a milder dish, replace the red jalapeño chiles with a second red bell pepper.

¼ cup extra-virgin olive oil
4 slices round Italian or French country bread (6 ounces)
1 medium onion, sliced
1 red bell pepper, seeded and sliced
1 pound button (white) mushrooms, sliced
2 large garlic cloves, finely chopped
4 large fresh red jalapeño chiles, seeded and sliced
1 teaspoon ground fennel seeds
Salt and freshly ground black pepper, to taste
1 pound beef tri-tip or flank steak, thinly sliced into 2 × 1-inch pieces
½ bunch fresh cilantro (coriander leaf), chopped

1. In a 12-inch nonstick pan, heat 1 tablespoon of the olive oil over high heat, then cook the bread slices until golden on both sides, about 5 minutes total. Transfer to individual ovenproof dinner plates or an ovenproof platter.

2. Add another 2 tablespoons of the olive oil to the pan, then add the onion, bell pepper, mushrooms, garlic, jalapeño chiles, and fennel seeds. Season with salt and pepper and cook, stirring, until softened, about 15 minutes. Divide equally among the bread slices, and keep warm in the oven or with aluminum foil loosely draped over the slices.

3. Add the remaining 1 tablespoon olive oil to the pan, then add the beef strips and cilantro and cook, stirring, until crispy brown but rare, about 3 minutes. Season lightly with salt and pepper. Spoon on top of the bread slices and serve hot.

He-Man Beef and Chile Stir-Fry

This exceedingly hot dish will put hair on your chest. However, it's not all about heat; the flavors are delicious and it's loaded with things good for you. You can tone down the dish by leaving out the Thai chiles or replacing them with a third poblano chile. The recipe can be doubled if desired.

2 fresh poblano chiles

¼ cup vegetable oil

¾ pound beef filet mignon or sirloin, cut into 1-inch cubes

10 ounces peewee fingerling potatoes (or Yukon gold potatoes cut into 1-inch cubes)

4 small white onions (about 5 ounces), peeled and halved

2 large garlic cloves, finely chopped

15 fresh green or red Thai chiles, left whole, or 4 fresh green serrano chiles, cut in half lengthwise

Salt and freshly ground black pepper, to taste

2 tablespoons finely chopped fresh oregano or tarragon

½ cup dry white wine, rice wine (mirin), or water

1. Place the poblano chiles on a wire rack set over a burner on high heat and roast until their skins blister black on all sides, turning occasionally with tongs. Remove the chiles and place in a paper or heavy plastic bag to steam for 20 minutes, which will make peeling them easier. When cool enough to handle, rub off as much blackened skin as you can and remove the seeds by rubbing with a paper towel (to avoid washing away flavorful juices) or by rinsing under running water (to remove more easily). Slice into thin strips and set aside.

2. In a wok, heat 2 tablespoons of the oil over high heat until smoking, then cook the beef, tossing, until it turns color, about 1 minute. Remove the beef and reserve.

3. Heat the remaining 2 tablespoons oil in the wok, then add the potatoes, cover the pan, and cook, tossing occasionally, until almost tender when pierced by a skewer and golden, about 7 minutes. Add the onions and garlic and cook, covered, tossing occasionally, for 3 minutes. Add the reserved poblano chiles and the Thai chiles and season with salt and pepper. Cook, tossing, for 4 minutes. Return the beef to the wok, add the oregano and wine, and cook, tossing, until the meat is rare, about 4 minutes. Serve immediately.

He-Man Beef and Potato Stir-Fry

I am by no means a meat-and-potatoes guy; however, I love meat and potatoes. So how do you do that in one pot and keep the elements distinct and not have the dish turn into a stew? The solution presented itself: the wok sitting on the stove from the night before. In this recipe, the trick is drying the potatoes and cooking them twice and cooking the beef very briefly.

5 tablespoons extra-virgin olive oil
1½ pounds Yukon gold or white potatoes, peeled, cut into ¾-inch cubes,
    and dried well with paper towels
Salt, to taste
¾ pound filet mignon or beef sirloin, sliced
Freshly ground black pepper, to taste
½ cup finely chopped fresh flat-leaf parsley

1. In a wok, heat 4 tablespoons of the olive oil over high heat, then add the potatoes and cook, tossing and stir-frying, until golden brown, about 8 minutes. Remove the potatoes with a slotted spoon and let cool completely.

2. Add the remaining 1 tablespoon olive oil to the wok and heat again over high heat. Cook the potatoes again until crispy on the outside and tender on the inside, about 5 minutes. Using a slotted spoon, transfer to a bowl and toss with some salt.

3. Maintain the heat on high, add the sliced beef, and spread it around the wok. Season with salt and pepper and let it cook without tossing for 1 minute. Begin tossing as you cook for another 15 seconds. Return the potatoes to the wok, add the parsley, and toss for 1 minute. Serve hot.

Steak Sandwiches with Tomato and Onion

Many supermarkets sell thin-sliced bottom cut of beef round as "sandwich steaks." These steaks are perfect for quick frying with some fresh tomatoes and onions. This is a dish you can make in the summer when you want dinner to be quick, simple, tasty, and fun. If you want it spicier, fry the steaks in chile oil. All it needs is a side salad of greens.

¼ cup extra-virgin olive oil
4 to 6 soft sub rolls
2 cups chopped onions
2 cups chopped or crushed canned or fresh tomatoes
3 garlic cloves, finely chopped
¼ cup finely chopped fresh flat-leaf parsley
2 pounds bottom round sandwich steaks, very thinly sliced into strips
Salt and freshly ground black pepper, to taste

1. In a 12-inch nonstick pan or cast-iron skillet, heat a film of olive oil over medium heat. Cut the rolls open and cook, cut side down, in batches until golden, about 4 minutes. Remove and set aside.

2. Heat the remaining olive oil over medium-high heat, then add the onions and cook, stirring occasionally, until translucent, about 5 minutes. Add the tomatoes, garlic, and parsley and continue cooking, stirring, for 3 minutes.

3. Add the sandwich steak strips to the pan, season with salt and pepper, and cook, stirring, until browned on both sides, about 5 minutes. Divide all the ingredients into 4 to 6 portions, spoon into the rolls, and serve immediately.

Steak, Corn on the Cob, and Peppers on the Grill

It was the beginning of a beautiful summer evening and I was loading a tray up with porterhouse steak, corn on the cob, and some Hatch chiles to bring to the barbecue grill where I had started a hardwood charcoal fire a little earlier. My son asked, "Is this a recipe test for the one-pot book?" I answered, "No, it's not." He said, "Why not, it's all being cooked on the grill, which is the one pot." Hmmm, I thought, I guess so; so here's the simplest and commonest one-pot dish. Although you don't have to prepare the corn as I suggest here (you can just throw it on the grill), I like to do it this way, as it takes on more flavor.

4 ears corn on the cob (unhusked)
4 tablespoons (½ stick) unsalted butter
Salt, to taste
8 large, fleshy fresh Hatch or Anaheim chiles or
    4 large, fleshy green bell peppers
One 2-pound beef porterhouse steak
Olive oil, as needed
Freshly ground black pepper, to taste

1. Prepare a hot charcoal fire or preheat a gas grill on high.

2. Pull the husks down the ears of corn, but don't remove; only remove the silky material. Butter the entire cob and season with salt, then replace the husks and wrap each in aluminum foil. Place the corn and chiles on the grill, cover, keeping all the air holes open, and grill the cobs for 15 minutes, turning once or twice. Remove the corn and set aside. Continue grilling the chiles until blistered black on all sides, then remove with tongs, place in a paper bag or a heavy plastic bag, and let rest with the corn.

3. Drizzle the porterhouse steak with olive oil and season with salt and pepper. Place on the grill, cook for 4 minutes, then turn and cook for another 4 minutes for very rare or for another 2 to 3 minutes on each side for rare. Transfer the steak to a cutting board.

4. Unwrap the ears of corn and peel and seed the chiles while the steak rests. Carve the steak into portions and serve with the corn and chiles.

Korean Braised Short Ribs and Kimchi Sandwiches with Wasabi Mayonnaise

The inspiration for this sandwich comes from the All Star Sandwich Bar in Cambridge, Massachusetts. I lived in Cambridge for nearly fifteen years and left before the new wave of eateries appeared on the scene. This kind of sandwich is popular in California, where I live now. You can cook the short ribs days beforehand if you want and then use them as needed for making sandwiches. The way I usually make this is to start the beef braise in the morning, place it on a simmer-controlled burner for 10 hours, and then serve it for supper. You could also leave it in a 250-degree oven or use a slow cooker if you have one. If your cooktop does not have a super-low simmer control, follow the instruction below.

For the beef
½ Asian pear, peeled, seeded, and finely chopped
½ medium onion, grated
3 scallions, trimmed and finely chopped
4 large garlic cloves, finely chopped
6 tablespoons soy sauce
5 tablespoons sugar
2 tablespoons rice wine (mirin)
1 tablespoon sesame seeds, crushed or whole
1 tablespoon sesame seed oil
2½ pounds boneless beef chuck short ribs or 4 pounds thick-cut short ribs

For the sandwiches and dressing
½ cup mayonnaise
Five 4.5-gram packets wasabi paste (about 1 ounce)
4 large brioche buns
Four ½-inch-thick slices iceberg lettuce
One 12-ounce jar kimchi, drained

1. In a bowl, mix together the Asian pear, onion, scallions, garlic, soy sauce, sugar, rice wine, sesame seeds, and sesame oil.

2. Place the short ribs in a large, heavy flameproof baking casserole and pour the marinating liquid over them. Toss and turn the ribs to coat. The liquid should come about one-third of the way up the ribs. Cover the casserole with a tight-fitting lid. Bring to a near boil over high heat, then reduce the heat to low and cook, turning several times, until the meat can be pulled apart easily with two forks, about 4 hours. Remove from the heat and keep warm.

3. Mix the mayonnaise and wasabi together. Slice the buns open and lay a slice of lettuce on the bottom, spread with the mayonnaise, then spoon some kimchi on top. Place some beef on top, close, and serve.

Griddled Beefsteak and Eggplant Wraps with Hummus and Avocado

This wrap is made with the very thin Middle Eastern flatbread called *lavash,* which is actually the Armenian name. It is also called *marquq* bread, and some supermarkets simply sell it labeled as "sandwich wrap bread." This recipe is all about assembly, so you can prepare everything ahead of time and then cook the meat and roll the sandwiches at the last minute. Of course, the meat doesn't have to be hot; you can cook it ahead of time, too. You could also use store-bought hummus but the recipe below is quick, easy, and better.

For the hummus
One 15-ounce can chickpeas, rinsed and drained
¼ cup extra-virgin olive oil
¼ cup water
2 large garlic cloves
½ teaspoon salt, plus more as needed
3 tablespoons tahini
3 tablespoons fresh lemon juice
Freshly ground black pepper, to taste

For the wraps
1 tablespoon extra-virgin olive oil, plus more as needed
2 tablespoons pine nuts
1 long Japanese eggplant, sliced lengthwise into 8 thin slices
1 pound filet mignon or sirloin steak
½ pound lavash bread (2 sheets)
2 ounces mixed baby greens
1 avocado, cut in half, pitted, flesh scooped out and sliced
1 small onion, chopped
1 large ripe tomato, chopped
2 tablespoons chopped fresh mint

1. For the hummus, place the chickpeas in a food processor with the olive oil and water and run until mushy.

2. In a mortar, pound the garlic with the salt with a pestle until it is a creamy mush.

3. In a small bowl, beat the tahini and lemon juice together slowly. Stir the tahini-juice mixture into the garlic-salt mixture. Stir this mixture into the chickpea purée in the food processor, adjust the salt, season with pepper, and process until smooth. Check the consistency; if it is too thick, like oatmeal, then add some water until it is smoother. Set aside.

4. For the wraps, preheat a cast-iron skillet over medium-high heat. Add 1 teaspoon of the olive oil and cook the pine nuts, stirring, until light brown, 1 to 2 minutes. Remove and set aside. Add another 1 teaspoon olive oil to the skillet and let it heat. Lay the eggplant slices in the skillet and cook, turning once, until golden brown, 3 to 4 minutes. Remove and set aside. Lay the filet mignon in the skillet and cook, turning once, until both sides are golden brown and crispy charred and rare, about 8 minutes in all. Remove and let rest on a cutting board for a couple of minutes, slice thinly, and then chop.

5. Lay one of the lavash sheets in front of you with the short side closest to you. Spread several tablespoons of the hummus on the bottom third. Lay some mixed baby greens on top. Lay half the eggplant slices down and half the avocado slices on top of the eggplant. Sprinkle with half the pine nuts, half the onion, and half the tomato. Drizzle with a little of the remaining olive oil. Lay half of the filet mignon pieces on top. Season with salt, pepper, and half the mint and roll up tightly. Divide into quarters, slicing on the diagonal. Set aside while you finish stuffing and rolling the remaining sandwich.

Skillet Shawarma

In Syria and Lebanon, there is a popular street food called *shawarma* consisting of marinated meat grilled on a vertical rotisserie that is sliced off into a wrap of thin Arabic bread with lettuce, tomatoes, onions, lamb fat, and a yogurt-cucumber and garlic sauce, sometimes with pickled turnip slices. Shawarma is found in other Near Eastern countries, all slightly different, including Turkey where it is known as *döner kebab* and in Greece as *gyro*. One doesn't make it at home because it requires the vertical rotisserie. But it's a delicious food and there's no reason you can't make a mock one at home as in this recipe. The recipe calls for lavash bread, which is the Armenian name often used in U.S. packaging for a very thin flatbread found throughout the Middle East under different names. Supermarkets carry it these days and certainly Middle Eastern markets do. It also goes by the names *marquq* bread, mountain bread, and sandwich wrap bread. It could be replaced with one large split pita bread.

For the spice mix
1 small onion, finely chopped
2 large garlic cloves, very finely chopped
2 teaspoons ground coriander
1½ teaspoons ground allspice
1¼ teaspoon dried summer savory
Salt and freshly ground black pepper, to taste

For the steak
2 pounds skirt steak, sliced

For the sauce
2 cups whole-milk plain yogurt
1 cucumber, peeled, seeded, grated, and squeezed of its excess water
4 garlic cloves, mashed in a mortar using a pestle with 1 teaspoon salt
1 teaspoon dried mint

For the assembly
   Lavash bread
   Shredded lettuce
   Chopped ripe tomatoes
   1 medium onion, chopped
   Pickled turnips, pickled okra, or sweet gherkins, for garnish

1. In a blender, process the spice mix of onion, garlic, coriander, allspice, savory, salt, and pepper until homogenous. Rub the steak with the spice mix. Place in a ceramic or glass bowl or pan and cover with plastic wrap. Leave in the refrigerator for 6 to 24 hours (preferably the longer time).

2. Make the sauce by stirring together the yogurt, cucumber, garlic, and mint until creamy. Reserve in the refrigerator until needed.

3. Lightly oil a large cast-iron skillet over high heat until smoking. Cook the skirt steak, turning once, until browned on the outside but medium-rare or medium on the inside, about 5 minutes. Transfer to a cutting board and slice thinly. Arrange a piece of lavash bread in front of you. Place some lettuce on the lavash bread and top with tomatoes, onion, pickles, and the skirt steak. Spoon some sauce on top. Fold the bottom portion over the stuffing, fold over the right side only, and continue rolling so it is wrapped up tightly. Leave the top end open. Serve with any remaining vegetables or sauce on the side.

Braised Beef Short Ribs

Beef short ribs are very popular in restaurants today, and increasingly home cooks are trying the dish in their own kitchens. But due to the nature of the short rib there is no way you will be cooking this when you come home from work because it will take too long. That's why short ribs are perfect for a wintery Saturday. There should not be any mystery behind short ribs, but some cooks seem at a loss. That's probably because they are unfamiliar with the cut and that different cuts come from different parts of the cow and require different cooking methods. Short ribs are a beef cut from the region of the cow's anatomy known as chuck, the portion of the cow running from the shoulders down a bit to include the shorter portion of the ribs, hence the name. This is a very tough piece of meat with lots of connective tissue. It needs long, slow cooking to break this down and create the melt-in-your-mouth result that we all love to replicate. There's one secret and that's to cook it for a ridiculously long time at a very low temperature. This means it should cook for between 5 and 6 hours. The most appropriate way to cook short ribs is by braising or stewing. Serve with crusty bread and a robust salad made from a variety of lettuces, watercress, and tomatoes.

4 tablespoons (½ stick) unsalted butter

2 tablespoons extra-virgin olive oil

3 pounds beef short ribs

All-purpose flour, for dredging

1 small onion, finely chopped

1 medium carrot, scraped and finely chopped

1 large garlic clove, finely chopped

3 cups red wine such as Cabernet Sauvignon or Zinfandel

Bouquet garni, tied in cheesecloth, consisting of 5 fresh flat-leaf parsley sprigs,
   1 teaspoon dried thyme, 1 teaspoon dried herbes de Provence,
   ½ teaspoon dried oregano, and 1 bay leaf

Salt and freshly ground black pepper, to taste

1. In a deep flameproof baking casserole, melt the butter with the olive oil over high heat until almost smoking. Dredge the short ribs in flour and tap off any excess. Cook the short ribs until golden brown on all sides, turning with tongs, about 8 minutes. Add the onion, carrot, and garlic and cook, stirring, until softened, about 3 minutes. Pour in the red wine, add the bouquet garni, reduce the heat to very low, and simmer, partially covered and turning occasionally with tongs, until very tender, about 6 hours. (If your simmer control doesn't go low enough, you can use a heat diffuser.) Season with salt and pepper.

2. Remove the short ribs from the casserole and serve; or if you want to serve the next day, remove and discard the bouquet garni, skim off the fat from the cooking liquid, and set the short ribs aside, let the liquid remaining in the casserole cool, then refrigerate until the remaining fat solidifies. Remove the fat, reheat the short ribs and the sauce, and serve.

Wine-Braised Beef Short Ribs with Mushrooms

Beef short ribs covered with a wine sauce, the meat nearly falling off the bone is a very appealing sight. The wafting aroma of well-cooked, aromatic short ribs having braised for hours is one of the most satisfying. Short ribs come from the short plate of the cow, the underside of the animal below where the rib roasts would be cut. They are sold in supermarkets labeled as "beef short ribs," so they should be easy to find. The short ribs need to cook for a long time, until very tender and the meat is barely clinging to the bones. The pancetta in this recipe is meant to replace the traditional *petit salé*, a lean salt pork used in French country cooking. Because the wine is an important part of this stew, you should use a good Merlot or Burgundy, something you would be pleased to drink, too. Serve with crusty French or Italian bread and a light green salad.

4 tablespoons (½ stick) butter
2 slices pancetta (about 1 ounce)
3 pounds beef short ribs
All-purpose flour, for dredging
1 large onion, coarsely chopped
2 carrots, scraped and cut into small pieces
2 parsnips, scraped and cut into small pieces
6 large garlic cloves, finely chopped
1½ pounds small button (white) mushrooms
1 bottle Merlot or Burgundy wine
Salt and freshly ground black pepper, to taste
1 tablespoon dried summer savory or oregano
¾ pound green beans, trimmed and cut into 1-inch pieces

1. In a large, heavy flameproof baking casserole, melt the butter over medium-high heat with the pancetta while stirring. Dredge the beef short ribs in flour, tapping off the excess. Once the pancetta is sizzling, add the short ribs to the casserole and cook, turning with tongs, until the beef is browned on all sides, about 8 minutes. Add the onion, carrots, parsnips, and garlic and cook, stirring frequently, until the vegetables are slightly softened, about 10 minutes. Add the mushrooms and cook, stirring, for 5 minutes. Pour in the wine, season with salt and pepper, add the summer savory, and stir everything in together.

2. Reduce the heat to very low and simmer, covered, until the beef is tender, about 4 hours. (If your simmer control doesn't go low enough, you can use a heat diffuser.)

3. Remove the cover, stir in the green beans, and continue cooking until the meat is falling off the bone and the sauce is syrupy, about another 1½ hours. Serve hot.

Braised Meatballs in Wine Gravy

I first published a variation of this recipe in *Bon Appétit* magazine about ten years ago. It is a favorite in our family partly because everyone loves meatballs, but it's the wine gravy that just makes it spectacular.

6 ounces day-old French bread (leave crust on if desired)

½ cup whole milk

2 pounds lean ground beef

1 large egg

1 medium onion, finely chopped

½ cup finely chopped fresh flat-leaf parsley

¾ teaspoon dried summer savory

2 teaspoons salt, or more as needed

1 teaspoon freshly ground black pepper, or more as needed

All-purpose flour, as needed

2 tablespoons unsalted butter

1½ teaspoons extra-virgin olive oil

1 pound Yukon gold potatoes, peeled and cut into ½-inch cubes

¾ cup dry red wine

1 tablespoon tomato paste

¾ cup beef broth

½ pound frozen peas

1. Soak the bread in the milk, then squeeze the liquid out as if making a snowball. In a bowl, mix the bread, beef, egg, onion, parsley (reserving 1 tablespoon for garnishing the finished dish), summer savory, salt, and pepper. Transfer to a food processor and process the beef mixture in batches until pasty looking, or mix in a bowl with your hands. Make 16 to 20 meatballs and dredge each in the flour, tapping off any excess flour, and place on a platter.

2. In a large 14-inch nonstick pan (or cook in batches if you don't have a skillet that large), melt the butter with the olive oil over medium-high heat. When it stops sizzling, add the meatballs as quickly as you can and shake the pan, then add the potatoes and cook until the meatballs are browned on all sides, about 10 minutes.

3. Mix the wine and tomato paste together. Add the wine mixture to the pan and let it evaporate for 2 minutes, stirring to make the gravy velvety. Reduce the heat to low, add the beef broth, season with salt and pepper, and simmer until the meatballs and potatoes are cooked through and the gravy is thicker, about 20 minutes. Add the peas and cook for another 10 minutes, adding water if the gravy is thickening too much. Transfer to a deep serving platter, sprinkle with the reserved parsley, and serve.

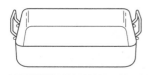

Baked Beef Brisket with Onions and Root Vegetables

This is a big family-style Sunday dinner where everything is meltingly tender, especially the vegetables. There's a nice aroma in the house when you make this. When my daughter was about sixteen years old, she asked me to put some leftovers aside for an after-school snack—it's that good.

1 tablespoon unsalted butter

2 ounces smoked slab bacon, cut into sticks

24 to 26 small white onions (about 1½ pounds), peeled

One 3-pound beef brisket

All-purpose flour, for dredging

Salt and freshly ground black pepper, to taste

1 cup dry white wine

¾ pound carrots, scraped and cut into large chunks

¾ pound small red potatoes (unpeeled)

¾ pound parsnips, scraped and cut into large chunks

Bouquet garni, tied in kitchen twine, consisting of 5 sprigs each
    fresh flat-leaf parsley and tarragon and 1 leafy celery stalk

2 teaspoons dried thyme

4 cups beef broth

1. Preheat the oven to 300°F.

2. In a large, heavy roasting pan, melt the butter with the bacon pieces and onions over medium-high heat and cook, stirring, until the bacon has rendered some fat and the onions are slightly golden, 7 to 8 minutes. Remove the onions and bacon and set aside.

3. Dredge the brisket in the flour, season with salt and pepper, and brown on both sides, about 8 minutes in all. Deglaze the pan with ½ cup of the wine. Add the carrots, potatoes, parsnips, and bouquet garni. Return the bacon and onions to the pan. Season with the thyme, salt, and pepper.

4. Place the roasting pan in the oven and bake until the meat is very tender, about 5 hours, moistening occasionally with the beef broth, using all of it, and the remaining ½ cup wine, and turning the meat and vegetables occasionally. Remove and discard the bouquet garni. Serve hot.

Daube Languedocienne

A *daube* (pronounced "dohb," with a long "o") is the classic French braise. The daube of Languedoc in southwestern France, *daube languedocienne*, is a slowly braised beef stew with tomatoes, garlic, and wild mushrooms. There are varieties of this dish prepared throughout southern and central France, although the origin of daube seems to be related to Italian cooking because *daube* derives from the Italian *addobbo* (which also gives us the Mexican *adobo*), meaning "seasoning" or "dressing." Some cooks insist that the beef come from two different parts of the cow, say, rump and shoulder. Some items for this preparation will have to be ordered from the butcher if your supermarket is not particularly well stocked. Some of the more unusual items such as the foot or the pork skin provide a depth of flavor to the stew that is not achievable without them, but you can treat them as optional if they prove hard to find. Dried juniper berries are available through www.penzeys.com, or you can use dried raspberries. The marc or grappa, a distillation of used grape skins and seeds, is a strong alcoholic liqueur that can be replaced with vodka. This stew cooks for hours, so this is ideally made on a weekend; but remember that the leftovers are heavenly. There are a lot of ingredients in this dish; however, it's all for a heavenly purpose that you'll shortly enjoy.

1 veal or beef foot (optional, but highly desirable)
6 ounces salt pork, cut into thin sticks
¼ pound pork or beef lard or 3 tablespoons extra-virgin olive oil
3 pounds beef chuck, cut into 2-ounce pieces
All-purpose flour, for dredging
½ pound carrots, scraped and cut into 1½-inch pieces
½ pound onions, chopped
½ pound leeks, white and light green parts, split lengthwise, washed well, and sliced
4 large garlic cloves, crushed
¼ pound pork skin
1 pound tomatoes, peeled, seeded, and coarsely chopped (see box page 47)
1 bottle dry red wine
¼ cup marc or grappa
2 ounces dried porcini or other dried wild mushrooms

Bouquet garni, tied in cheesecloth, consisting of 8 fresh flat-leaf parsley sprigs,
    8 fresh thyme sprigs, 3 fresh tarragon sprigs, 2 fresh sage sprigs,
    1 fresh rosemary sprig, 1 fresh lavender sprig (optional), and 1 bay leaf
2 whole cloves
1 whole nutmeg
1 cinnamon stick
10 whole dried juniper berries
Grated zest of ½ orange
1 tablespoon salt
2 teaspoons freshly ground black pepper
¼ pound pitted green olives
½ pound pitted black olives

1. In a large, heavy flameproof baking casserole, bring enough water to cover the veal foot to a boil over high heat, then add the foot and blanch for 5 minutes. Remove and set aside. Add the salt pork and blanch for 5 minutes. Remove and reserve. Discard the water.

2. Add the salt pork to the casserole and cook, stirring, over medium heat until golden and crispy, about 5 minutes. Remove and set aside.

3. Melt the lard in the casserole over high heat. Dredge the beef pieces in the flour, tapping off any excess, then add to the casserole with the carrots, onions, leeks, and garlic and cook, stirring and turning, until browned, about 8 minutes. Add the reserved veal foot, pork skin, tomatoes, red wine, marc, mushrooms, bouquet garni, cloves, nutmeg, cinnamon, juniper berries, and orange zest. Bring to a boil over high heat, then reduce the heat to very low and simmer, covered, until fork-tender, about 4 hours. (If your simmer control doesn't go low enough, you can use a heat diffuser.)

4. When the beef is tender, remove and discard the bouquet garni, cloves, nutmeg, and cinnamon stick. Add the reserved salt pork, season with the salt and pepper, add the olives, and simmer for 15 minutes. Serve hot, although it may be kept warm for 2 hours before serving.

Spicy Beef and Sweet Potato Braise

This preparation begins as a stew and ends as a braise, and it is very, very spicy-hot. However, that heat will be tempered by the sour cream and chopped scallions that go on top when serving. If you decide to serve something with the dish, a simple tossed green salad would be best.

¼ cup extra-virgin olive oil

1 pound beef chuck, cut into bite-size cubes

1 medium onion, chopped

2 fresh habanero chiles, halved

2 small fresh green serrano chiles, chopped

1 roasted poblano chile (page 193), chopped

3 large garlic cloves, finely chopped

3 cups water, plus more as needed

One 12-ounce can evaporated milk

2 pounds sweet potatoes

1 teaspoon dried oregano

½ teaspoon ground cumin

Salt and freshly ground black pepper, to taste

1 cup sour cream

3 scallions, chopped

3 tablespoons chopped fresh cilantro (coriander leaf)

1. In a large, heavy flameproof baking casserole, heat the olive oil over medium-high heat, add the beef and cook until browned on all sides, about 3 minutes. Add the onion, habanero chiles, serrano chiles, and poblano chiles and cook, stirring, until softer, about 3 minutes. Add the garlic and cook, stirring, for 2 minutes. Add the water and evaporated milk, reduce the heat to low, and simmer, partially covered, until almost tender, about 2½ hours.

2. Add the sweet potatoes, oregano, cumin, salt, and pepper and simmer until the sweet potatoes are tender, about 30 minutes. It should be thick and gooey. If it is too liquidy, remove the meat and vegetables with a skimmer and reduce the liquid until saucy, then return the food to the casserole. Serve with the sour cream, chopped scallions, and cilantro.

Braised Beef with Onions

This recipe is the classic Greek beef stew known as *stifado*. It's a family dish made all over Greece, but is typical of rustic Greek mountain cooking. The Greek name comes from the Italian and is probably an influence from the Venetians, who ruled Greece in the Middle Ages. The Turks, who also ruled Greece for a long time, seem to have contributed the spicing of clove and cinnamon, as well as the walnuts and currants. This is an ideal stew for cold weather, and you can be free-form with it too: Replace the walnuts with carrots or potatoes if you like.

5 tablespoons (½ stick plus 1 tablespoon) unsalted butter

2 pounds boneless beef stew meat, cut into 1-inch cubes, or
    4 pounds beef short ribs

1 medium onion, chopped

10 garlic cloves, lightly crushed

1 cup tomato purée (canned or fresh)

½ cup dry red wine

2 tablespoons red wine vinegar

2 bay leaves

1 cinnamon stick

4 whole cloves

1 teaspoon sugar

Salt and freshly ground black pepper, to taste

2 pounds small white onions, both ends sliced off and peeled

2 tablespoons currants

1 cup walnut halves

1 cup crumbled large-chunk Greek or Bulgarian (preferably) feta cheese

1. In a large, heavy flameproof baking casserole, heat 3 tablespoons of the butter over medium-high heat, then add the beef and brown on all sides, about 5 minutes. Add the chopped onion and garlic cloves to the casserole with the remaining 2 tablespoons butter and cook, stirring, until the onions are translucent, about 4 minutes. Add the tomato purée, wine, and wine vinegar and deglaze the casserole. Add the bay leaves, cinnamon, cloves, and sugar and season with salt and pepper.

2. Cover the casserole and simmer over low heat for 1 hour. Add the small onions and currants and cook until the meat falls off the bones (if using short ribs), about 1 hour more. Add the walnuts and cook for 20 minutes more. Add the feta cheese, cook for 5 minutes, remove and discard the bay leaves, cinnamon stick, and cloves, and then serve.

Hungarian Goulash

This famous dish from Hungary has thousands of variations, but this recipe is based not only on what I had in Budapest many years ago but also on George Lang, the famous gastronome, restaurateur, and cookbook author who wrote the best book on Hungarian cuisine, *The Cuisine of Hungary*. He tells us that goulash was originally a soup with origins that trace back to the ninth century, when shepherds slowly cooked their meat in an iron kettle until the liquid evaporated. The remnants they dried in the sun, and then they put this pemmican in a bag made of sheep's stomach. When they needed to eat, they took a piece of dried meat out and reconstituted it with a lot of water, in which case it was a soup (*gulyásleves*), or a little water was added and it became a meat stew, *gulyáhús*, that is, goulash. First, an authentic goulash *never* has sour cream in it. The authentic Hungarian dish we call goulash, with the sour cream, is what the Hungarians call *paprikás*. In Hungarian restaurants (in Hungary), goulash will appear on menus under soups, because that is what it originally was. The word *goulash* itself means something like "cowboy." So, this was cowboys' soup. In Hungarian, goulash is actually called *bográcsgulyás*, which means "kettle goulash," because it was traditionally cooked by the drovers in a black kettle called a *bogrács*.

2 tablespoons rendered bacon fat or pork lard
2 medium onions, very coarsely chopped
2 pounds beef chuck or rump, cut into ¾-inch cubes
½ pound beef heart, diced
1 large garlic clove, crushed
1 teaspoon caraway seeds
Salt, to taste
2 tablespoons sweet Hungarian paprika
4 cups warm beer (lager)
4 cups warm water
1 large ripe tomato, peeled, seeded, and chopped (see box page 47)
2 green bell peppers, seeded and sliced into rings
1 pound boiling potatoes, peeled and cut into ¾-inch cubes

1. In a large, heavy flameproof baking casserole or stewpot, heat the fat or melt the lard over medium-low heat. Add the onions and cook, stirring, until translucent, about 10 minutes. Add the beef and beef heart and cook, stirring, until brown, about 8 minutes. Add the garlic and caraway seeds, season with salt, stir, and remove from the heat.

2. Add the paprika, beer, and water and stir to mix everything. Return to the heat, bring to a gentle boil over medium heat, then reduce the heat to low, cover, and simmer for 2 hours.

3. Add the tomato and peppers and taste the stew to see if it needs any salt. Increase the heat to medium-low and cook until the peppers are softened, about 1 hour. Add the potatoes and cook, stirring occasionally, until everything is tender, about 1 hour longer. The goulash will be thicker, the soup now looking more like a gravy that you will still need to eat with a spoon.

Goulash Dos and Don'ts

One of the most famous cookbooks about Hungarian cuisine is George Lang's *The Cuisine of Hungary*. Here's what he recommends about cooking goulash:

"*Never* use any flour. *Never* use any other spice besides caraway [I guess he doesn't consider paprika a spice, because it's essential]. *Never* Frenchify it with wine. *Never* Germanize it with brown sauce. *Never* put in any other garniture besides diced potatoes or *galushka* [egg dumplings]."

Cocido

This beef and vegetable stew may be Colombia's best-known dish, although that name also refers to Spain's national dish, too. The Colombian stew is made with fresh corn on the cob that is cut into 2-inch lengths. The potatoes, carrots, and celery are all cut up into sticks to cook in the stew. There is not much meat used, but feel free to double the amount if you like. The spicing, too, is light and not overpowering, just enough to provide a delightful flavor. Serve the stew with corn tortillas. This recipe is adapted from one in the *Time-Life* series about the cooking of Latin America.

2 tablespoons extra-virgin olive oil

1 small onion, coarsely chopped

1 medium tomato, peeled, seeded, and coarsely chopped (see box page 47)

1 pound boneless stew beef, preferably chuck, cut into 1½-inch cubes

3 large garlic cloves, finely chopped

1 small bay leaf

1 teaspoon freshly ground cumin seeds

1 teaspoon salt

4 whole black peppercorns

½ teaspoon dried oregano

¼ teaspoon ground turmeric

1½ cups cold water

1 teaspoon apple cider vinegar

½ pound Yukon gold or white potatoes, peeled and cut lengthwise into ¼-inch slices and then into ½-inch strips

2 medium carrots, scraped and cut lengthwise into ¼-inch slices and then into ½-inch strips

4 celery stalks, cut into 2-inch lengths

½ cup fresh or frozen peas

2 ears corn on the cob, cut into 2-inch lengths

1. In a large, heavy flameproof baking casserole, heat the oil over medium heat, then add the onion and cook, stirring frequently, until it is translucent, about 5 minutes. Add the tomato and cook for 3 minutes, then add the beef, garlic, bay leaf, cumin, salt, peppercorns, oregano, and turmeric. Stir, then add the water and vinegar. Reduce the heat to very low, cover, and simmer, stirring occasionally, for 2 hours. (If your simmer control doesn't go low enough, you can use a heat diffuser.)

2. Add the potatoes, carrots, and celery and stir. Cover and continue cooking for 1 hour. Add the peas and corn, cover, and cook until the beef is tender and the vegetables are softened, about 20 minutes longer. Taste and correct the seasoning, remove and discard the bay leaf, and serve.

Dumplings for Beef Stew

Here is a simple recipe for flour dumplings for beef stews. For light dumplings, don't use eggs and don't take the lid off while they cook.

2 cups all-purpose flour
1¼ teaspoons baking powder
¾ teaspoon salt
2 tablespoons unsalted butter, cut into pieces
⅔ cup milk

In a bowl, sift the flour, baking powder, and salt together. Work the butter into the flour with a pastry knife or fork. Add the milk to make a soft dough. Turn the dough out onto a floured surface and roll about ½ inch thick. Cut into 12 squares. When cooking dumplings, it is important that they be cooked under a tight-fitting lid or they will be become heavy. Place them on top of the stew being cooked, cover tightly, and cook for 20 minutes without lifting the cover.

Makes 12 dumplings

Beef Stew

This recipe is the old-fashioned American beef stew that can probably be traced to early New England. There are thousands of different recipes for beef stew, but this one is old-fashioned in the sense that it's meant to serve a hungry family on a cold night when the windows are steamed up and the flavors of the stew beckon the kids playing in the snow and Dad shoveling the walk. Typically, old-fashioned beef stews are served with dumplings (see box page 132), which are simply spoon-dropped on top of the covered stew.

1¾ pounds boneless beef chuck, cut into large bite-size pieces
¼ cup all-purpose flour
Salt and freshly ground black pepper, to taste
3 tablespoons unsalted butter or beef suet
1 medium onion, chopped
2 cups cold water
1 pound red rose, white, or Yukon gold potatoes, peeled and cubed
1½ carrots, scraped and diced
1 large parsnip, scraped and diced
1 medium turnip, peeled and diced
½ recipe Dumplings (optional) (see box page 132)

1. Dredge the beef in the flour and season with salt and pepper. In a large, heavy flameproof baking casserole or stewpot, melt the butter over medium-high heat, then brown the meat on all sides, about 8 minutes total. Add the onion and cook, stirring and scraping the bottom of the pot, until softened, about 4 minutes. Pour in water to barely cover, reduce the heat to low, stir a bit, then simmer, partially covered, until tender, about 2 hours.

2. Add the potatoes, carrots, parsnip, and turnip and continue cooking, stirring occasionally, until everything is very tender, about 1 hour. Add the dumplings if desired, cover, and cook for 20 minutes longer, never removing the cover while the dumplings cook. Serve immediately.

Beef Stew in Beer

In the cold autumn of 1977 I was living in Salzburg, Austria, and many a cozy Austrian restaurant had *rindfleisch in bier*, beef cooked in beer and vegetables, on the menu. This stew cooks for a long time, until the beef is falling apart. The vegetables flavor the broth and don't actually get eaten—you wouldn't want to, either, since they are by that time totally demolished, having given up their entire flavor to the stew. Serve it with thick-cut warm rye bread and a cucumber salad. Dried juniper berries are available through www.penzeys.com, or you may use dried raspberries instead.

6 slices thick-cut bacon

2 large onions, sliced ¼ inch thick

3 carrots, scraped and sliced ¼ inch thick

1 leek, split in half lengthwise, washed well, and sliced ½ inch thick

2 medium turnips, peeled and sliced ¼ inch thick

12 whole black peppercorns

6 lightly crushed dried juniper berries

6 leafy fresh flat-leaf parsley sprigs

2 bay leaves

Six 1-inch-long slices lemon peel, without any white pith

One 4-pound piece boneless beef rump steak, cut into 8 pieces

Two 12-ounce bottles beer (lager)

Salt and freshly ground black pepper, to taste

2 tablespoons unsalted butter

2 tablespoons all-purpose flour

1. In a large, heavy flameproof baking casserole, layer the bacon, onions, carrots, leek, and turnips, in that order, and sprinkle with the peppercorns, juniper berries, parsley, bay leaves, and lemon peel. Lay the pieces of beef on top. Pour in the beer so it reaches the top of the meat but does not cover it. Season with salt and pepper. Bring to a boil over high heat, reduce the heat to low, and simmer until the beef is tender, 4 to 5 hours. Check for doneness by gently pulling on the beef with a fork. Once it pulls apart very easily, it is done; cook it longer if necessary. If you have to cut it with a knife, it is not done. Remove the meat from the casserole and keep warm; discard the vegetables and bay leaves. Strain the broth and reserve 2 cups.

2. Melt the butter in the casserole over medium-high heat, then add the flour and cook, stirring, until a light brown roux is formed, 2 to 3 minutes. Slowly add the 2 cups reserved broth, stirring or whisking constantly, and simmer over low heat until a smooth gravy forms, about 30 minutes. Taste and correct the seasoning if necessary, then pour over the beef and serve hot.

Beef Stew of La Mancha

Here's a stew that Don Quixote would love. It's called *tojunta* in Spanish, which means that everything is thrown together. It's got beef and potatoes and bell peppers and onions simmered in white wine and saffron, and it's just delicious. And most important, it's very easy to cook. Serve the stew with crusty bread. Meat departments often have packages of meat labeled "beef stew meat," but if they don't, look for beef chuck or bottom round.

½ cup extra-virgin olive oil
2 large green bell peppers, seeded and sliced
1 medium onion, sliced
6 large garlic cloves, finely chopped
2¼ pounds boneless beef stew meat, cut up into irregular shapes
1¾ pounds Yukon gold potatoes, peeled and cut up into irregular shapes
1 tablespoon salt
1 teaspoon freshly ground black pepper
¼ teaspoon ground cloves
1 bay leaf
Big pinch of saffron, crumbled in a mortar using a pestle
1 cup dry white wine

Put the olive oil, bell peppers, onion, garlic, and beef in the stewpot in that order. Layer the potatoes on top of the beef. Add the salt, pepper, cloves, bay leaf, and saffron. Add the wine and enough water to cover and bring to a boil. Reduce the heat to low, cover, and cook until the meat is very tender, about 2½ hours. Remove and discard the bay leaf. Serve immediately.

Pot Roast with Cranberries

This is a wonderful way to get rid of that extra bag of cranberries you bought for Thanksgiving. Actually, it's just a great pot roast with a delightful tangy flavor from the cranberries, which melt into the sauce from long cooking. It sounds sweet, but it isn't.

One 2½-pound beef bottom round
All-purpose flour, for dredging
Salt and freshly ground black pepper, to taste
2 tablespoons vegetable oil
One 1-pound bag fresh cranberries
1½ cups water
½ cup sugar
1 cup beef broth
3 whole cloves
1 cinnamon stick
8 small onions (about 1 pound), peeled
12 small carrots (about 1 pound), scraped
1½ pounds turnips, cut into 2-inch pieces
1 teaspoon fresh lemon juice

1. Dredge the beef in the flour, tapping off any excess, and season lightly with salt and pepper.

2. In a large, heavy flameproof baking casserole, heat the oil over medium heat, then brown the beef all over, about 10 minutes in total. Add the cranberries, water, and sugar and cook, stirring, for 8 minutes. Add the beef broth, cloves, and cinnamon stick, reduce the heat to low, and cook, covered, turning occasionally, for 2½ hours.

3. Add the whole onions, carrots, and turnips, cover, and continue cooking until tender, 45 minutes. Remove and discard the cinnamon stick. Add the lemon juice and let rest for 15 minutes before serving.

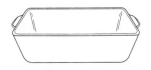

Beef, Yam, and Pecan Casserole

I like to use yams in this casserole because the orange color is so attractive. It's important that the yams be sliced as instructed, or they will not cook through in the time suggested. If you like, you can replace the beef steak with ground beef. You'll also be using a lot of chives in this dish.

1¼ pounds yams, peeled and cut into ¼-inch slices
Salt and freshly ground black pepper, to taste
1½ cups chopped fresh chives (from about 3 bunches)
1¼ pounds skirt steak, flap steak, or flank steak, sliced into
   ½-inch-thick slices with the grain
1 cup pecan halves (about ¼ pound)
3 tablespoons unsalted butter, cut into thin slices
1 cup heavy cream

1. Preheat the oven to 375°F.

2. Arrange the yam slices on the bottom of a buttered 13 × 9 × 2-inch (or similar) baking casserole. Season with salt and pepper. Sprinkle the chives over the sweet potatoes. Lay the beef slices on top of the chives and sprinkle with the pecans and a little salt and pepper. Lay the butter slices over the beef. Pour the cream over everything, cover with aluminum foil, and bake until the yams are soft and the sauce is bubbling vigorously, about 1¼ hours. Serve hot.

Spicy Beef and Onion Stew

This stew is so common in Algeria that it is called *tabikha*, which means something like "cooked dish." When the Arabs arrived in the mid-seventh century A.D., Algeria was a Berber land where they also found a population of Jews, for whom this stew was a wedding-day stew. It also is made for the bar mitzvah. For these reasons, among Algerian Jews the dish is a prestigious one. The only vegetable in the dish is the onion, to symbolize the sweetness of the marriage and the hope that it may not turn sour, to vinegar.

¼ cup extra-virgin olive oil
2 large onions, grated with a box grater
3 garlic cloves, chopped
1 tablespoon harīsa (see box page 140)
Salt and freshly ground black pepper, to taste
1 pound beef chuck or bottom round, trimmed of excessive fat and cubed
1 pound ripe tomatoes, peeled, seeded, and chopped (see box page 47)
2 cups water
¼ cup finely chopped fresh cilantro (coriander leaf)
Flatbread, for serving

1. In a large, heavy flameproof baking casserole or stewpot, heat the olive oil over medium-high heat, then add the onions and cook, stirring occasionally, until translucent, about 10 minutes.

2. Add the garlic and harīsa, season with salt and pepper, and stir to mix well. Add the beef and brown on all sides, 2 to 4 minutes. Add the tomatoes and water. Stir, reduce the heat to medium, cover, and cook for 45 minutes.

3. Add the cilantro and cook until the meat is tender, another 45 minutes. Serve hot with flatbread.

Harīsa

The spicy chile paste known as *harīsa** is the single most important condiment used in the North African cooking of Algeria and Tunisia. It is made commercially and you might find it sold in tubes or small cans in supermarkets. However, there's nothing like your own, and given how easy it is to make, here's a recipe for you to try. I'll wager that you'll start using it far beyond the North African dishes that call for it. I call for specific dried chiles, but these are not rare or hard to find; they're simply the names of some commonly found chiles whose exact names you may not have noticed before.

4 ounces dried guajillo chiles
1 ounce dried árbol chiles
5 large garlic cloves
2 tablespoons water
2 tablespoons extra-virgin olive oil
½ teaspoon freshly ground caraway seeds
¼ teaspoon freshly ground coriander seeds
1½ teaspoons salt
Extra-virgin olive oil, for topping off

1. Soak the chiles in tepid water to cover until softened, about 1 hour.

2. Drain and remove the stems and seeds. Place in a blender or food processor with the garlic, water, and olive oil and process until completely smooth, stopping occasionally to scrape down the sides.

3. Transfer the mixture to a bowl and stir in the caraway, coriander, and salt. Store in a jar and top off with a layer of olive oil covering the surface of the paste. Unless you use all the harīsa within 2 weeks, whenever the paste is used you must always top off with olive oil, making sure that no paste is exposed to air; otherwise it will spoil.

Makes 1 cup

*Often, and incorrectly, spelled as *harissa*; the correct transliteration uses the macron diacritical mark.

Ground Beef and Mung Beans

There's a secret to this dish: do not stir it after it starts to cook. Not only is this an easy preparation but you'll also be amazed at how flavorful it is from so little beef and spices. The resulting dish is like a big pilaf except that you've got legumes in it. Remember not to stir as it finishes cooking.

2 tablespoons unsalted butter
2 medium onions, thinly sliced
½ pound ground beef
2 teaspoons salt
½ teaspoon ground turmeric
½ teaspoon freshly ground black pepper
4 cups water
⅔ cup dried mung beans
½ cup long-grain rice
½ cup dried pinto or red kidney beans

In a large, heavy flameproof baking casserole, melt the butter over medium heat, add the onions, and cook, stirring, until golden, 12 to 15 minutes. Add the beef, salt, turmeric, and pepper, and cook, stirring, until the meat is browned, about 5 minutes. Add the water, mung beans, rice, and beans and cook, *without stirring*, over medium heat until tender, about 50 minutes. Serve hot.

Catalan Beef Stew

Some years ago while writing a book, I rented an apartment in Barcelona in order to research Catalan food and fell in love with the various stews and braises of Catalonia—not to mention all of its other marvelous food. This is a recipe from Catalonia that cooks for a long time and is flavored with garlic and chocolate. It can be made with beef (known as *estofado de buey*) or veal (*estofado de ternera*), but in either case it is made with *morcillo* (foreknuckle, the fleshy part from the shoulder to the elbow) or *espalda* (shoulder or back meat). Please don't shy away from using pork lard; it's a make-or-break ingredient for this stew.

2 tablespoons all-purpose flour
4 ounces (½ cup) pork lard
1¾ pounds small Yukon gold or fingerling potatoes, peeled
1 pound small white onions
5 ounces lean bacon
2¼ pounds boneless beef shoulder clod and shank, cut into large chunks
1 large onion, chopped
1 carrot, scraped and cut into rounds
2 heads garlic, outer skin rubbed off but cloves left attached
Bouquet garni, tied in cheesecloth, consisting of 4 fresh flat-leaf parsley sprigs,
    3 fresh thyme sprigs, and 1 bay leaf
2 large tomatoes
1 cup very dry sherry
¼ cup brandy
1 cinnamon stick
1 ounce dark bitter unsweetened chocolate
Salt and freshly ground black pepper, to taste
2 tablespoons finely chopped fresh parsley

1. In a large, heavy flameproof baking casserole, cook the flour without any fat or liquid until browned, a few minutes. Remove and set aside. Add 1 ounce (2 tablespoons) of the lard and melt over medium-high heat. Add the potatoes and small white onions and cook, stirring, until golden, about 5 minutes. Remove with a slotted spoon and set aside.

2. Add the remaining 3 ounces (6 tablespoons) lard to the casserole, reduce the heat to medium, and once it melts, add the bacon and cook, stirring, until golden. Add the beef and cook until browned on all sides, about 10 minutes.

3. Add the chopped onion, carrot, garlic heads, and bouquet garni, stir, and simmer for 15 minutes over low heat, adding a few tablespoons of water if it is drying out. Add the tomatoes and cook, stirring, for 5 minutes, then add the sherry, brandy, and cinnamon stick. Sprinkle with the browned flour and add water to cover. Bring to a boil over high heat, then reduce the heat to low, cover, and cook for 1 hour.

4. Add the reserved potatoes and onions and the chocolate. Add some hot water, if necessary, to keep everything covered with liquid. Cook over low heat, partially covered, until the beef is tender, about 4 hours.

5. Season with salt and pepper. Remove and discard the bouquet garni and cinnamon stick. Serve from the casserole with the parsley sprinkled on top.

Stove-Top Casseroled Beef, Beans, and Rice

The ideal vessel for this dish is an enameled cast-iron flameproof baking casserole. The beans get cooked first, and as their water evaporates the other ingredients are added and everything melds together with wonderful and enticing flavors. At the end, you add the rice. You may use peas instead of the spinach, in which case cook it for 3 to 4 minutes more.

½ cup dried red kidney beans

10 to 12 cups water

2 teaspoons salt

½ cup dried black-eyed peas

3 tablespoons extra-virgin olive oil

1 pound ground beef

4 canned plum tomatoes, chopped

1 celery stalk, chopped

1 medium onion, chopped

2 large garlic cloves, finely chopped

1 cup long-grain rice, rinsed well

5 ounces spinach leaves, coarsely chopped, or 1 cup fresh or frozen peas

¼ cup chopped fresh flat-leaf parsley

¼ cup chopped fresh dill

⅛ teaspoon cayenne pepper

Freshly ground black pepper, to taste

1. Put the red beans in large, heavy flameproof baking casserole and cover with 8 cups of the water. Bring to a boil over high heat, add 1 teaspoon of the salt, and cook for 15 minutes. Add the black-eyed peas and continue cooking for 45 minutes longer, replenishing with more water when it has almost evaporated.

2. When the beans are almost tender, let the last addition of water nearly evaporate. Add the olive oil and then the ground beef, tomatoes, celery, onion, and garlic and cook, stirring and breaking up the meat, until the vegetables are softened, about 4 minutes. Reduce the heat to low, cover, and simmer for 10 minutes. Add 1 cup of water and the rice and cook, covered, until the rice has absorbed the water, about 15 minutes.

3. Add the spinach, parsley, and dill and cook, stirring and tossing until wilted, about 3 minutes. Season with the cayenne, the remaining teaspoon salt, and the black pepper and serve hot.

Fragrant Rice Pilaf with Bison, Carrots, and Peas

A Middle Eastern rice pilaf with bison is of course an American invention, as bison are not found in the Middle East. But there's no reason why we shouldn't use this wonderful lean and light-tasting meat in such a dish. A perfect rice pilaf is achieved by soaking long-grain rice in water, frying the grains in fat, and finally, never touching or stirring the rice while it cooks. In this recipe, inspired by the cooking of the small Emirates of the Persian Gulf, the fragrance comes from the spices that are used whole rather than ground. The whole dried lime can be found in Middle Eastern markets or you can dry your own by leaving Key limes out for a month to dry. The optional Aleppo pepper can be found at www.penzeys.com and in Middle Eastern markets.

2 tablespoons unsalted butter or clarified butter
1 small onion, finely chopped
1 large garlic clove, finely chopped
2 cups long-grain rice such as basmati, soaked in water for 30 minutes, rinsed, and drained
1 pound ground bison or ground beef
1 large carrot, scraped and finely diced
1 cup frozen peas
¼ cup golden raisins
Seeds from 3 cardamom pods
1 cinnamon stick
1 bay leaf
2 whole cloves
1 dried lime (*lūmī* or *loomi*) or 1 tablespoon fresh lime juice
2 teaspoons salt
3½ cups water
1 teaspoon Aleppo pepper (optional)
Whole-milk plain yogurt, for garnish

1. In a large, heavy flameproof baking casserole, melt the butter over medium-high heat, then add the onion and garlic and cook, stirring constantly, until translucent, 1 to 2 minutes. Add the rice and cook, stirring, for 2 minutes. Add the bison, carrot, peas, raisins, cardamom, cinnamon, bay leaf, cloves, dried lime, and salt and stir, breaking up the ground bison with a wooden spoon as you do.

2. Add the water, bring to a furious boil over high heat so everything in the casserole is bubbling, then turn the heat off, cover with a kitchen towel, replace the lid, and let rest to absorb all the liquid, about 1 hour. Remove and discard the cinnamon stick, bay leaf, and cloves. Transfer the rice pilaf to an oval or round platter, mound attractively with your hands, and sprinkle with Aleppo pepper, if using. Serve hot with some yogurt on the side.

Spinach, Mustard, and Prune Stew

This stew will give you a definite tang from the sharp taste of mustard. However, it is all delightfully moderated by the prunes, which eventually disintegrate in the stew. The stew is thick and green and most attractive. This Persian-influenced dish should be accompanied by warm flatbread.

4 tablespoons (½ stick) unsalted butter

1 large onion, halved and then thinly sliced

¼ cup finely chopped fresh mint

1 pound beef round, cut into small cubes

1 teaspoon ground cinnamon

1 teaspoon salt

4 cups water

1 pound dried pitted prunes

2 tablespoons sugar

2 teaspoons ground turmeric

½ teaspoon freshly ground black pepper

1 pound fresh spinach, coarsely chopped

1 pound fresh mustard greens, coarsely chopped

1 bunch fresh cilantro (coriander leaf), coarsely chopped

½ cup fresh lemon juice

1. In a large, heavy flameproof baking casserole, melt 2 tablespoons of the butter over medium heat and cook the onion, stirring, until golden, about 10 minutes. Remove from the casserole with a slotted spoon and set aside. Stir the mint into the onion.

2. Add the remaining 2 tablespoons butter to the casserole and let it melt over medium heat. Add the meat to the casserole, season with the cinnamon and salt, and cook, stirring, until it is golden on all sides, about 5 minutes. Add the water and bring to a boil over high heat, then reduce the heat to medium and cook, stirring occasionally, until the beef chunks are a bit tender, about 1 hour.

3. Add the prunes and cook until the sauce is gravy-like and the prunes are very soft, about 45 minutes.

4. Add the sugar, turmeric, and black pepper and stir into the meat. Add the spinach, mustard, and cilantro in handfuls, stirring as each batch wilts, and then cook, stirring, for 10 minutes. Remove from the heat, stir in the onion-mint mixture and the lemon juice, and serve hot.

Baked Rice Casserole with Veal and Cabbage

This preparation is best cooked in a Spanish-style earthenware *cazuela*, but any baking casserole will do. This is a hearty and easy casserole to make since everything goes into the casserole with no precooking, and then it just bakes slowly until done. It's not a Spanish dish, but serving it with a Spanish *allioli* (page 388) improves it remarkably.

1 pound ground veal
2½ cups chicken broth, vegetable broth, or water
1 cup medium-grain rice such as Calrose or short-grain rice such as Arborio
1 large Yukon gold potato (10 ounces), peeled and diced
1 large turnip (10 ounces), peeled and diced
1 pound green cabbage, cored and coarsely chopped
1 medium onion, chopped
½ green bell pepper, seeded and chopped
4 large garlic cloves, finely chopped
¼ cup extra-virgin olive oil
4 whole cloves
1 tablespoon hot paprika
1 bay leaf, finely crumbled
2 teaspoons salt
Freshly ground black pepper, to taste
¼ cup chopped fresh cilantro (coriander leaf) or fresh flat-leaf parsley
Allioli, for garnish (see box page 388)

1. Preheat the oven to 350°F.

2. In a large earthenware casserole (preferably) or any baking casserole, stir together the veal, broth, rice, potato, turnip, cabbage, onion, bell pepper, garlic, olive oil, cloves, paprika, bay leaf, salt, and pepper. (If using earthenware and it is not flameproof, you will need to use a heat diffuser. Earthenware heats up slower but retains its heat longer than other casseroles. When using earthenware, food may cook slower at first and then cook very quickly while retaining its heat.) Break up the ground veal further with your fingers, place the casserole in the oven, and bake until the liquid is absorbed and the rice tender, about 2 hours. Sprinkle with the cilantro and serve hot with the allioli.

Veal, Cabbage, and Pumpkin Ragoût

In this preparation, which may be made with summer or winter squash depending on the season, the pumpkin (or zucchini in the summer) and the cabbage nearly disintegrate after the long cooking and thicken the ragoût in a most pleasant way. This stew is ideally made in an earthenware tagine, but if you don't have one then a heavy enameled flameproof cast-iron or similar casserole is fine.

¾ cup extra-virgin olive oil
1 pound boneless veal shoulder, cut into bite-size pieces
Salt and freshly ground black pepper, to taste
1 medium onion, chopped
2 teaspoons harīsa (see box page 140)
1½ teaspoons freshly ground coriander seeds
1½ teaspoons cayenne pepper
1 teaspoon ground turmeric
1½ pounds pumpkin flesh, cut into bite-size chunks
½ pound (about ½ a small head) green or savoy cabbage, cored, cut in half,
    and leaves separated

1. In a tagine or a large, heavy flameproof baking casserole, heat the olive oil over medium-high heat. Season the veal with salt and black pepper and add to the pan along with the onion, harīsa, and coriander. Cook, stirring, until it loses its pink color, about 8 minutes.

2. Add the cayenne pepper and turmeric and stir. Add the pumpkin and then the cabbage leaves. Cover and cook until the cabbage is wilted enough to dissolve into the ragoût, about 10 minutes.

3. Reduce the heat to low, cover, and cook, stirring and turning the ingredients occasionally, until everything is very tender, about 2½ hours. Mash the pumpkin and cabbage further using two forks to shred them. Let rest, covered, for 30 minutes before serving. Taste and correct the seasoning and serve hot.

Pork

I first came across the Iowa Pork Tenderloin Sandwich (page 154) when I was writing this book. I wanted to find a pork dish from America's heartland that I could include, but I wanted something famous locally and not something generic that could be attributed to more than one state. Here it was, a wonderful sandwich that not only met the one-pot criteria but was unique and utterly delicious. As a huge fan of sausages, I've included a good number of sausage recipes, but I think the relatively simple Greens Platter with Sausage (page 184) is probably my favorite. Strips of pork beg to be stir-fried, and I think Stir-Fried Pork and Golden Tofu with Chiles (page 198) fits the bill; easy to make and satisfying on all fronts.

Iowa Pork Tenderloin Sandwiches

An Iowa pork tenderloin sandwich is traditionally prepared from a thinly sliced piece of pork tenderloin that is pounded very thin so it is larger than the hamburger bun in which it will be enclosed. When served that way it's called a "hang over" because it hangs over the bun. The tenderloin is marinated in buttermilk and eggs, then dredged in bread crumbs or cracker crumbs before being fried in oil. The fried breaded tenderloin is served on a hamburger bun with condiments—typically mustard, iceberg lettuce, white onions, pickles, and mayonnaise—placed either on top, or traditionally under, the tenderloin. You will need to buy one long piece of pork tenderloin and slice from it four 5-ounce pieces. This recipe is based on the criteria used in a contest by the Iowa Pork Producers Association in awarding their Best Breaded Pork Tenderloin.

Four 5-ounce pieces pork tenderloin
½ cup buttermilk
1 large egg, beaten
3 tablespoons all-purpose flour
Salt and freshly ground black pepper, to taste
3 cups vegetable oil, for frying
2 to 3 cups Japanese-style panko bread crumbs
Four ¼-inch-thick slices iceberg lettuce
4 hamburger buns
½ cup mayonnaise
Four ¼-inch-thick slices tomato
Four ¼-inch-thick slices white onion
2 large pickles, sliced thinly lengthwise
4 tablespoons mustard
Coleslaw, for garnish

1. Lay the pieces of pork tenderloin in front of you on a work surface. Butterfly each piece of tenderloin with a sharp knife by placing your guide hand on top of the piece and slicing in the middle with the knife, making sure you do not cut all the way through. Open the sliced meat, place the meat between two sheets of plastic wrap, and pound gently with a mallet until about 10 × 5 inches.

2. In a glass or ceramic casserole, stir together the buttermilk, egg, flour, and salt and pepper. Lay the pounded cutlets in the marinade and marinate for 6 hours.

3. Preheat the frying oil in a large cast-iron skillet to 360°F using a deep-fry/candy thermometer to measure the temperature.

4. Remove the pork, let the marinade drip off, then dredge in the bread crumbs on both sides. Deep-fry the breaded pork cutlets in the oil until golden brown, about 3 minutes. Keep the cooked tenderloin warm in a low oven or near the stove while you prepare the sandwiches if you haven't done so already.

5. Lay a slice of lettuce on the bottom portion of a hamburger bun, cover with 2 tablespoons of mayonnaise, then lay a slice of tomato, a slice of onion, 2 pickle slices, and finally the mustard on the bun. Place the cutlet on top and cover with the top of the hamburger bun. Serve with coleslaw, if desired.

Pork Carnitas Tacos

Carnitas, meaning "little meats," is the name of a pork preparation in Mexico that usually finds its way into a soft corn taco. Pork shoulder is cut into slightly smaller than bite-size pieces and boiled in water until the water evaporates. Then the pieces continue to brown in the resulting fat until crispy on the outside. It's fun to set up all the ingredients and condiments on a platter and let diners serve themselves.

2 pounds boneless pork shoulder, cut into 1-inch pieces

2 quarts water

4 garlic cloves, crushed

1 large fresh habanero chile, cut in half

1 teaspoon cumin seeds

Salt and freshly ground black pepper, to taste

½ cup fresh orange juice

½ cup whole milk

12 white corn tortillas, warmed in the oven or over a burner

½ cup chopped fresh cilantro (coriander leaf)

1 medium red onion, chopped

2 avocados, cut in half, pitted, flesh scooped out and diced

¼ pound Mexican queso cotija, queso fresco, queso ranchero, or
    Greek feta cheese, crumbled

1 cup sour cream

1 cup salsa verde (green salsa), fresh or from a jar

6 lime wedges, for serving

1. In a large, flameproof baking casserole, combine the pork, water, garlic, habanero, and cumin seeds. Season with salt and pepper. Cover and bring to a boil over high heat. Reduce the heat to medium and cook, uncovered, until the water has evaporated, about 45 minutes. Attend to the pork as the water evaporates and it gets closer to frying in its own fat. Once it does, add the orange juice and milk and cook, stirring occasionally, until the liquid has evaporated, about 8 minutes. The pork will start browning after the liquid has evaporated. Cook, stirring constantly, until golden brown and crispy, about 3 minutes. Season well with salt and pepper.

2. Hold a corn tortilla and spoon some pork on top. Sprinkle with cilantro and spoon some onion, avocado, cheese, sour cream, and salsa verde on top. Squeeze some lime juice over the meat and serve.

Pork Belly and Kimchi Tacos

Itinerant food trucks serving gourmet fusion fast food were one of the great food novelties of the aughts in Los Angeles. One of the most popular trucks was the Kogi Korean BBQ with their Mexican-Korean fusion. This kind of preparation was born in the polyglot immigrant communities of southern California, and their offerings are true fusion, as is this Korean taco. Although the possibilities seem endless and younger diners with adventurous palates are eagerly horrifying the parents from the old country, these aren't random combinations but rather combinations based on an understanding of what will work taste-wise. This particular taco I've adapted from Long Beach, California, denizen Julie Kang, from her Korean American women's blog Kimchimamas.

¾ pound pork belly slices (fresh bacon)
Salt and freshly ground black pepper, to taste
¼ pound oyster mushrooms, sliced
1 teaspoon sesame oil
One 12-ounce jar prepared kimchi, coarsely chopped
1 teaspoon Korean chile flakes (preferably) or chile flakes,
    or to taste (optional)
12 corn tortillas
1 cup chopped green cabbage
1 small tomato, chopped
1 cup Simple Guacamole (see box page 159)
¼ pound Mexican queso fresco cheese (optional)

1. Place the pork belly strips in a large sauté pan and cook, turning occasionally, over low heat, covered, until a bit golden, about 10 minutes. Uncover and continue cooking until tender, about 30 minutes longer. Season with salt lightly (because the kimchi may be salty) and pepper. Cut the pork belly into 1-inch pieces while they're still in the sauté pan. Add the mushrooms and sesame oil and cook, stirring, for 4 minutes.

2. Add the kimchi and chile flakes and cook until tender, 30 minutes.

3. Wrap the corn tortillas in aluminum foil and warm in an oven or warm each individually over a burner.

4. Mix the cabbage and tomato together. Spread some guacamole on a tortilla. Sprinkle on some cabbage and then lay some pork belly strips and kimchi on the tortilla and top with the cheese, if desired. Serve hot.

Simple Guacamole

2 ripe avocados, cut in half, pitted, flesh scooped out
2 fresh green serrano chiles, seeded or not, finely chopped
1 medium tomato, chopped
½ cup chopped red onion
¼ cup finely chopped fresh cilantro (coriander leaf)
3 tablespoons fresh lime juice
1 teaspoon ground cumin
Salt and freshly ground black pepper, to taste

Place all the ingredients in a deep bowl and mash with a fork until mushy with little chunks. Check the seasoning and adjust. Transfer to a serving bowl. Serve immediately or cover and refrigerate for later.

Makes 2 cups

Sausage, Fennel, and Potato Tortillas

This simple preparation is perfect when you want a dinner with a lot of flavor in a short amount of time that is easy to do. Chipotle chiles en adobo are sold in small cans in supermarkets. Once opened, cover and refrigerate and they will last several weeks, or freeze for several months.

1 tablespoon extra-virgin olive oil
½ pound Yukon gold potatoes, peeled and diced small
2 shallots, finely chopped
2 large garlic cloves, finely chopped
1 fennel bulb, trimmed of stalk, chopped
1 pound mild Italian sausage or fresh Mexican chorizo sausage,
    casing removed and crumbled
½ pound tomatoes, peeled, seeded, and chopped (see box page 47)
3 tablespoons chopped chipotle chiles en adobo
1 teaspoon ground red chile powder
½ teaspoon ground cumin
Salt and freshly ground black pepper, to taste
Six 8-inch flour tortillas
1 cup crumbled queso fresco or feta cheese
Sour cream, for garnish

1. In a large, flameproof baking casserole, heat the olive oil over medium-low heat, then add the potatoes, shallots, garlic, and fennel and cook, covered and stirring occasionally, until softer, about 10 minutes. Add the sausage and cook, breaking it up with a wooden spoon as you stir, until it begins to turn color in a few minutes.

2. Add the tomatoes, chipotle chiles en adobo, ground chile, cumin, salt, and pepper, reduce the heat to low, cover, and simmer, stirring occasionally, until cooked through and tender, about 10 minutes.

3. Heat the tortillas in an oven or over a burner and divide the stuffing ingredients among them. Sprinkle the cheese on top and roll them up tightly. Serve hot with the sour cream.

Braised Pork Shoulder with Hominy

This recipe and the next, Braised Pork Spareribs with Hominy and Black Beans (page 162), seem identical, but a close look will show that they are very different. This delicious braised pork shoulder is based on the same cooking concept used in Pork Carnitas Tacos (page 156), namely the meat is first stewed until tender; then once the liquid has evaporated, the meat fries in its own fat. It's a substantial meal and although you don't need an accompaniment, I do like to serve some very simple broccoli slaw on the side, using the precut broccoli slaw bags I find in the supermarket mixed with vinegar and mayonnaise.

1¼ pounds boneless pork shoulder, with its fat, cut into 1-inch cubes
1 medium onion, quartered
2 large garlic cloves, chopped
4 fresh jalapeño chiles, 2 red and 2 green, seeded and cut into rings
1 bay leaf
1 teaspoon ground cumin
1 teaspoon dried oregano
4 cups chicken broth
One 29-ounce can hominy, rinsed and drained
One 15-ounce can black beans, rinsed and drained
Freshly ground black pepper, to taste
2 tablespoons finely chopped fresh cilantro (coriander leaf)
2 scallions, chopped
½ cup sour cream

1. In a large, flameproof baking casserole, place the pork, onion, garlic, chiles, bay leaf, cumin, and oregano and cover with the chicken broth. Bring to a boil over high heat, then reduce the heat to low and simmer, stirring occasionally, until all the liquid has evaporated, about 3¼ hours.

2. Add the hominy and black beans, cover, and simmer, stirring occasionally, for 20 minutes. Season with pepper. Remove and discard the bay leaf. Serve topped with the cilantro, scallions, and sour cream.

Braised Pork Spareribs with Hominy and Black Beans

In this preparation the spareribs are separated into their individual ribs and then braised in onion, bell pepper, and their own juices. The aromas of this dish emanating from the slow-cooked ribs are very enticing, and the ribs give their flavor to the hominy and refried black beans.

2 tablespoons extra-virgin olive oil
1½ pounds pork spareribs, separated into individual ribs
½ cup water
1 medium onion, sliced
½ green bell pepper, seeded and cut in half
3 large garlic cloves, finely chopped
3 fresh green serrano chiles, seeded or not, sliced
1 bay leaf, finely crumbled
1 teaspoon ground cumin
Salt, to taste
One 29-ounce can Mexican-style hominy, rinsed and drained
One 16-ounce can refried black beans with jalapeño chiles
Freshly ground black pepper, to taste
¼ cup chopped fresh cilantro (coriander leaf)
2 ounces Mexican queso ranchero cheese, crumbled

1. In a flameproof baking casserole, heat the olive oil over low heat. Add the ribs, water, onion, bell pepper, garlic, chiles, bay leaf, cumin, and salt and cook, stirring occasionally, until softened, about 2 hours. Remove the ribs with a slotted spoon.

2. Add the hominy to one end of the casserole and the refried black beans to the other. Lay the spare ribs on tips, season with pepper, and cook until hot, bubbling, and tender, about 30 minutes. Serve with a sprinkling of cilantro and cheese.

Pork with Sweet Peppers

All the different colored bell peppers make this dish look very pretty and colorful. The peppers are mounded atop a large toasted piece of French country bread that acts as a trencher for the flavorful juices. The pork is seared very quickly with the peppers and onion.

Four 7 × 5 × ¾-inch slices Italian or French country bread (about 7 ounces)
6 tablespoons extra-virgin olive oil
1 pound boneless pork sirloin, cut into small bite-size pieces
1 medium onion, finely chopped
2 red bell peppers, seeded and cut into 1-inch pieces
2 green bell peppers, seeded and cut into 1-inch pieces
2 orange or yellow bell peppers, seeded and cut into 1-inch pieces
2 garlic cloves, finely chopped
¼ cup dry white wine
Salt and freshly ground black pepper, to taste
¼ cup finely chopped fresh marjoram or ½ teaspoon dried marjoram (optional)
¼ cup finely chopped fresh flat-leaf parsley

1. Preheat the oven to 350°F.

2. Brush the bread slices with 2 tablespoons of the olive oil and toast in the oven until lightly browned.

3. In a large, flameproof baking casserole, heat the remaining 4 tablespoons olive oil over medium-high heat. Add the pork and cook, stirring or shaking the casserole often so all sides of the pork brown evenly, about 4 minutes. Add the onion, bell peppers, and garlic and cook, stirring frequently, until much softer, about 8 minutes. Add the white wine, season with salt and pepper, and cook for 2 minutes while the wine reduces. Sprinkle with marjoram and parsley, stir again, and serve hot, spooning it on top of the bread slices.

Bacon, Cabbage, and Chickpea Stew

This one-pot farm meal from Andalusia in southern Spain has the distinctive smell and taste of cumin. These kinds of stews are called *olla* in Spain, after the stewpot, and this simple recipe is representative of *cocina pobre*, the cuisine of the poor, from the hilly farmlands around Córdoba. This stew can be frozen and is excellent later in the week. Although you could use cooked chickpeas from a can, cooking them takes only 10 minutes in step 1, and you would miss out on a lot of flavor. Serve with crusty bread.

5 quarts cold water
2 cups dried chickpeas (about 1 pound), soaked in cold water for 8 hours,
     then drained, or 4 cups cooked chickpeas (from about three 15-ounce cans),
     rinsed and drained
1 large onion, chopped
3 large garlic cloves
3 tablespoons extra-virgin olive oil
1 teaspoon ground cumin
Salt, to taste
½ pound Irish or Canadian bacon, diced
1 small head green cabbage (about 1¾ pounds), cored and chopped

1. Bring the water to a boil in a stewpot. If using soaked dried chickpeas, add them, along with the onion, garlic, olive oil, cumin, and salt, and cook for 2 hours.

2. Reduce the heat to medium and add the bacon. Cook until the chickpeas are softened, about 1 hour.

3. Add the cabbage to the pot and cook for 1 hour. Taste and correct the seasoning and serve.

Pork and Cabbage Stew

The snowy white and cold winter of Salzburg, Austria, is charming. The air is crisp. The smell of the forest is close and as you gaze over the rooftops, smoke glides lazily upward from countless chimneys. When I lived in Salzburg through the chilly fall of 1977, my hausfrau introduced me to *Wienereintopf*, Viennese stew, made with pork and cabbage and seasoned with ground caraway seeds. This stew always reminds me of that lovely time.

6 tablespoons (¾ stick) unsalted butter
1 large onion, sliced
1½ pounds Yukon gold potatoes, peeled and sliced ¼ inch thick
2 pounds boneless pork shoulder, cut into 1½-inch cubes
2 large carrots, scraped and sliced
½ small savoy cabbage (about ¾ pound), cored and chopped
2 teaspoons freshly ground caraway seeds
Salt and freshly ground black pepper, to taste
2 cups chicken broth

1. Preheat the oven to 350°F with the rack set in the lower third of the oven.

2. In a large, flameproof baking casserole, melt the butter over medium-high heat. Add the onion and cook, stirring, until translucent, about 10 minutes. Remove the onion with a slotted ladle and reserve. Pour off all the butter and reserve it, leaving enough to coat the bottom of the casserole.

3. Layer the potatoes, pork, carrots, and cabbage, in that order, in the casserole, sprinkling each layer with caraway, salt, and pepper. Make the final layer one of potatoes and top with the reserved sautéed onions. Again, sprinkle with caraway, salt, and pepper. Pour the reserved butter over the top. Pour the chicken broth over the potatoes. Cover the casserole tightly.

4. Bake until the pork and potatoes are tender, about 2½ hours. Remove the lid, increase the heat to broil, and cook until the top potato layer is browned, 3 to 4 minutes. Serve immediately.

Pumpkin and Cabbage Stew

This is a wonderfully enriched pork and pumpkin stew based on minestrone that is perfect for the fall. The main event here is the pumpkin and cabbage, but there's plenty of meat and even macaroni to create a soul-satisfying dish. The amount of herbs is quite copious and all of that goes to make this such a delicious stew. This is a recipe to make in October and November when pumpkins are plentiful.

¼ cup extra-virgin olive oil, plus more for drizzling
1 medium white onion, finely chopped
4 large garlic cloves, finely chopped
1 carrot, scraped and finely chopped
1 celery stalk, finely chopped
2 ounces pancetta, chopped
¼ cup finely chopped fresh flat-leaf parsley
¼ cup finely chopped fresh basil leaves
3 tablespoons finely chopped fresh mint leaves
2 fresh rosemary sprigs, leaves chopped
2 tablespoons fresh thyme leaves
1 pound ground pork
1¾ pounds pumpkin flesh, cubed small
1 pound green cabbage, cored and shredded
6 cups water
¾ pound veal or beef marrow or soup bones (preferred, but optional)
1 piece Parmigiano-Reggiano cheese rind (optional)
Salt and freshly ground black pepper, to taste
¼ pound small macaroni such as tubetti, ditalini, pennette,
    or small elbow macaroni
Freshly grated pecorino cheese, for sprinkling

1. In a large stewpot, heat the olive oil over medium-high heat, then add the onion, garlic, carrot, celery, pancetta, parsley, basil, mint, rosemary leaves, and thyme and cook, stirring occasionally so the garlic doesn't burn, until the onions are softened, about 6 minutes.

2. Add the pork and cook, breaking it up with a wooden spoon, until browned, about 3 minutes. Add the pumpkin and cabbage and toss a few times so all the ingredients are mixed well. Add the water and bring to a boil, then immediately reduce the heat to low, add the veal marrow bones and Parmigiano-Reggiano cheese rind, if using, and cook until the pumpkin is tender, about 1 hour.

3. Season with salt and pepper, return the stew to a boil, add the pasta, and cook until al dente, about 10 minutes. Turn off the heat and let sit for 10 minutes. Taste and correct the seasoning and serve with pecorino and a drizzle of olive oil.

Bean and Cabbage Stew

This humble bean and cabbage stew is one of the famous dishes of the French region of Roussil-lon, which borders Spain. The stew is called *ouillade* in French, derived from the Old French verb meaning "to replenish the cask or cauldron," implying that this stew was perpetually cooking.

½ cup dried small white beans

6 quarts water

Bouquet garni, tied in cheesecloth, consisting of several fresh thyme sprigs
   and 1 bay leaf

¾ pound leeks, white and light green parts only, halved lengthwise,
   washed well, and sliced

6 ounces salt pork, diced small

Salt and freshly ground black pepper, to taste

1 pound Yukon gold potatoes, peeled and diced

¾ pound savoy cabbage (about ½ small head), damaged outer leaves
   removed, cored, and sliced

1 tablespoon goose fat or duck fat (preferably), pork lard, or butter

1. Place the beans in a large stewpot and cover with the water. Bring to a boil over medium-high heat, then add the bouquet garni, increase the heat to high, and boil, stirring occasionally, for 1 hour.

2. Add the leeks and salt pork and cook for 30 minutes. Don't wander away, because you need to stir occasionally. Remove and discard the bouquet garni. Check the seasoning, adding salt and pepper as desired. Add the potatoes and cabbage and cook, stirring frequently, until tender, about 10 minutes. Add the goose fat and cook for 3 minutes. Serve hot.

Pork, Pumpkin, and Fennel Ragoût

Normally, a stew or ragoût would cook slowly, but in this recipe you'll cook everything quickly. In order to get full flavor given how few ingredients there are, the first step is to create a crusty aromatic film on the bottom of the stewpot that you will lift up by simply deglazing with water.

¼ cup extra-virgin olive oil, plus more for drizzling
1 pound pork tenderloin, cut into bite-size pieces
2 ounces salt pork, chopped
5 large garlic cloves, finely chopped
2 quarts water
2½ pounds fennel, trimmed of all stalks except one, quartered lengthwise
1½ pounds pumpkin flesh, diced or cubed
Salt and freshly ground black pepper, to taste
1½ cups small elbow macaroni

1. In a stewpot, heat 3 tablespoons of the olive oil over high heat, then add the pork and cook, stirring constantly and vigorously, until browned on all sides, about 2 minutes. The pork will stick but that's all right; the bits will pull off when you deglaze later. Remove the pork with a slotted spoon and reserve. Add the remaining tablespoon olive oil and cook the salt pork and garlic, stirring constantly and vigorously so the garlic doesn't burn, until the salt pork is beginning to get a little crispy, 1 to 2 minutes. Remove the saucepan from the heat and deglaze with ¼ cup of the water, scraping the bottom and sides of the pot with a wooden spoon. Return the pot to the heat and let the water reduce by half. Add the fennel and pumpkin and, with the heat still on high, cook, tossing frequently, until well coated, about 6 minutes.

2. Add the remaining 7¾ cups water, scrape up any remaining bits from the bottom and sides of the stewpot, and cook over high heat until the vegetables are al dente, about 20 minutes, partially covering the pot once the broth begins to boil. Season with salt and pepper, add the macaroni and pork, and cook until the pasta is al dente and the vegetables are softened, about 10 minutes. Turn the heat off and let the stew sit for 5 minutes so everything settles down and the flavors meld. Serve in individual soup bowls with a drizzle of olive oil, if desired.

Spicy Pork and Squash Stew

This spicy stew needs to be eaten with something bland, and warmed flour tortillas are perfect. Serve the stew in bowls and rip off pieces of tortilla to pick up the pork. Chimayó chile is a chile produced in Chimayó, New Mexico, with a particularly desirable taste. You can order it from www.savoryspiceshop.com or the gourmet food and grocery section of www.amazon.com.

1¾ pounds boneless pork shoulder, cubed
All-purpose flour, for dredging
3 tablespoons pork lard or butter
1 medium onion, chopped
4 garlic cloves, finely chopped
2 fresh green serrano chiles, seeded or not, finely chopped
1½ cup dry white wine
1½ cups water
1 acorn squash (about 2 pounds), peeled, seeded, and cubed
2 tablespoons finely chopped fresh tarragon
2 tablespoons finely chopped fresh cilantro (coriander leaf)
1 tablespoon Chimayó chile powder or any red chile powder
3 whole cloves
1 teaspoon dried oregano
1½ cups (about ½ pound) fresh or frozen lima beans
Salt and freshly ground black pepper, to taste
Eight 6-inch flour tortillas

1. Dredge the pork in the flour and tap off any excess.

2. In a stewpot, melt the lard over medium-high heat, then add the onion, garlic, serrano chiles, and pork and cook, stirring, until the meat has turned color, about 5 minutes. Add the wine and water, bring to a boil over high heat, then reduce the heat to low and simmer, partially covered, for 2½ hours.

3. Add the squash, tarragon, cilantro, chile powder, cloves, and oregano, and continue cooking until tender, about 1 hour.

4. Add the lima beans, salt, and pepper and continue cooking for 45 minutes. Serve hot with the flour tortillas.

Garbure

I first published this recipe in my book *Real Stew* but feel compelled to reprint it here since it's the French one-pot meal par excellence. Garbure is the classic peasant farmer's stew from Béarn and Gascony in southwest France. It is the regional version of the stew known nationwide as *potée*. The main difference between the two is that a garbure contains dry white haricot beans and a ham bone. A garbure contains cabbage, a little meat such as bacon, salt pork, sausage, ham hock, or confit of duck and a variety of seasonal vegetables and it is less solid than a potée, being more stewy. It is said that the most famous garbure comes from the little town of Oloron-Sainte-Marie in the Pyrénnées Atlantiques, which hosts an annual Garburade, a festival of the local cooks' best garbures. The smoked bacon piece, which in some ways is the most critical ingredient, is best found in a German, Hungarian, or Polish delicatessen, of which there are plenty in this country. Notice that I do not take the peels off the fava beans. That's because the stew cooks so long that you will not need to, and the beans will keep their textural integrity and taste. This garbure is so good that you may want to double it. If you do, double all the ingredients listed except the ham bone and the bouquet garni.

3 quarts water

1 pound smoked bacon in one piece, preferably on the bone with its skin

2 tablespoons goose or duck fat (preferably), pork lard, or butter

1¼ pounds fresh ham hock

½ pound leeks, washed well and sliced

½ pound carrots, scraped and cut into rounds

½ celery stalk, chopped

6 large garlic cloves, finely chopped

1 ham bone

2 fresh pork sausages (about ½ pound), cut into 1-inch pieces

½ pound turnips, peeled and cubed

1 cup fresh fava beans

½ cup dried white haricot beans

4 Yukon gold, red, or white potatoes (about 1 pound), peeled and
    cut in half lengthwise
1 small green cabbage (about 1¼ pounds), cored and quartered
2 small onions, each studded with a clove
Bouquet garni, tied in cheesecloth, consisting of fresh flat-leaf parsley and
    thyme sprigs, celery leaves, and bay leaf
Salt and freshly ground black pepper, to taste
6 large slices Italian or French bread (about ½ pound), toasted and rubbed
    with cut garlic

1. In a large stewpot, bring 1 quart of the water to a boil and blanch the bacon piece for 30 minutes. Drain, saving the water, and reserve the bacon. Dry the pot with paper towels.

2. In the same large stewpot, melt the goose fat over medium-high heat, then add the remaining 2 quarts water, reserved bacon cooking water, the reserved bacon piece, ham hock, leeks, carrots, celery, and garlic and cook, stirring frequently so the garlic doesn't burn, about 5 minutes. Add the ham bone, sausages, turnips, favas, haricot beans, potatoes, cabbage, onions, and bouquet garni and season with salt and pepper. Bring to a boil, then reduce the heat to low and cook until the meats are tender, about 4 hours.

3. Remove the meats, remove all the meat from the bones, and return the meat to the stew. Discard the bones, skin, and fat of the ham hock, but keep the skin and fat of the bacon piece and return them to the stew. Remove and discard the ham bone and bouquet garni. Continue cooking until the stew is thick and a spoon could almost stand upright in it, about 30 minutes. If it is still soupy, remove extra liquid with a soup ladle.

4. Place a slice of bread at the bottom of each soup bowl, then ladle the broth and vegetables on top, and serve the meat on the side of the bowl.

The Lore of Garbure

The origin of garbure is controversial. The first mention of a garbure in French is apparently from the playwright Molière in 1655. The word *garbure* is of obscure origin too, although in Gascon it is *garburo*, perhaps derived from the Spanish word *garbías*, meaning a ragoût. This is how the sixteenth-century Spanish chef Ruperto de Nola used the word in his *Libro de guisados* from 1525 to describe a preparation called *fruta llamada garbias a la catalana* made of borage, Swiss chard, fresh cheese, and fine spices. So it seems as if the garbure might have Catalan origins. Another idea, which I don't accept, is that the word derives from the Basque *garbe*, meaning "sheaf" or "bunch," it being a bunch of vegetables. Sometimes the soupy part of the stew is served first with toasted or dried bread and the meat and vegetables are served afterward. And an authentic garbure requires that a piece of confit of duck, goose, or pork be thrown in half an hour before it's done. In the Béarn, the Basques make *chalorot* by blending a bit of red wine into the broth.

Pork, Pumpkin, and Bean Stew

This is a very simple family-style meal for the fall enhanced by the use of different cuts of pork. If you can't procure a prosciutto bone, use a ham hock, smoked or fresh. The final dish is an attractive white stew that you can season—and color—with black pepper and parsley.

1¾ cups (about ¾ pound) dried white beans
2 quarts water
2 pounds various cuts of pork such as shoulder, ribs, sausage, etc.,
      cut into pieces
One ¼-pound piece prosciutto bone or ⅛-inch-thick slice prosciutto
1 bay leaf
3 fresh thyme sprigs
2 medium onions, coarsely chopped
1 pound pumpkin flesh, coarsely chopped
½ cup medium-grain rice such as Calrose or short-grain rice such as Arborio
1 tablespoon salt
1 tablespoon freshly ground black pepper
¼ cup chopped fresh flat-leaf parsley

1. Place the beans in a stewpot with the water, pork meat, prosciutto bone, bay leaf, and thyme. Bring to just below a boil over high heat, then reduce the heat to very low and simmer the beans for 30 minutes. Add the onions and pumpkin and continue cooking, stirring occasionally, until the beans are almost breaking apart and the meat is very tender, about 3 hours.

2. Add the rice and salt, and cook until the rice is tender, 15 to 18 minutes. Remove and discard the bay leaf. Stir in the pepper and parsley and serve immediately.

Hotpot

This famous dish from the Lorraine region of France is called *potée Lorraine*. In 1954 my mom and dad moved us to Toul, near Nancy, the capital of Lorraine, and we ate *potée* that they learned how to make from their neighbors, as it was never a restaurant dish. It was almost the daily fare of the peasants. Variations of this hotpot are known throughout Europe, such as *hochepot*, Garbure (page 172), and Pot-au-Feu (page 252). What makes them distinctive is that they are not stews, but hotpots, which means the foods cooked retain their identity and are served in discrete portions as if they were cooked separately.

3 tablespoons unsalted butter

2 medium onions, thinly sliced

4 fat carrots, scraped and cut into small chunks

½ pound turnips, scraped and cut into small chunks

1 pound pork shoulder or smoked pork shoulder or chops

4 cups water

1 large garlic clove, crushed

Bouquet garni, tied in cheesecloth, consisting of fresh flat-leaf parsley and
      thyme sprigs, celery stalk with leaves, and bay leaf

3 whole cloves

½ cup dried white beans

1 small green cabbage (about 1 pound), cored and leaves separated

¼ pound smoked bacon piece, cut into thin strips

¾ pound fresh pork sausages, bratwurst, or smoked kielbasa

½ pound Yukon gold potatoes, peeled and sliced ¼ inch thick

¼ pound fresh green beans, trimmed

1 cup fresh or frozen peas

4 leeks, white part only, split lengthwise, washed well, and sliced ½ inch wide

Salt, to taste

1. In a large flameproof baking casserole, melt the butter over medium-high heat. Add the onions, carrots, and turnips and cook, stirring, until the onions are translucent, about 10 minutes. Put the pork shoulder on top of the vegetables. Add the water to cover along with the garlic, bouquet garni, and cloves. Reduce the heat to low, cover, and simmer for 30 minutes.

2. Add the beans and continue cooking without stirring for another 30 minutes.

3. Remove and discard the bouquet garni. Cover the meat with the cabbage leaves, lay the bacon strips on top of the cabbage, and cook for another 30 minutes.

4. Prick the sausages with a fork and place them on top of the cabbage leaves. Scatter the potatoes, green beans, peas, and leeks over the sausages and season with salt. Cook until the green beans are tender, 30 to 45 minutes. Serve hot.

Kassler Rippchen with Sauerkraut, Caramelized Onions, and Apples

Popular throughout Germany, *Kassler rippchen* is a smoked pork loin brined in salt. It is also readily available in American supermarkets sold already smoked, but without its German name. The meat of a smoked pork loin looks and tastes a bit like ham. In this preparation, you'll cook the onions and apples for a long time, until caramelized, and then put in the meat and sauerkraut, which only need to be heated through.

4 tablespoons (½ stick) unsalted butter
2½ pounds sweet onions such as Vidalia or Maui, cut in half and thinly sliced
1 Gala or Red Delicious apple, cored and sliced or chopped
1 Fuji or McIntosh apple, cored and sliced or chopped
1 pound sauerkraut, drained
4 smoked pork chops

For the mustard sauce
6 tablespoons sour cream
2 tablespoons Dijon mustard
1 tablespoon prepared horseradish

1. In a large sauté pan, melt the butter over low heat, then add the onions and apples and cook, stirring occasionally, until very soft and caramelized, about 1½ hours.

2. Push the onion-apple mixture to one side of the pan. Add the sauerkraut to the pan and place the smoked pork chops on top of the onion-apple mixture and the sauerkraut. Cover and cook until heated through, about 15 minutes.

3. For the mustard sauce, in a small bowl, stir together the sour cream, mustard, and horseradish. Serve on the side with the pork, sauerkraut, and onions.

Spanish Sausage with Chickpeas and Tomato

This recipe is best when you use a highly flavored sausage. I sometimes purchase from www.donajuana.com, which is a nice Internet source for a variety of sausages and salamis. Look for *butifarra* or *chorizo bilbao* sausages, but if they are not to be found then you can use hot Italian sausage, Cajun andouille sausage, or kielbasa. Blood sausage works well, too. Some cooks add pine nuts and hard-boiled eggs to the dish as a garnish once it's finished.

2 tablespoons extra-virgin olive oil
1 very large onion, chopped
½ pound Spanish *butifarra* sausage or hot Italian sausage, casing removed and sliced
4 slices prosciutto or *jamón serrano*, chopped
8 ripe plum tomatoes, peeled and chopped
Four 15-ounce cans chickpeas, rinsed and drained
¾ cup water
2 bay leaves
Salt and freshly ground black pepper, to taste
2 tablespoons chopped fresh flat-leaf parsley

1. In a large flameproof baking casserole (preferably earthenware), heat the olive oil over medium heat, then add the onion, sausage, and prosciutto and cook, stirring occasionally, until the onion is softened, about 10 minutes. (If using earthenware and it is not flameproof, you will need to use a heat diffuser. Earthenware heats up slower but retains its heat longer than other casseroles. When using earthenware, food may cook slower at first and then cook very quickly while retaining its heat.)

2. Add the tomatoes, chickpeas, water, and bay leaves, season with salt and pepper, reduce the heat to low, and cook, covered, until the meat is tender, about 35 minutes. Remove and discard the bay leaves. Sprinkle with the parsley and serve from the casserole.

Sausage with Chickpeas and Spinach

This combination of foods—sausage, chickpeas, and spinach—is typically found in both Italy and Spain. I love it cooked this way, as it's easy, simple, and delicious. One could find this mixture on top of pizza or stuffed into empanadas.

¼ cup extra-virgin olive oil
1¼ pounds mild Italian sausage
1 medium onion, cut in half and then sliced
3 large garlic cloves, finely chopped
¼ cup dry white wine
One 15-ounce can chickpeas, rinsed and drained
One 10-ounce bag spinach leaves
2 tablespoons finely chopped fresh basil leaves
Salt and freshly ground black pepper, to taste

In a large sauté pan, heat the olive oil with the sausage, onion, and garlic over high heat and cook, stirring, until the sausage is slightly browned and the onion a bit softer, about 6 minutes. Reduce the heat to medium, add the wine and chickpeas, and simmer until the sausage is cooked through, about 15 minutes. Add the spinach in handfuls and as each handful wilts, add another. Once all the spinach has been added and wilted, add the basil and cook, stirring, for 2 minutes. Season with salt and pepper and serve hot.

Sausage with Chickpeas and Napa Cabbage

In this preparation you'll want to use two kinds of fresh sausage. For example, you could use a hot Italian sausage and a chicken-cilantro sausage. Just use whatever two are the best quality where you shop.

6 tablespoons extra-virgin olive oil
¼ pound slab bacon, cut into matchsticks
½ pound celery, chopped
½ pound carrots, peeled and chopped
8 large garlic cloves, finely chopped
2 fresh thyme sprigs
2½ pounds fresh sausage (choose 2 or 3 types)
Two 15-ounce cans chickpeas, rinsed and drained
6 dried red chiles
2 pounds napa cabbage, cored and sliced
½ cup finely chopped fresh flat-leaf parsley
4 scallions, trimmed and chopped
Salt and freshly ground black pepper, to taste

1. In a large flameproof baking casserole, heat the olive oil with the bacon over medium heat and cook until the bacon starts turning translucent, about 2 minutes. Add the celery, carrots, garlic, and thyme sprigs and cook, stirring, until softer, about 4 minutes. Add the sausage and cook for 3 minutes, then add the chickpeas and chiles, reduce the heat to very low, and simmer, stirring occasionally, until the sausage is cooked through, about 40 minutes.

2. Add the napa cabbage and cook, stirring, until it has wilted, about 30 minutes. Season with the parsley, scallions, salt, and pepper and continue cooking for 5 minutes. Serve hot.

Kielbasa and Cabbage with Horseradish Sauce

This preparation is a standard in many Polish-American homes. Ideally, the dish is made with fresh kielbasa, but if you can only find smoked, then try fresh bratwurst or mild Italian sausage instead.

3 tablespoons pork lard or butter
1 pound fresh kielbasa (preferably), fresh bratwurst, or mild Italian sausage
¼ pound slab bacon, diced
1 large onion, cut in half and then sliced
1 large garlic clove, finely chopped
2½ pounds green cabbage, cored and shredded
2 teaspoons caraway seeds
Salt and freshly ground black pepper, to taste

For the horseradish sauce
1 cup sour cream
⅓ cup grated fresh horseradish
2 tablespoons Polish or Dijon mustard
½ teaspoon salt
½ teaspoon sugar

For accompaniment
Black bread or rye bread

1. In a large, flameproof baking casserole, melt the pork lard or butter over low heat, then add the sausage, bacon, and onion and cook, stirring, until the sausage loses its pink and is golden, about 25 minutes. Add the garlic and cook for 1 minute. Add the cabbage and caraway seeds and cook until wilted, about 35 minutes.

2. Meanwhile, prepare the horseradish sauce. Stir together the sour cream, horseradish, mustard, salt, and sugar in a bowl and reserve in the refrigerator until needed.

3. Season the cabbage with salt and pepper and serve hot with the horseradish sauce on the side and warm bread.

Garlic Sausages with Red Cabbage

If you have ever traveled in the lands of the old Austro-Hungarian Empire—Austria, Czech Repub-lic, Hungary, Croatia—you will run across hearty meals of sausage and cabbage like this recipe. Having traveled in Austria, Hungary, and the Czech Republic, I make this when I have a yearning for the food of the Hapsburgs. Short of a trip to Central Europe, you should try this recipe. For a starch, a potato dish would be typical, but cooking up some orzo would be nice, too. Warm rye bread or paprika-sprinkled dinner rolls are nice as well. Juniper berries sound exotic, but most good spice sections have them. They are also available through www.penzeys.com, or you can use dried raspberries.

2 tablespoons pork lard
1 medium white onion, peeled and thinly sliced
1 pound fresh garlic sausage or chicken sausage
2 pounds red cabbage, cored and shredded
10 dried juniper berries, coarsely ground in a mortar
½ teaspoon freshly ground caraway seeds
2 teaspoons paprika
1 teaspoon freshly ground black pepper
½ teaspoon salt
8 ounces sour cream (optional)

1. In a large sauté pan or flameproof baking casserole, melt the lard over medium-low heat. Add the onion and sausages and gently cook, stirring, until the onions are softened and the sausages are lightly browned, about 20 minutes.

2. Add the cabbage, juniper berries, caraway seeds, paprika, pepper, and salt and toss well to combine all the ingredients. Cover and cook, stirring occasionally, until the cabbage is softened, about 1 hour.

3. Stir in the sour cream (if using) and cook, tossing a bit, until it is blended, about 5 minutes. Serve immediately.

Greens Platter with Sausage

This platter of cooked mixed greens is quite familiar in southern Italy, where they would use wild greens, too. Feel free to substitute all the greens called for with prewashed bags of greens sold in supermarkets, and use any choice of greens that you wish. If using broccoli rabe, in particular, make sure you remove the heaviest portion of the stems. Serve with warm and crusty Italian or French bread.

¼ cup extra-virgin olive oil, plus more for drizzling (optional)
2 large garlic cloves, finely chopped
2 hot Italian sausage links (about ¾ pound), casing removed and crumbled
1 pound broccoli rabe, heavy stems removed, coarsely chopped
1 pound mustard greens, heavy stems removed, coarsely chopped
1 pound Swiss chard, coarsely chopped
1 pound spinach, heavy stems removed, coarsely chopped
Salt and freshly ground black pepper, to taste
Freshly grated Parmesan cheese

In a large, flameproof baking casserole that can hold all of the greens, heat the olive oil over medium heat, add the garlic, and cook, stirring, until sizzling. Add the Italian sausage and cook, stirring and breaking it up further with a wooden spoon, until it is cooked through, about 5 minutes. Add the broccoli rabe and cook until it starts to wilt, about 2 minutes. Add the mustard greens and Swiss chard and cook until they wilt, about 6 minutes. Add the spinach and cook until all the greens are wilted but still bright green, 2 to 3 minutes. Season the greens with salt and pepper, transfer to a serving platter, drizzle with more olive oil, if desired, and the cheese, and serve immediately.

Pan-Roasted Sausage, Potatoes, and Grapes

This unusual preparation, all finished in a single cast-iron skillet, will not seem so unusual once you've cooked and eaten it. The sweetness of the grapes acts as a wonderful foil for the heat of the spicy ingredients. It's quite satisfying and easy to do. Cook over a low heat the whole time. You might want to have a green salad on the side. I originally published this recipe in the *Lodge Cast Iron Cookbook* but wanted to include it here because it's a real winner.

6 tablespoons extra-virgin olive oil

2 large garlic cloves, crushed

3½ pounds potatoes (any kind), peeled and cubed small, dried well with
    paper towels

Salt, to taste

1 mild Italian sausage link (about ½ pound), casing removed and crumbled small

2 hot Italian sausage links (about 1 pound), casing removed and crumbled small

1 teaspoon red chile flakes (preferably Chimayó chile flakes; page 170)

2½ cups (about 1¼ pounds) green grapes

Freshly ground black pepper, to taste

1. In a 12- or 14-inch cast-iron skillet, heat the olive oil over low heat with the garlic cloves. Once the garlic turns light golden, remove and discard. Add the potatoes and shake the skillet so they cover the bottom. Season lightly with salt. Place the sausages on top of the potatoes, sprinkle with the chile flakes, and cook until the potatoes are sticking and golden on the bottom, about 15 minutes. Turn by scraping with a spatula and continue cooking, stirring occasionally, until golden brown, about 1 hour.

2. Add the grapes, season with salt and pepper, and cook until the grapes are softened, about 20 minutes. Serve hot.

Pan-Roasted Sasusage, Brussels Sprouts, and Potatoes

This is an attractive dish, as the potatoes will be golden and the Brussels sprouts will have an appetizing crispy look. The key to this dish is making sure you cook the ingredients in the proper order, then that you cook the Brussels sprouts with their cut side down until crispy and golden in the bacon fat. These are like no Brussels sprouts you've ever had. You will then add the kielbasa to finish the dish. If fresh kielbasa is not available, then use the more commonly found smoked kielbasa or whatever fresh sausage is readily available to you.

2 ounces bacon, cut into ½-inch strips or squares
2 tablespoons vegetable oil
1 pound all-purpose potatoes, peeled and cut into ½-inch cubes
1 small onion, thinly sliced
1 pound fresh kielbasa, smoked kielbasa, or other fresh sausage,
    cut into 1½-inch pieces
2 teaspoons finely chopped fresh sage
1 pound Brussels sprouts, trimmed and cut in half lengthwise
3 tablespoons chopped fresh flat-leaf parsley
Salt and freshly ground black pepper, to taste

1. Preheat a large cast-iron skillet over medium-high heat for 10 minutes.

2. Add the bacon and oil and cook, turning once, until the bacon is just beginning to become crispy, about 3 minutes, then add the potatoes and cook, stirring once or twice and scraping with a metal spatula when necessary, until they become light golden, 6 minutes. Add the onion and cook, stirring, until it begins to wilt, about 2 minutes.

3. Add the kielbasa and sage, then add the Brussels sprouts, cut side down, pushing other food aside if you have to. Cook, stirring occasionally and scraping the bottom of the skillet with a metal spatula to lift and turn, until the cut sides of the Brussels sprouts are golden brown and crispy, the kielbasa is cooked through, and the potatoes are tender, about 10 minutes. Season with the parsley, salt, and pepper, tossing a few times to mix well, then serve hot.

Smoked Sausage and Lentil Stew

This German stew is a rich, hearty one-pot meal that is perfect in cold weather. There are a couple of ingredients that you may not have used before. The first, lovage, is a musty herb that is used in stews, but it's rarely found outside of a farmers' market, so consider it optional. Celeriac is also known as celery root, which it is not; that is, it's not a root. It is a form of celery in which the lowest part of the stem, or corm, has been developed into a swollen state. You should be able to find it in the supermarket. Last, one piece of advice: Be careful you do not overcook the lentils, and stir them gently to keep them intact; otherwise the dish will look mushy.

> 2½ cups beef broth
> One ¾-pound smoked bacon piece
> 1 tablespoon tomato paste
> 1 pound black (beluga) lentils (preferably) or green or brown lentils,
>   rinsed and drained
> 2 carrots, scraped and diced
> 2 medium onions, coarsely chopped
> 2 leeks, white and light green part only, split lengthwise, washed well,
>   and sliced
> 1 celeriac (1½ to 2 pounds), trimmed, peeled, and diced
> ¾ pound Yukon gold, red, or white potatoes, peeled and diced
> 4 smoked kielbasa links (about 1½ pounds), sliced
> Leaves from 1 bunch fresh flat-leaf parsley, finely chopped
> 2 bushy fresh lovage sprigs, chopped (optional)
> 2 tablespoons white wine vinegar
> Salt and freshly ground black pepper, to taste

1. In a large, flameproof baking casserole, combine the broth, bacon, and tomato paste and bring to a gentle boil over medium-high heat, covered. Reduce the heat to low and add the lentils, carrots, onions, leeks, celeriac, and potatoes. Cover, and cook, gently stirring occasionally, until almost tender, about 1¼ hours.

2. Remove the piece of bacon and dice it; return the bacon to the casserole. Add the sausages, parsley, and lovage, if using, to the casserole. Cook until the sausage is heated through, about 10 minutes. Sprinkle with the vinegar, season with salt and pepper, and serve hot.

Italian Sausage, Broccoli Rabe, and Mustard Greens

This very flavorful dish will surprise you both with its beautiful color and delicious flavor. Ideally, you can use a package of prewashed mustard greens.

1 pound Italian sausage (mild or hot), casing removed and crumbled
2 large garlic cloves, finely chopped
2 tablespoons extra-virgin olive oil
1 pound broccoli rabe, heavy stems removed, coarsely chopped
½ pound Brussels sprouts, quartered
¾ pound mustard greens, heavy stems removed
Leaves from 1 bunch fresh flat-leaf parsley, coarsely chopped
1 bunch fresh cilantro (coriander leaf), coarsely chopped
Salt and freshly ground black pepper, to taste

In a large sauté pan or flameproof baking casserole, cook the sausage with the garlic over medium heat until the sausage turns color, breaking it up further with a wooden spoon. Add the olive oil, broccoli rabe, Brussels sprouts, mustard greens, parsley, and cilantro. Partially cover and cook, stirring occasionally, until all the greens are wilted and tender, about 7 minutes. Season with salt and pepper and serve hot.

Mock Pozole

Pozole is a Mexican stew of pork and hominy. I call this a "mock pozole" because I added things that aren't in a traditional pozole. It's great, though, and easy to make; however it does require long simmering. Nixtamal is a Mexican-style hominy often available in supermarkets around Christmastime. If you can't find it you'll have to use canned nixtamal-style hominy.

6 ounces dried pasilla or ancho chiles, soaked in tepid water for 1 hour
One 3½-pound pork butt, cut into 6 pieces
1 pound fresh Mexican chorizo sausage, coarsely chopped
1 pound kale, cut into strips
1 small eggplant, cubed
1 pound nixtamal white corn hominy
1 large onion, chopped
1 green bell pepper, seeded and chopped
8 large garlic cloves, finely chopped
1 large fresh red chile, seeded and finely chopped
2 ounces prosciutto fat, chopped
¼ cup extra-virgin olive oil
2 teaspoons freshly ground cumin seeds
1 teaspoon cayenne pepper
1 tablespoon dried oregano
Salt and freshly ground black pepper, to taste
2 pig's feet, split

1. In a food processor or blender, process the pasilla chiles with ½ cup of their soaking water until a paste forms.

2. In a large stewpot, add the pork, sausage, kale, eggplant, nixtamal, onion, bell pepper, garlic, red chile, prosciutto fat, olive oil, cumin seeds, cayenne, oregano, salt, and black pepper. Cover with water, place the pig's feet on top, and bring to a boil. Reduce the heat to low and simmer until the meat is falling off the bone and the hominy is al dente, about 4 hours. Serve hot.

Chorizo Sausage and Nixtamal Hominy

I fell in love with fresh Mexican-style hominy, called nixtamal, when I bought a bag from a super-market in Los Angeles. I thought, wow. However, recently I couldn't find it readily anymore and, not willing to explore why, I decided the canned nixtamal would have to do to satisfy my cravings. This meal is hot, wonderful, rich, and delicious, and I suggest you eat it with corn tortillas and beer.

2 fresh poblano chiles

1 large fresh jalapeño chile

2 tablespoons pork lard (preferably) or vegetable oil

1 pound (2 or 3 links) fresh Mexican chorizo sausage

1 medium onion, chopped

2 large garlic cloves, finely chopped

One 29-ounce can Mexican-style hominy, rinsed and drained

2 ripe tomatoes, peeled and chopped (see box page 47)

1 fresh sage sprig

1 bay leaf

2 teaspoons dried oregano

1 teaspoon dried epazote (optional)

1 teaspoon ground cumin

2½ cups water

Salt and freshly ground black pepper, to taste

1. Place the poblano and jalapeño chiles on a wire rack set over a burner on high heat and roast until their skins blister black on all sides, turning occasionally with tongs. Remove the chiles and place in a paper or heavy plastic bag to steam for 20 minutes, which will make peeling them easier. When cool enough to handle, rub off as much blackened peel as you can and remove the seeds by rubbing with a paper towel (to avoid washing away flavorful juices) or by rinsing under running water (to remove more easily). Chop and reserve.

2. In a flameproof baking casserole, melt the pork lard over medium-high heat. Add the sausage, onion, and garlic and cook, stirring frequently, until the onion is golden, about 12 minutes. Add the hominy, tomatoes, roasted chiles, sage, bay leaf, oregano, epazote, if using, and cumin. Add the water, reduce the heat to low, and simmer, uncovered, until the liquid is saucy and the hominy very tender, about 2 hours. Season with salt and pepper. Remove and discard the bay leaf. Serve or keep warm in a 200-degree oven until ready to serve.

Stir-Fried Shredded Pork and Bok Choy

Pork tenderloin is a very tender and lean piece of meat and ideal for wok cookery, since it cooks fast. In this recipe with bok choy, it's spiced up considerably by the chiles. Feel free to add more bok choy to the mix. The pequin chiles and Chinkiang black vinegar can be purchased from the groceries and gourmet foods section of www.amazon.com.

2 tablespoons peanut oil

2 large garlic cloves, finely chopped

One 1-inch cube fresh ginger, peeled and finely chopped

2 teaspoons dried pequin chiles or 6 dried red chiles, broken in half, seeds shaken out

1 pound pork tenderloin, cut into 2 × ¼-inch slices

4 bok choy (about 1 pound), green parts sliced ¼ inch thick, white parts sliced into 2 × ¼-inch pieces

1 scallion, trimmed and cut into ½-inch sections on the diagonal

½ cup vegetable or chicken broth or water

2 green bell peppers, seeded and cut into squares

1 tablespoon cornstarch

1 tablespoon soy sauce

2 teaspoons sesame oil

1 teaspoon Chinkiang black vinegar or rice vinegar

1 teaspoon rice wine (mirin)

½ teaspoon sugar

1. In a wok, heat the peanut oil over high heat until smoking and very hot. Add the garlic, ginger, and chiles and cook, tossing constantly, for 30 seconds. Add the pork and cook, tossing constantly, until the pork loses its pink color, about 3 minutes. Remove the pork with a skimmer and reserve. Add the white parts of the bok choy and scallion and cook, tossing, for 1 minute. Add the broth, cover, and cook for 3 minutes. Add the bell peppers and green portions of the bok choy and cook, uncovered, tossing and stirring frequently, for 3 minutes.

2. Meanwhile, blend the cornstarch, soy sauce, sesame oil, vinegar, rice wine, and sugar in a small bowl. Add the pork back to the skillet, stir the cornstarch mixture into the wok, and cook for 2 minutes while stirring. Serve hot.

Stir-Fried Pork, Summer Squash, and Chile

This is an exceedingly hot dish, spicy from the habanero chile and very flavorful. If you don't like spicy food, forget it. However, if you do like spicy-hot experiences, you'll love this extraordinary combination of pork and summer squash that seems to jump out of the pan.

2 tablespoons extra-virgin olive oil
3 yellow summer squash, trimmed, quartered lengthwise, and diced
1 large white onion, cut into eighths, then each eighth cut in half and separated
3 large garlic cloves, finely chopped
5 fresh serrano chiles, thinly sliced
1 fresh habanero chile, seeds and membranes removed, finely chopped
1 pound ground pork
¼ cup finely chopped fresh cilantro (coriander leaf)
Salt and freshly ground black pepper, to taste
Corn tortillas, warmed, for serving (optional)

In a large nonstick pan, heat the olive oil over medium-high heat, then add the summer squash, onion, garlic, serrano chiles, and habanero chile and cook, stirring frequently, until softened, about 10 minutes. Add the pork and cook, stirring frequently, until it turns color, about 5 minutes. Add the cilantro, stir to mix, and cook for 2 minutes. Season with salt and pepper. Serve hot with corn tortillas, if desired.

Stir-Fried Pork and Tofu

The easiest way to cook Chinese food is by having all your ingredients prepared and ready to go. So look down the ingredient list, prepare them as required, and put those items that go into the wok at the same time all together. For example, you can put the ginger, garlic, chile-garlic sauce, and chile flakes together in a little bowl because they go in together. There will likely be a number of brands of chile-garlic sauce available in your supermarket's international food aisle. A common one is the Lee Kum Kee brand. If you like you can serve this with steamed rice, leftover rice, buns, or salad.

¼ cup peanut oil or vegetable oil
1 pound boneless raw or roasted pork loin, cut into 3½ × ¼-inch strips
One 1½-inch piece fresh ginger, peeled and finely chopped
5 large garlic cloves, thinly sliced
3 tablespoons chile-garlic sauce
1½ teaspoons red chile flakes
7 scallions, trimmed and cut into 1½-inch lengths
6 tablespoons soy sauce
1 pound extra-firm tofu, drained and cut into 16 cubes
5 teaspoons cornstarch dissolved in ½ cup water

1. In a wok, heat the peanut oil over high heat until smoking, then add the pork and stir-fry, tossing constantly, until it turns color, about 3 minutes if raw, 1 minute if cooked. Add the ginger, garlic, chile-garlic sauce, and red chile flakes and stir-fry, tossing constantly, for 30 seconds. Add the scallions and soy sauce and continue cooking, tossing and stirring, for another 30 seconds.

2. Add the tofu and, when the liquid in the wok reaches a boil, cook, uncovered, stirring occasionally, until nearly evaporated, about 2½ minutes. Add the cornstarch-water mixture and toss the mixture in the wok until syrupy, about 2½ minutes. Serve hot.

Stir-Fried Pork and Golden Tofu with Chiles

Although there is a lot of preparation in this dish even before you begin any cooking, as is typical of Chinese cooking, this Sichuan-inspired recipe is packed with flavor and the tofu remains the equal of the pork. Tofu, a highly processed bland food made from soy beans, benefits immensely from all the contrasting flavors and chiles. The actual cooking goes very quickly, so you'll need everything prepared beforehand. The chile-garlic sauce called for will be found in your supermarket's international aisle. A common one is the Lee Kum Kee brand. The Chinkiang black vinegar can be purchased from the grocery and gourmet foods section of www.amazon.com.

¾ pound extra-firm tofu

¼ cup peanut oil

1 large egg white

1 pound pork sirloin, cut into thin 2-inch-long strips

8 large garlic cloves, 4 finely chopped, 4 thinly sliced

3 tablespoons rice wine (mirin)

2 teaspoons cornstarch

1 teaspoon salt

½ teaspoon sugar

Freshly ground black pepper, to taste

1 tablespoon soy sauce

2 teaspoons Chinkiang black vinegar or balsamic vinegar

½ red onion, thinly sliced

1 red bell pepper, seeded and cut into 1½-inch squares

1 fresh habanero chile, seeded and thinly slivered

3 fresh poblano chiles, cut into 1½-inch squares

1 tablespoon peeled and finely chopped fresh ginger

1 tablespoon chile-garlic sauce

½ cup unsalted cashews

1. Cut the tofu into 1-inch cubes and lay on a paper towel–lined plate. Cover with more paper towels and place a plate or bowl on top to press down. Let it drain for 15 minutes.

2. Pour 3 tablespoons of the peanut oil into the wok and let it heat up over high heat. Add the tofu, spread it around the wok, and let it cook, undisturbed, for 1 minute to sear. Stir-fry for 1 more minute, until light golden, then remove the tofu and set aside.

3. In a bowl, beat the egg white until frothy. Combine the pork with the egg white and chopped garlic, 1 tablespoon of the rice wine, the cornstarch, salt, sugar, and pepper. In another small bowl, combine the remaining 2 tablespoons rice wine, soy sauce, and vinegar.

4. Pour the remaining 1 tablespoon peanut oil into the wok, let it heat to smoking over high heat, then add the red onion, bell pepper, habanero chile, poblano chiles, sliced garlic, and ginger and cook for 2 minutes while stir-frying. Push the vegetables to the side, add the pork, and cook without stirring for 1 minute to sear. Add the chile-garlic sauce and cook for 2 minutes while stir-frying. Add the rice wine mixture and cook, stir-frying, until the pork is cooked through, about 2 minutes. Return the reserved tofu to the wok, add the cashews, stir, and serve.

Paella with Sausage, Peas, and Lima Beans

In Spain, especially in Valencia and Catalonia, there are two basic kinds of rice dishes, *paelles* and *arrosses al forn*—paellas (*paelles* is the Spanish plural) and oven-baked rice, respectively. This preparation is a paella, and ideally you'll cook it in the pan of the same name with its two handles. If you don't have a paella pan, you can use your 10-inch or larger sauté pan.

2 tablespoons extra-virgin olive oil

1 pound smoked or fresh Spanish-style chorizo sausages or kielbasa, cut into ¾-inch pieces

1 small onion, chopped

4 large garlic cloves, finely chopped

3 tablespoons finely chopped fresh flat-leaf parsley

1 cup medium-grain rice such as Calrose or short-grain rice such as Arborio

2 cups water

½ cup fresh or frozen peas

½ cup fresh or frozen baby lima beans

1 teaspoon hot paprika

1 teaspoon salt

½ teaspoon freshly ground black pepper

½ teaspoon dried thyme

1 bay leaf

In a 10-inch paella pan or large sauté pan, heat the olive oil over medium heat, then add the sausage and cook, stirring, until lightly browned, about 2 minutes. Add the onion, garlic, and parsley and continue cooking, stirring, until softened, about 4 minutes. Add the rice, stir to coat with the oil, and cook for 1 minute. Pour in the water, add the peas, lima beans, paprika, salt, pepper, thyme, and bay leaf, and bring to a boil. Reduce the heat to low and simmer until all the liquid is absorbed and the rice is tender, about 25 minutes. Remove and discard the bay leaf. Serve hot.

Rice with Sausage and Brussels Sprouts

This rib-sticking dish has full flavors and is most appreciated on cold days. The sage adds a rustic taste to the dish that is appealing.

2 tablespoons unsalted butter
¾ pound mild Italian sausage, casing removed and crumbled
2 tablespoons finely chopped onion
2 garlic cloves, finely chopped
1 cup short-grain rice such as Arborio, rinsed in a strainer
1½ cups water
1 teaspoon finely chopped fresh sage
½ teaspoon salt
¼ pound Brussels sprouts, trimmed and chopped
Freshly ground black pepper, to taste
Freshly grated Parmesan cheese

1. In a large sauté pan, melt the butter over high heat. Add the sausage, onion, and garlic and cook, stirring frequently, until the sausage turns color, about 10 minutes, breaking up the sausage with a wooden spoon.

2. Add the rice and cook, stirring, for 1 minute. Add the water, sage, and salt and bring to a boil. Once it reaches a boil, reduce the heat to low and cook for 5 minutes without stirring.

3. Add the Brussels sprouts and fold into the rice, then cook over low heat until the rice and Brussels sprouts are al dente and all the water is absorbed, 10 to 20 minutes, so keep checking.

4. Place a paper towel over the rice, cover with the lid, and let it stand for 5 minutes before serving. Serve with a sprinkle of pepper and the cheese.

Lamb

||||||||||||||||||||||||||||||||||||||||||||||||||||||||||||||||||||||||||||||||||||||||||||||||||||||||||||||||||||||||

Lamb was once an all-American meat, hugely popular in the West, but it has receded in popularity. There's no good reason for that, as lamb has the kind of distinctive taste that avoids the "tastes like chicken" epithet that befalls so much interesting cooking. A nice place to start in the world of lamb cookery is with the cultures that favor lamb, such as Greece—the Braised Lamb and Eggplant (page 207) will provide a meltingly delicious taste that will remind you of your trip to Greece or inspire you to take one. You could go more exotic and try the North African–inspired Meatball Tagine (page 230), which will provide a dish I'm sure you've never eaten, let alone cooked all by your lonesome.

Braised Leg of Lamb with Potatoes

This meal requires a large flameproof baking casserole. If you don't have one, you can use a roasting pan and cover it with aluminum foil. It's a big one-pot meal that will feed a good amount of people and it's utterly easy to do: Just layer everything and cook for 5 hours, until the meat falls off the bone. It's impossible to screw it up. Traditionally, this Sardinian dish is made with mutton, which you could order from a butcher if you like.

4 small onions, quartered
5 celery stalks, coarsely chopped
4 carrots, scraped and cut into ½-inch pieces
6 sun-dried tomatoes, coarsely chopped
12 fresh flat-leaf parsley sprigs
One 8-pound bone-in leg of lamb, cut into 6 large pieces
    (ask the butcher to do this)
2 pounds small fingerling potatoes, peeled
Grated zest of 1 lemon
Salt, to taste

In a large earthenware casserole (preferably) or any large flameproof baking casserole, arrange the onions, celery, carrots, sun-dried tomatoes, and parsley on the bottom, then lay the lamb pieces on top. (If using earthenware and it is not flameproof, you will need to use a heat diffuser. Earthenware heats up slower but retains its heat longer than other casseroles. When using earthenware, food may cook slower at first and then cook very quickly while retaining its heat.) Pour in enough water to not quite cover the meat. Arrange the potatoes on top, along with the lemon zest and salt. Push the potatoes and lemon zest down slightly into the water. Bring to a boil over high heat, cover, reduce the heat to low, and cook until the lamb is falling off the bone, about 5 hours.

Tomato and Lamb Stew

In Arab cookery, stews usually take the name of the most important vegetable in the stew. The reason for this is that the meat acts as a condiment to the vegetable rather than being the center of the dish. This stew is popular among families in Lebanon and is called "tomato stew" because of the amount of tomatoes used. There will be a lot of liquid from the tomatoes and it will have to evaporate over the many hours that the stew simmers. The stew is ever so slightly sweet, too, from the natural sweetness of the onions and the sweet spicing of cinnamon. Serve with warm pita bread and a green salad if desired.

¾ cup clarified butter or unsalted butter
¼ cup pine nuts
1¼ pounds boneless leg or shoulder of lamb, chopped small
2 pounds onions, coarsely chopped
2 teaspoons salt
1½ teaspoons freshly ground black pepper
1 teaspoon bahārāt (see box page 206)
½ teaspoon ground cinnamon
4 pounds ripe tomatoes, cut in half, seeds squeezed out, and grated against the
largest holes of a grater

1. In a large flameproof baking casserole, melt the clarified butter over medium-high heat, then add the pine nuts and cook, stirring occasionally, until they turn light brown, about 2 minutes. Remove the pine nuts with a slotted spoon and reserve.

2. Add the lamb and onions to the casserole and season with the salt, pepper, bahārāt, and cinnamon and cook, stirring, until the onions are softened, about 8 minutes. Reduce the heat to very low, add the tomatoes, stir, cover, and cook for 1 hour, then uncover and cook until the sauce is thicker and the meat very tender, about another 3 hours. Serve with the pine nuts sprinkled on top.

Bahārāt

Bahārāt means "spice" in Arabic, derived from the word *bahār*, which means "pepper," but in the Levant it also refers to a very specific all-purpose spice mix whose basic foundation is a mixture of black pepper and allspice with the addition of cinnamon, paprika, coriander seeds, cassia bark, sumac, nutmeg, cumin seeds, and/or cardamom seeds as the spice merchant or cook desires. An American spice company has recently begun selling packages of bahārāt, so you might find it in the spice section of your supermarket or at Middle Eastern groceries. You could also search in the groceries and gourmet foods section at www.amazon. com. I encourage you to make this easy recipe fresh for yourself and keep it stored in a spice jar. You can fiddle with the recipe and add some of the other spices mentioned, using much smaller ratio proportions.

¼ cup whole black peppercorns
¼ cup whole allspice berries
2 teaspoons ground cinnamon
1 teaspoon freshly grated nutmeg

In a spice grinder or mortar, grind the peppercorns and allspice together, then blend with the cinnamon and nutmeg. Store in a jar in your spice rack, away from sunlight. It will lose pungency as time goes by, but properly stored, it will keep for many months.

Makes about ½ cup

Braised Lamb and Eggplant

Lamb is a popular meat in Greece, and around Easter many famous lamb dishes are prepared. It doesn't seem to matter how you cook the lamb—it just tastes great. I first had this preparation at the Taverna Pantheon in the market of Iraklion on Crete about twenty years ago. The lamb was braised and particularly luscious, with the eggplant cooked along with the lamb instead of being fried beforehand. I like to cook Greek lamb dishes in a manner similar to how you would encounter them in a taverna—long and slow.

6 ounces (1½ sticks) unsalted butter
4 pounds bone-in lamb shoulder and neck, cut up into large pieces,
    excess fat removed
1 pound onions, chopped
1½ pounds ripe tomatoes, cut in half, seeds squeezed out, and grated against
    the largest holes of a box grater down to the peel, or one 29-ounce can
    crushed tomatoes
Salt and freshly ground black pepper, to taste
3½ pounds eggplant, peeled and cut into 2-inch cubes
3 large garlic cloves, finely chopped

1. In a large earthenware (preferably) casserole or a large flameproof baking casserole, melt the butter over high heat, then add the lamb and onions and cook, stirring, until browned, about 12 minutes. (If using earthenware and it is not flameproof, you will need to use a heat diffuser. Earthenware heats up slower but retains its heat longer than other casseroles. When using earthenware, food may cook slower at first and then cook very quickly while retaining its heat.)

2. Add the tomatoes, salt, and pepper. Bring to a boil over high heat, then cover, reduce the heat to low, and simmer until some of the shoulder bones are protruding, 2 hours. Add the eggplant and garlic and continue cooking until everything is fork-tender, about 2 hours. The casserole can be kept warm on top of the stove for 2 to 3 hours longer without the cover. Serve hot.

Braised Lamb Patties in Ragoût

This delicious preparation will perfume the house as it cooks, and the patties themselves are quite aromatic. Don't be turned off by the long list of ingredients because it's just stuff going into the patties and it doesn't represent a lot of work for you. The patties may also be made long ahead of time and kept refrigerated for a day or frozen until you want to make the dish.

For the lamb patties
2 ounces Italian or French bread without the crust
½ cup whole milk
1½ pounds ground lamb
1 large egg
2 ounces mortadella, chopped
½ cup freshly grated Parmesan cheese (about 1½ ounces)
2 tablespoons pine nuts
2 tablespoons raisins, soaked in tepid water for 15 minutes, then drained
2 tablespoons finely chopped fresh flat-leaf parsley
2 teaspoons grated lemon zest
Pinch of freshly grated nutmeg
Salt and freshly ground black pepper, to taste

For the ragoût
3 tablespoons extra-virgin olive oil
2 ounces pancetta, chopped
1 small onion, finely chopped
2 garlic cloves, finely chopped
2 tablespoons finely chopped fresh flat-leaf parsley
½ cup dry white wine
2 tablespoons tomato paste, dissolved in ½ cup water
Four 1-inch-thick slices Italian or French bread (about ¼ pound),
    toasted and buttered
12 flat-leaf spinach leaves
Freshly grated Parmesan cheese, for serving (optional)

1. For the lamb patties, soak the bread in the milk, then squeeze out the excess as if you were forming a snowball.

2. In a bowl, mix together the soaked bread, lamb, egg, mortadella, cheese, pine nuts, raisins, parsley, lemon zest, nutmeg, and salt and pepper. Knead it very well so it is blended. Form the lamb into patties 4 × 2 × 1 inch thick.

3. For the ragoût, in a large sauté pan, heat the olive oil with the pancetta over medium-high heat. Add the lamb patties and cook, turning once, until browned on both sides, about 6 minutes total. Add the onion, garlic, and parsley and continue cooking, stirring, until softened, about 3 minutes. Add the wine and let it nearly evaporate. Reduce the heat to low, add the tomato paste and water mixture, and cook, stirring the sauce and turning the patties occasionally, until the meat is firm and the sauce is dense, 20 to 30 minutes.

4. Lay a slice of buttered toast in each bowl. Cover each with 3 leaves of spinach, then spoon the patties and sauce on top. Let rest for a couple of minutes, then serve with more cheese, if desired.

Istanbul Pilaf

This rice pilaf from Istanbul is usually made with lamb or chicken liver, but you can also use the milder sirloin I suggest, which I find people like quite a bit. If you like liver, the original is spectacular. The method of rice cookery in this recipe is written if you want to serve the dish relatively quickly. But alternatively, you can bring the water to a boil with the rice, then cover the pot with some paper towels, replace the lid, and turn the heat off and let it sit for an hour; it will be just perfectly cooked and heavenly. I often use this latter method when I have other things to do or want to relax and not actively attend to cooking.

3 tablespoons clarified butter or extra-virgin olive oil

2 cups long-grain rice, soaked in warm water for 30 minutes, then rinsed and drained in a strainer

½ pound lamb or chicken liver, lamb or chicken hearts, arteries removed and diced small, or diced lamb sirloin

20 whole blanched almonds

1 tablespoon pistachios

2½ cups chicken broth

1 cup frozen or fresh peas

2 teaspoons salt

½ teaspoon sugar

Pinch of saffron, crumbled slightly

In a heavy saucepan with a heavy lid, melt the clarified butter over medium-high heat. Add the rice and cook, stirring constantly, until it is sticking to the bottom and fragrant, about 5 minutes. Add the meat, almonds, and pistachios and cook, stirring, for 5 more minutes. Add the chicken broth, peas, salt, sugar, and saffron. Bring to a boil, stirring occasionally, then reduce the heat to medium, cover, and cook without stirring or looking under the cover for 5 minutes. Reduce the heat to low and simmer for another 5 minutes, then reduce the heat to very low and simmer until the liquid is absorbed, never stirring or removing the lid, until the end, about another 5 minutes. Remove from the heat and let stand for 20 minutes with the cover on. Transfer to a serving platter, fluff the rice, and serve.

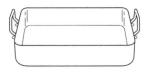

Garlic-Stuffed 9-Hour
Roast Leg of Lamb

My former wife, Najwa, recently asked me for this recipe and I exclaimed, "But I got it from you!" She had no recollection of giving it to me and furthermore couldn't remember how to make it. However, this Palestinian preparation is one she remembers fondly from her childhood. It is a special dish in that it is usually made only for special occasions such as a family reunion or to celebrate an event. It's more typical of rural Palestinian cooking than city cooking, but once you taste it you will see why everyone loves it. The secret is really long, really slow cooking. If you find yourself fiddling with the oven temperature, which I seem to do no matter how many times I cook it, just remember to keep your fiddling over 240°F and under 275°F. The reason you might fiddle with the temperature is that you don't want the roast to blacken too soon and your oven might not be calibrated correctly. The strategy I use when I make this is to start the preparation early in the morning and, if it is done by five or six in the afternoon, that's okay, because it can sit in a turned-off oven for another couple of hours, making it an ideal party dish. The roast will be crusty black on the outside from the spice rub and succulent and tender on the inside, so much so that you don't carve the meat—you just pull it apart with your fork. Serve with warm pita bread.

One 5- to 7-pound leg of lamb
20 to 30 fresh mint leaves
8 large garlic cloves, slivered
¼ cup extra-virgin olive oil
2 tablespoons bahārāt (see box page 206)
1 teaspoon ground allspice
1 teaspoon ground cloves
½ teaspoon ground cinnamon
½ teaspoon salt
½ teaspoon freshly ground black pepper
6 baking potatoes (3 pounds), cut in half
1 cup water

1. Preheat the oven to 250°F.

2. Pierce the lamb in several places with a thin boning knife and push some mint leaves into each incision, followed by a sliver of garlic. Rub the leg of lamb on all sides with the olive oil. Mix the bahārāt, allspice, cloves, cinnamon, salt, and pepper together in a small bowl and then sprinkle the entire amount on the lamb on all sides, rubbing it in with your fingers.

3. Place the lamb, fat side up, and potatoes in a large roasting pan, preferably earthenware, add the water, and roast until falling off the bone, about 9 hours. Adjust the temperature of the oven if necessary. Baste the lamb periodically with its own fat.

Lamb with Orzo Pasta

This Greek dish is traditionally made in an earthenware casserole called a *youvetsi* (or *giouvetsi*), which gives the preparation its name. Although orzo is thought of as an Italian pasta (and *orzo* is Italian for "barley"), it's actually more typically a Greek pasta. The Greeks don't call it orzo but rather *manestra*, which means "cantaloupe seeds," or *kritharaki*, which does mean "barley." You can replace the lamb with veal knuckle, shank, or shoulder.

½ cup extra-virgin olive oil

4 pounds bone-in lamb shoulder, trimmed of fat and cut into chunks

3 cups hot water

3 cups fresh or canned crushed tomatoes or tomato purée

1 medium onion, chopped

2 garlic cloves, finely chopped

1 teaspoon dried savory

Salt and freshly ground black pepper, to taste

1 pound orzo

1 cup grated kefalotyri cheese or cheddar cheese

1. Preheat the oven to 350°F.

2. In a large earthenware (preferably) casserole or a large flameproof baking casserole, heat the olive oil over medium heat. Add the lamb and cook, stirring, until browned on all sides, about 12 minutes total. (If using earthenware and it is not flameproof, you will need to use a heat diffuser. Earthenware heats up slower but retains its heat longer than other casseroles. When using earthenware, food may cook slower at first and then cook very quickly while retaining its heat.) Add the water, tomatoes, onion, garlic, and savory and season with salt and pepper. Mix well, cover, and place in the oven. Bake until the lamb is tender, about 1¼ hours.

3. Remove 2 cups of liquid from the casserole and reserve. Add the orzo to the casserole, stir, and return to the oven to bake for 15 minutes, uncovered. If the liquid in the casserole has dried out and the orzo is not yet cooked, add some of the reserved liquid. Sprinkle the casserole with the cheese and continue baking, uncovered, until brown specks form on top, about 15 minutes, then serve.

Farro with Lamb

Farro is the vernacular Italian word used interchangeably for several kinds of antique wheat species popular in medieval and ancient times that have been making a comeback, namely spelt, emmer, and einkorn. Farro is popular among chefs because it has a rich, earthy taste and is very satisfying as a grain. In this preparation, the spelt is in the form of wheat berries and it is cooked as a *farrotto*, an Italian neologism that means something that's cooked like risotto. I prefer a long and slow method of simmering, but that can take 3 to 4 hours, so I've written this recipe so that it cooks quicker. You may need to use 2 or 3 quarts of water throughout the cooking process.

2 tablespoons extra-virgin olive oil

½ pound boneless lamb shoulder or leg, diced

1 small onion, finely chopped

2 large garlic cloves, finely chopped

1 cup spelt wheat berries (farro)

1 large ripe tomato, halved, seeds squeezed out, and grated against the largest holes of a box grater

1 teaspoon salt, or more as needed

6 cups water, plus more as needed

1 cup fresh or frozen peas

¼ to ½ cup freshly grated pecorino cheese or ricotta salata

2 tablespoons finely chopped fresh mint

Freshly ground black pepper, to taste

1. In a medium flameproof baking casserole or heavy saucepan, heat the olive oil over medium-high heat. Add the lamb, onion, and garlic and cook, stirring, until the lamb turns color, about 4 minutes. Add the spelt and tomato and stir to coat, then add the salt and water and bring to a boil over high heat. Reduce the heat to low and cook, stirring frequently and adding water in ½-cup increments, until the farro is tender, about 1½ hours. (Check the farro occasionally because it could become tender earlier or later.)

2. Add the peas, cook for 5 minutes, then season with the cheese, mint, and pepper and serve hot.

Rice Pilaf with Spicy Lamb

Once I learned how to make rice pilaf (about forty years ago), that fluffy light separated-grain rice you can find in Indian restaurants, and all those fabulous dishes using it in so many Middle Eastern, Central Asian, and Indian subcontinent cuisines, I went wild putting together all kind of combinations, as the possibilities seemed endless—and they are! One delicious combination is with ground beef and leeks. I usually serve this highly spiced pilaf with a chopped salad and warm pita bread. A little plain yogurt on the side is nice, too.

¼ cup extra-virgin olive oil

1 medium onion, finely chopped

1 leek, trimmed of green leaves, split, washed well, and chopped

1 large garlic clove, finely chopped

2 tablespoons finely chopped carrots

1 pound boneless lamb sirloin or leg, chopped (not ground)

Salt and freshly ground black pepper, to taste

1 teaspoon harīsa (see box page 140)

¼ teaspoon ground coriander

¼ teaspoon hot paprika

¼ teaspoon Aleppo pepper (optional)

⅛ teaspoon ground caraway

⅛ teaspoon ground cumin

2⅔ cups veal, chicken, or vegetable broth

½ cup medium-grain rice such as Calrose or short-grain rice such as Arborio, soaked in water for 30 minutes, then rinsed and drained

1 tablespoon unsalted butter

1 large loaf Arabic flatbread, split open, ripped into pieces, and fried in olive oil until light golden and crisp (frying optional)

1. In a flameproof baking casserole, heat the olive oil over medium-high heat. Add the onion, leek, garlic, and carrots and cook, stirring frequently, until softened, about 8 minutes. Turn the heat to high and brown the lamb for about 2 minutes. Season with salt and pepper.

2. Add the harīsa, coriander, paprika, Aleppo pepper, if using, caraway, and cumin and cook, stirring and mixing well so the meat and vegetables are coated, 1 minute. Pour in 2 cups of the broth and cook on high heat for 10 to 12 minutes. Add the rice, butter, and the remaining ⅔ cup broth. Continue cooking on high heat for 5 minutes. Reduce the heat to very low and cook until the rice is tender and most of the liquid has evaporated, about 20 minutes. Check the seasoning. Transfer the rice to a serving platter and serve with the fried Arabic bread on the side or on top of the rice.

Rice Pilaf with Lamb and Nuts

This rice pilaf is typical of the cooking of Lebanon and Syria. It is usually served with roast lamb or roast chicken and is always accompanied by yogurt, but in this recipe it works as a one-pot meal. You need to pay particular attention to the cooking of the nuts, as they can blacken rather quickly, which you don't want to have happen. Remove the nuts, especially the pine nuts and almonds, as they turn golden, turning off the heat if necessary.

½ cup clarified butter (preferably), unsalted butter, or extra-virgin olive oil
2 tablespoons pine nuts
½ cup whole or slivered blanched almonds
2 tablespoons pistachios
½ pound ground lamb
2 teaspoons salt
1 teaspoon ground cardamom
½ teaspoon ground cinnamon
½ teaspoon hot paprika
½ teaspoon saffron, crumbled
3 cups water
2 cups long-grain rice such as basmati, soaked in water to cover for
    30 minutes, then rinsed and drained
1 cup frozen or fresh peas

1. In a large flameproof baking casserole, melt the clarified butter over medium-high heat. Add the pine nuts and cook, stirring, until light brown, about 1 minute. Quickly remove with a skimmer and set aside. Add the almonds to the casserole and cook, stirring, until light brown, about 2 minutes, then quickly remove and set aside with the pine nuts. Now add the pistachios and cook, stirring, for 1 minute, then remove and set aside with the other nuts. The clarified butter will be golden and smell nutty.

2. Add the ground lamb to the casserole and cook, stirring with a wooden spoon and breaking it up, until it loses its pink color, about 3 minutes. Add the salt, cardamom, cinnamon, paprika, and saffron and stir, then add the water, reduce the heat to low, and simmer, stirring occasionally, for 10 minutes.

3. Add the rice and peas, stir to mix well, cover, and let simmer over low heat until all the water is absorbed, about 30 minutes. Turn off the heat and let the rice sit, covered, for 15 minutes. Fluff the rice with a fork, then mound and mold the rice attractively on a serving platter. Sprinkle the nuts on top and serve.

Lamb Stew with Chickpeas

One Spanish food writer said that this lamb stew was made by drovers on market day in Andalusia a century ago. Whatever its origins, today it's a typical family stew that can be made with goat as well. It's a delicious one-pot dish, and you'll find the addition of almonds and saffron makes it just a little more exotic.

⅓ cup extra-virgin olive oil
2¼ pounds boneless leg of lamb, cubed
½ pound onions, finely chopped
4 large garlic cloves, finely chopped
1 green bell pepper, seeded and finely chopped
2 tablespoons sherry wine vinegar
2 cups cooked chickpeas (from two 15-ounce cans), rinsed and drained
1 cup dry white wine
3 tablespoons finely chopped fresh flat-leaf parsley
1 dried red chile (optional)
2 bay leaves
1 tablespoon hot paprika
1 teaspoon dried thyme
1 teaspoon dried oregano
½ teaspoon saffron, crumbled
½ cup whole blanched almonds, roasted until golden

1. In a heavy stewpot, preferably earthenware, heat the olive oil over medium-high heat, then add the lamb and cook, stirring, until browned, about 8 minutes. (If using earthenware and it is not flameproof, you will need to use a heat diffuser. Earthenware heats up slower but retains its heat longer than other casseroles. When using earthenware, food may cook slower at first and then cook very quickly while retaining its heat.)

2. Add the onions, garlic, bell pepper, and vinegar and continue cooking, stirring, until bubbling, about 5 minutes. Add the chickpeas, wine, parsley, chile, if using, bay leaves, paprika, thyme, oregano, and saffron, bring to a boil, then reduce the heat to low and simmer, covered, until the lamb is tender, about 1¼ hours.

3. Add the almonds, cook for another 15 minutes. Remove and discard the bay leaves. Serve hot.

Slow-Cooked Lamb Shank and White Bean Stew

This is a slow-cooked Turkish stew with little liquid, so if your burner heat doesn't go low enough you may need to use a heat diffuser. It's ideally made in an earthenware casserole, and if you have a new clay pot this stew is perfect for breaking it in. A lid is essential to keep all the moisture in the casserole, which will turn the tough shank into succulent pieces of lamb melting off the bone. The beans will cook in the juices and fat of the lamb and by the time it's ready they too will be soft and melt in your mouth. The Aleppo pepper called for in the ingredient list refers to an unusually dark-colored, not-too-hot ground chile used in Turkish and Syrian cooking and typically found in Middle Eastern markets. You can also find it at www.penzeys.com. In its place, you could make a blend of three parts sweet paprika to one part ground red chile.

8 tablespoons (1 stick) unsalted butter
5 pounds lamb shanks
2 medium onions, chopped
8 large garlic cloves, finely chopped
5 cups peeled and chopped tomatoes
4 cups dried white beans, soaked overnight in cold water to cover,
     then drained
4 cups water
2 tablespoons tomato paste
2 tablespoons Aleppo pepper
Salt and freshly ground black pepper, to taste
6 peperoncini chiles (Italian frying peppers) or New Mexico/Anaheim chiles,
     seeded and cut into rings
¼ cup finely chopped fresh flat-leaf parsley

1. In a large earthenware (preferably) casserole or any large flameproof baking casserole, melt the butter over medium-high heat, then add the lamb and cook, turning occasionally, until browned on all sides, about 8 minutes. (If using earthenware and it is not flameproof, you will need to use a heat diffuser. Earthenware heats up slower but retains its heat longer than other casseroles. When using earthenware, food may cook slower at first and then cook very quickly while retaining its heat.) Add the onions and garlic and cook, stirring, for 4 minutes. Add the water, bring to a boil, then reduce the heat to medium-low and simmer at a gentle boil for 1½ hours, skimming the surface of foam if necessary.

2. Add the tomatoes, beans, tomato paste, and Aleppo pepper. Season with salt and pepper, cover, bring to a boil, then reduce the heat to very low and simmer for 3½ to 4 hours, moistening with more water if it is drying out.

3. Add the peperoncini chiles, cover, and continue cooking until the meat falls off the bone and the beans could melt in your mouth, about 1 hour longer. The liquid in the casserole should be slightly bubbling at the most. Serve with a sprinkling of parsley.

Lamb and Almond Stew

This fragrant one-pot meal from Tunisia is a stew usually made with mutton, a stronger-tasting adult sheep. It is made with chickpeas, sugar, raisins, and almonds and is typically made for a special occasion. You could replace the almonds with chestnuts and add plums, prunes, and fresh apricots instead of raisins, too. Serve with warm Arabic bread or instant couscous soaked in some of the broth from the stew. The dried rosebuds can be purchased by searching the grocery and gourmet foods section of www.amazon.com.

1 teaspoon ground cinnamon

2 teaspoons ground dried rosebuds or ¾ teaspoon rose water

2 teaspoons freshly ground black pepper

2 pounds boneless leg of lamb, cut into 1½-inch cubes

Salt, to taste

¾ cup extra-virgin olive oil

4 cups cooked chickpeas (from one 35-ounce and one 16-ounce can),
    rinsed and drained

1 cup whole blanched almonds

2 cups water

1½ cups raisins

⅔ cup sugar

1. On a plate, stir together the cinnamon, 1 teaspoon of the ground rosebuds (or all the rose water), and 1 teaspoon of the pepper. Roll the lamb pieces in the spice mix and sprinkle on the remaining pepper and some salt.

2. In a flameproof baking casserole or stewpot, heat the olive oil over medium-high heat. Add the lamb and cook, stirring, until browned on all sides, 8 to 10 minutes. Add the chickpeas and almonds, cover with the water, bring to a boil, reduce the heat to low, and simmer, stirring occasionally, until the liquid has evaporated by about half, about 1½ hours.

3. Add the raisins, sugar, and remaining 1 teaspoon ground rosebuds, stir into the stew, and cook, stirring occasionally, until the liquid has reduced by half again, about 1 hour. Serve immediately.

Braised Lamb, Beans, and Mushrooms

Succulent lamb and earthy mushrooms seems to me to be one of those natural combinations that everyone enjoys. The taste of this braise is rich and full-bodied and is perfect in the winter.

2 tablespoons extra-virgin olive oil
2 large garlic cloves, crushed
2 medium onions, quartered and separated
2 pounds boneless lamb sirloin or leg, cubed small
1 pound button (white) mushrooms, sliced
2 tablespoons tomato paste
1½ cups dry red wine
One 15-ounce can white beans, rinsed and drained
Salt and freshly ground black pepper, to taste
Finely chopped fresh flat-leaf parsley, for garnish

1. In a flameproof baking casserole, heat the olive oil over medium-high heat with the garlic until it just begins to turn brown. Remove the garlic and discard.

2. Add the onions and cook, stirring, until translucent, about 4 minutes. Add the lamb and mushrooms and cook, stirring, until the lamb browns, about 5 minutes. Dissolve the tomato paste in the wine and pour into the casserole along with the white beans; season with salt and pepper. Cook until the wine evaporates, about 20 minutes. Transfer to a serving platter, sprinkle with parsley, and serve.

Lamb and Haricot Bean Stew

In Algeria, this stew is called a bean stew, not a lamb stew, because the traditional ratio of ingredients should be two parts beans to one part lamb. I use a smaller ratio than that in this recipe. This one-pot meat is family fare and would typically be found at the lunch table, the main meal of the day in Algeria. The stew is made with lamb or often mutton and dried white haricot beans with lots of onions and tomatoes. It is seasoned in a spicy-hot way with dried chile powder, fresh chile, and the ubiquitous chile paste of North Africa called *harīsa*. You might like to accompany it with a platter of fresh salad greens, seeded and sliced cucumbers, and ripe tomatoes all chopped up and dressed with a drizzle of extra-virgin olive oil, very finely chopped garlic, a dusting of cayenne, and fresh lemon juice.

¼ cup extra-virgin olive oil

1¾ pounds boneless leg or shoulder of lamb or mutton, cut into
   smaller than bite-size pieces

1 tablespoon salt, or more as needed

2 teaspoons freshly ground black pepper, or more as needed

1 teaspoon cayenne pepper

1 tablespoon harīsa (see box page 140)

3 large onions, coarsely chopped

3 large ripe tomatoes (about 1½ pounds), peeled, seeded,
   and chopped (see box page 47)

4 cups water

2 cups dried white beans

½ cup finely chopped fresh cilantro (coriander leaf)

1. In a stewpot, preferably earthenware, heat the oil over high heat. Season the meat with the salt, black pepper, and cayenne, add to the pot, and cook, stirring occasionally, for 5 to 10 minutes. (If using earthenware and it is not flameproof, you will need to use a heat diffuser. Earthenware heats up slower but retains its heat longer than other casseroles. When using earthenware, food may cook slower at first and then cook very quickly while retaining its heat.) Add the harīsa, stir, then add the onions and tomatoes, reduce the heat to low, cover, and let simmer for 15 minutes.

2. Add the water, beans, and cilantro, bring to a boil, reduce the heat to low, and simmer until the beans are tender, 2 to 2½ hours, stirring occasionally. Taste and correct the seasoning, then serve hot.

Meatball Tagine

A tagine is an earthenware casserole with a conical cover used in North Africa for braising, dry stewing, and wet stewing. *Tagine* also refers to the prepared dish cooked in the vessel of the same name, and there are many hundreds of different tagines. This adaptation of an Algerian dish called *maḥūt* (transliterated often from the French style as *mhaouete*) is a slow-cooking tagine made with meatballs of lamb and chunks of lamb. In this recipe, I've dispensed with the whole chunks and added some vegetables to the tagine to complete the meal.

For the meatballs
- 1 pound ground lamb
- 1 large egg, beaten
- 2 large garlic cloves, very finely chopped
- 1 tablespoon all-purpose flour
- 1 teaspoon ground cumin
- 1 teaspoon salt

For the tagine
- 2 tablespoons extra-virgin olive oil
- 2 tablespoons unsalted butter
- 1 tablespoon tomato paste, diluted with 5 tablespoons water
- 2 tablespoons white wine vinegar
- 1 teaspoon harīsa (see box page 140)
- 1 teaspoon cayenne pepper
- 1 teaspoon salt
- 1 pound Yukon gold potatoes, peeled and cubed
- ½ pound green beans, trimmed and cut in half
- ½ teaspoon freshly ground black pepper
- 2 tablespoons finely chopped fresh flat-leaf parsley
- Lemon wedges, for serving

1. In a bowl, mix together the ground lamb, egg, garlic, flour, cumin, and salt and form into about twenty 1-inch diameter meatballs with your hands, dipping your hands in cold water so they don't stick.

2. In an earthenware tagine or flameproof baking casserole, heat the olive oil over medium heat, then add the meatballs and cook, turning, until they turn color, about 5 minutes. (If using earthenware and it is not flameproof, you will need to use a heat diffuser. Earthenware heats up slower but retains its heat longer than other casseroles. When using earthenware, food may cook slower at first and then cook very quickly while retaining its heat.) Remove the meatballs from the tagine with a slotted spoon and reserve. Add the butter to the tagine and let it melt, then add the diluted tomato paste, vinegar, harīsa, cayenne, and salt and stir to mix well. Add the potatoes and green beans and toss slightly so the vegetables are coated.

3. Place the meatballs on top and cover. Reduce the heat to low and simmer, without lifting the cover, until the potatoes are tender, about 1½ hours. Sprinkle with the black pepper and the parsley and serve with the lemon wedges.

Moroccan Tagine of Lamb and Onions

The wonderful thing about a tagine, the earthenware casserole used in North Africa, is that its conical lid captures all the steam produced by the food to circulate the flavors, letting it drip down onto the simmering lamb and onions. The ideal tagine is made of earthenware, but if you don't have a tagine, this dish can be prepared in a heavy casserole with a heavy lid, such as an enameled cast-iron casserole with 4-inch sides. There is no need to add any liquid because all the food will generate plenty of its own. If you decide to use the optional grains of paradise (its name was given to it by medieval spice traders) it can be bought at www. thespicehouse.com.

2 large onions, thinly sliced
2 large garlic cloves, thinly sliced
1 cup golden raisins
4 tablespoons (½ stick) unsalted butter, slivered
½ teaspoon ground ginger
½ teaspoon ground cumin
½ teaspoon ground cinnamon
½ teaspoon grains of paradise (optional)
½ teaspoon ras el hanout (see box page 60)
½ teaspoon salt
Pinch of saffron, crumbled
2 pounds bone-in lamb shoulder

1. In a large bowl, toss together one of the onions, the garlic, raisins, butter, ginger, cumin, cinnamon, grains of paradise (if using), ras el hanout, salt, and saffron.

2. Lay the remaining sliced onion on the bottom of an earthenware tagine (preferably) or a flameproof baking casserole. Lay the lamb on top of the onion, then cover with the remaining ingredients. (If using earthenware and it is not flameproof, you will need to use a heat diffuser. Earthenware heats up slower but retains its heat longer than other casseroles. When using earthenware, food may cook slower at first and then cook very quickly while retaining its heat.) Place the cover on the tagine and place over high heat. Once you hear some sizzling, in about 10 minutes with an earthenware tagine but less with metal, reduce the heat to low and simmer until very tender, about 2½ hours. Serve hot.

Lamb and Pumpkin Stew

This Turkish stew is traditionally made in an earthenware casserole called a *güveçi*, which gives the dish its name. There are many kinds of *güveçi*—ones for winter, ones for summer—and every family makes their own version, so there is no one recipe. However, this preparation is the one I make when I want that melodious taste of the eastern Mediterranean with its luscious flavor of lamb and a sweetness and deep red color derived from pomegranate molasses. Aleppo pepper can be found in Middle Eastern markets and at www.penzeys.com.

6 tablespoons extra-virgin olive oil

1½ pounds boneless leg of lamb, fat removed, cubed small

1 medium onion, chopped

2 large garlic cloves, finely chopped

One 6-ounce can tomato paste, dissolved in 4 cups water

14 ounces pumpkin flesh, cut into finger-size bâtons

1 tablespoon pomegranate molasses

1 tablespoon Aleppo pepper

1 teaspoon ground allspice

½ pound green beans, cut into 2-inch lengths

Salt and freshly ground black pepper, to taste

3 tablespoons finely chopped fresh mint leaves

1. In a large earthenware casserole (preferably) or large flameproof baking casserole, heat the olive oil over medium-high heat. Add the lamb and cook on all sides, stirring, until browned, about 8 minutes. (If using earthenware and it is not flameproof, you will need to use a heat diffuser. Earthenware heats up slower but retains its heat longer than other casseroles. When using earthenware, food may cook slower at first and then cook very quickly while retaining its heat.) Add the onion and garlic and cook, stirring, for 4 minutes.

2. Reduce the heat to low, stir in the dissolved tomato paste mixture, then add the pumpkin, pomegranate molasses, Aleppo pepper, and allspice. Simmer for 30 minutes.

3. Add the green beans, salt, and black pepper and continue cooking until all is tender, 1½ to 2 hours. Sprinkle on the mint, stir, let it rest for 5 minutes, and then serve immediately.

Lamb, Cauliflower, and Pomegranate Molasses Stew

There are many cauliflower stews in Lebanese and Syrian cooking, as each family makes their own version. Usually, the ratio of cauliflower to meat will be about two to one. In this recipe, the sweet and rich pomegranate molasses gives the stew a luscious flavor. The *lūmī* (or *loomi*) called for is nothing but a small dried lime, available in Middle Eastern markets or at www.daynasmarket.com (they call it sun-dried lime). If you can't access one, use a whole fresh lime and remove it at the end of the cooking. You can serve the stew with some warm pita bread and a light tomato salad if you like.

6 tablespoons extra-virgin olive oil
1 large onion, coarsely chopped
1 celery stalk, finely chopped
4 large garlic cloves, finely chopped
1¼ pounds boneless leg of lamb, fat removed, cut into small cubes
1 teaspoon bahārāt (see box page 206)
Salt and freshly ground black pepper, to taste
One 2-pound cauliflower, trimmed and broken into florets
1 pound tomatoes, peeled, seeded, and chopped (see box page 47)
2 tablespoons tomato paste
2 cups frozen or fresh peas
2 tablespoons pomegranate molasses
1 dried lime (*lūmī* or *loomi*) or fresh lime

1. In a stewpot, heat the olive oil over medium-high heat, then add the onion, celery, and garlic and cook, stirring, until softened, about 5 minutes. Add the lamb, cook until it turns color, then add the bahārāt, salt, and pepper.

2. Add the cauliflower, tomatoes, tomato paste, peas, pomegranate molasses, and dried lime, reduce the heat to low, cover, and cook, stirring occasionally, until the meat is a bit tender, about 1 hour. Remove the cover and continue cooking until the sauce is syrupy, about 1 hour longer. Serve hot.

Zucchini and Lamb Shank Stew

One-pot meals such as stews are typical home fare in Lebanon; no one would order a stew in a restaurant since Mom makes it better. In Arabic cooking, many stews take their name from the predominant vegetable in the stew and not from the meat. The meat is meant to take a secondary role. So in this *yakhnat al-kusa*, or zucchini stew, medium-size zucchini are cut into largish chunks. Lebanese cooks will cook the zucchini right along with the meat from the start, and as a result the zucchini will be very soft. This is how they like it. Lamb shanks are usually sold whole, but you can ask the butcher to slice them for you to expose more bone. This way the stew will have a lot more flavor. Serve with a salad and warm Arabic flatbread.

6 tablespoons (¾ stick) unsalted butter or clarified butter
1 medium onion, chopped
2½ pounds lamb shank, cut into 1½-inch pieces (if possible)
2 teaspoons bahārāt (see box page 206)
½ teaspoon ground allspice
⅛ teaspoon ground cinnamon
3 pounds medium zucchini, cut into 1-inch-thick slices
2½ pounds ripe tomatoes, cut in half, seeds squeezed out, and grated against the
    largest holes of a grater
10 large garlic cloves, lightly crushed
Salt and freshly ground black pepper, to taste

In a large flameproof baking casserole, melt the butter over medium-high heat, and once it stops sizzling, add the onion and cook, stirring, until light brown, about 8 minutes. Add the lamb, bahārāt, allspice, and cinnamon, and cook, stirring, until browned, about 6 minutes. Add the zucchini, tomatoes, garlic, salt, and pepper, bring to a boil, then reduce the heat to very low, using a heat diffuser if necessary, cover, and simmer until the lamb is falling off the bone, about 4 hours. Serve hot.

Lamb and Chicory Stew

When I first had this dish, years ago in Apulia, the region of Italy called the heel of the Italian boot, it was served directly from the earthenware cauldron that gives the dish its name, *calderotto*. The amount of chicory called for in the recipe seems excessive, but it's not. The finished dish is very green and very tender, the flavorful lamb surrounded by the almost melted texture of the chicory, which loses a lot of its bitterness in the cooking. If you can't find chicory you may use escarole.

2 pounds boneless lamb shoulder or leg, trimmed of any large pieces of fat
  and cut into bite-size pieces
1 large onion, sliced
½ pound ripe tomatoes, peeled, seeded, and chopped (see box page 47)
¾ cup coarsely chopped fresh flat-leaf parsley
½ cup dry white wine
5 tablespoons extra-virgin olive oil
Pinch of saffron, crumbled
1 cup water
3½ pounds chicory, coarsely chopped
Salt and freshly ground black pepper, to taste

1. Put the lamb, onion, tomatoes, parsley, wine, olive oil, and saffron in an earthenware casserole (preferably) with a cover or in a large flameproof baking casserole. (If using earthenware and it is not flameproof, you will need to use a heat diffuser. Earthenware heats up slower but retains its heat longer than other casseroles. When using earthenware, food may cook slower at first and then cook very quickly while retaining its heat.) Turn the heat to medium-low and cook until the liquid has evaporated, about 1½ hours. Stir occasionally and check to see that the liquid is not evaporating too fast. If it is, add a few tablespoons of water each time you stir.

2. Add the water and chicory, a handful at a time, stirring continuously and letting the chicory wilt so more handfuls can be added. Reduce the heat to low and season with salt and pepper. Cover and cook until the stew is thick and inviting, about 1 hour. If the stew remains very liquid, uncover for the last 30 minutes of cooking. Serve hot.

Lamb, Potato, and Pecorino Stew

This stew comes from the Basilicata region of Italy, the instep of the Italian boot, and is cooked in an earthenware vessel called a *pignatta*, a kind of jug-like earthenware pot that also gives the dish its name, *pigneti*. Traditionally, *pigneti* are hermetically sealed with clay and then placed in the embers of a fire to cook. Serve this with a salad.

3 pounds boneless leg of lamb, trimmed of fat and cut into 2-inch cubes
2 pounds Yukon gold potatoes, peeled, halved, and sliced
6 large ripe tomatoes (about 3 pounds), peeled, seeded, and
    coarsely chopped (see box page 47)
1 large onion, peeled, cut into eighths, and pieces separated
1½ cups water
⅓ pound pecorino cheese, diced
¼ pound spicy salami or pepperoni, cut into small pieces
1 teaspoon red chile flakes
Salt, to taste
All-purpose flour, for making a sealing rope (optional)

1. Add the lamb, potatoes, tomatoes, onion, water, cheese, salami, chile flakes, and salt in a large earthenware casserole with a heavy lid (preferably) or a large flameproof baking casserole with a heavy lid. (If using earthenware and it is not flameproof, you will need to use a heat diffuser. Earthenware heats up slower but retains its heat longer than other casseroles. When using earthenware, food may cook slower at first and then cook very quickly while retaining its heat.) Toss well and cover. If you would like to seal the cover (it's not absolutely necessary), make a paste from flour and water and form it into a rope: Place 1 cup of flour in a bowl and add enough water to form a dough, then roll out with your hands to form a long snake to fit around the circumference of the casserole. Seal the pot and lid together.

2. Turn the heat to medium-low and cook, shaking the casserole occasionally, for 2¼ hours. Check to see if the lamb is tender and the potatoes cooked. If the potatoes aren't cooked, continue cooking a bit longer after reforming a flour-and-water seal. Serve immediately.

Mixed Meats

||||||||||||||||||||||||||||||||||||||||||||||||||||||||||||||||||||||||||||||||||||||||||||||||||||||||||||||||||||||||||||||||||||||||||||||

The fun thing about mixed meats is just that—they're mixed. And the whole is greater than the sum of its parts, as these various meats combine their flavors with each other in unique and sometimes unexpected ways. You might think that the Pork, Duck, and Shrimp Pot Roast with Coca-Cola (page 258) is the most ridiculous thing you've ever heard, but this Southern-inspired preparation is full of surprises, the first being that it doesn't taste like Coca-Cola. Ever since making up the Santa Monica Fatboy (page 262), originally invented to be a massive dinner sandwich, I get regular requests to make it even though I tell people who eat it for the first time "you can make it yourself." Beware: They're incredibly delicious. There are many Asian stir-fries that use multiple meats and I've included some here, but you just can't go wrong by trying the Stir-Fried Green Beans with Ground Pork and Shrimp (page 268). Many mixed meat one-pot dishes are found in Spanish cuisine, from paella to the dishes they call *arroz al forno*, which includes the rich and complex-tasting Rice Casserole with Shrimp, Ham, and Chicken (page 282).

Catalan Chicken and Seafood Paella

Although the most famous Spanish paella is from Valencia, Barcelona in Catalonia can hold its own when it comes to paella, as exemplified in this fabulous dish *paella amb pollastre i marisc* (paella with chicken and seafood). Properly speaking, one must refer to *paelles*, the plural of *paella*, for there are hundreds of varieties of these rice dishes cooked in the flat low-sided metal pan known as a paella pan. In Catalonia, one will also find many rice dishes cooked in an earthenware *cazuela* or casserole, a cooking vessel that is deeper than a paella pan, making for slightly moister rice. This recipe is based on the making of a *sofregit*, a mixture based on red bell pepper, garlic, onion, and tomato that is the foundation to the flavors. The dish combines seafood and chicken, and the rice is cooked in a chicken broth.

> 5 tablespoons extra-virgin olive oil
> 1 Cornish game hen, cut into small pieces (on the bone), liver chopped separately
> ¾ pound squid, cleaned and cut into strips, tentacles cut in half if large
> 4 large spot prawns or 10 ounces jumbo shrimp (with their heads, if available), shelled with heads left on (shells saved for making Quick Seafood Stock, see box page 380, if desired)
> 6 ounces bluefish, mackerel, yellowtail, or mahimahi, diced large
> 1 medium onion, finely chopped
> 1 large tomato, peeled, seeded, and chopped (see box page 47)
> 2 roasted red bell peppers, 1 finely chopped, 1 cut into strips
> 5 large garlic cloves, finely chopped
> 3 tablespoons finely chopped fresh flat-leaf parsley
> 1 cup medium-grain rice such as Calrose or short-grain rice such as Arborio
> 10 ounces fresh peas or chopped green beans
> 2 cups chicken broth
> ¼ teaspoon saffron, crumbled in a mortar using a pestle with 1 teaspoon salt
> 12 mussels, debearded and cleaned
> Salt and freshly ground black pepper, to taste
> Allioli (see box page 388), for serving (optional)

1. In a medium paella pan (about 11 inches in diameter), heat 3 tablespoons of the olive oil over medium-high heat, then add the game hen and its gizzards (but not the chopped liver) and cook on all sides, turning them with tongs, until golden brown, about 5 minutes. Remove and set aside.

2. Add the squid, prawns, and fish and cook until the shrimp turns orange, the squid curls up, and the fish turns opaque, about 4 minutes. Remove with a slotted ladle, leaving the liquid in the pan, and transfer the seafood to the reserved chicken on the side.

3. Prepare the *sofregit*. Add the remaining 2 tablespoons olive oil to the paella pan, then add the onion and cook, stirring, until it is translucent, about 5 minutes. Add the tomato, chopped roasted pepper, garlic, and parsley, reduce the heat to low, and cook, stirring occasionally, until dense, about 30 minutes. Add the chopped game hen liver, rice, and peas and stir until coated with the *sofregit*. Pour in the broth and the saffron mixture.

4. Bring to a boil, stir, and lay the game hen and seafood along with the mussels on top, pushing them down slightly into the broth and rice. Season lightly with salt and pepper. Reduce the heat to low. Add the roasted pepper strips to the top, and cook, never stirring, until the rice is tender and no liquid is left, 45 to 50 minutes. Serve hot with Allioli, if desired.

Chicken with Sausage

Combining chicken and sausage is typical of home cooking in southern Italy. Every household has a different recipe. This is the way I like it—as a perfect quick one-pot meal that only needs a simple salad on the side. The peperoncini chiles are often sold under many different names; they are mild tasting, thin pale yellowish-green chiles 6 to 8 inches long.

¼ cup extra-virgin olive oil
2 large garlic cloves, lightly crushed
1 pound mild Italian sausage, casing removed and crumbled into bite-size pieces
1 medium onion, quartered, pieces separated
2 ounces prosciutto, cut into thin strips
1½ pounds boneless, skinless chicken breasts, cut into bite-size pieces
8 peperoncini chiles (Italian frying peppers) or New Mexico/Anaheim chiles,
　　seeded and sliced into long strips
Salt and freshly ground black pepper, to taste
¾ cup tomato purée
¾ cup dry red wine
8 fresh rosemary sprigs, tied together with kitchen twine

1. In a large flameproof baking casserole, heat the olive oil over medium-high heat, then add the garlic cloves and cook, stirring, until they begin to turn light brown. Remove and discard the garlic. Add the sausage, onion, and prosciutto and cook, stirring occasionally, until the onion is softened, about 10 minutes. Tilt the casserole and remove any excess fat with a spoon.

2. Increase the heat to high, add the chicken and peperoncini, and season with salt and pepper. Cook, turning the chicken often, for 3 minutes. Pour in the tomato purée, wine, and rosemary and continue cooking, stirring, until the sauce is as thick as you like it, 10 to 17 minutes. Remove and discard the rosemary and serve immediately.

Kale and Sausage Stew

This is a flavorful and easy stew to make and, if you like, an opportunity to use black kale, the very dark green crinkly-leaved Italian-style kale with a hearty taste. I usually serve this stew with slices of buttered, toasted bread.

2 tablespoons extra-virgin olive oil

2 ounces slab bacon, cut into bâtons

1 small onion, chopped

4 large garlic cloves, finely chopped

½ pound hot Italian sausage or fresh andouille sausage, casing removed and crumbled

¼ pound beef chuck, diced

10 cherry tomatoes

1½ cups red wine

1 cup water

¾ pound kale, heaviest portion of stems removed

1 bay leaf

Salt and freshly ground black pepper, to taste

In a stewpot, heat the olive oil with the bacon, onion, and garlic and cook, stirring, until softened, about 5 minutes. Add the sausage, beef, tomatoes, red wine, water, kale, and bay leaf, reduce the heat to low, cover, and cook, stirring occasionally, until the meat and vegetables are tender, about 2 hours. Remove and discard the bay leaf. Season with salt and pepper and serve hot.

Sancocho

Although this best-known Puerto Rican stew is thought of as a vegetable stew, it does contain meat. It would seem that some of the ingredients would be hard to find, but my experience was that if you look at some of the vegetables sold in your supermarket that you typically never look at, you're likely to find them. I did. Malanga (*Xanthosoma sagittifolium*), for instance, used in Caribbean cooking, is the corm of a plant related to taro. Many supermarkets in the Atlantic states and in Florida will carry these roots vegetables that are used in much Caribbean cooking.

1 pound beef flank steak, cut into cubes
½ pound pork shoulder, cubed
2 ounces cooked ham, chopped
1 medium onion, chopped
2 tomatoes, chopped
2 green bell peppers, seeded and chopped
1 fresh green chile, seeded and chopped
1 leafy fresh cilantro (coriander leaf) sprig
1 tablespoon salt
2 quarts water
½ pound malanga, peeled and cut into 1-inch cubes
½ pound pumpkin flesh, cut into 1-inch cubes
½ pound yams, peeled and cut into 1-inch cubes
½ pound small red or white potatoes, peeled and halved
1 green plantain, cut into ½-inch slices
1 ripe or red plantain, cut into ½-inch slices
2 ears corn on the cob, kernels scraped off

1. Add the beef, pork, ham, onion, tomatoes, bell peppers, chile, cilantro, and salt in a large flameproof baking casserole. Cover with the water and bring to a boil. Reduce the heat to low and simmer until the meat is somewhat tender, about 1 hour.

2. Add the malanga, pumpkin, yams, potatoes, plantains, and corn kernels and continue to cook over low heat for 1¼ hours.

3. Cover, raise the heat to medium, and cook until the meat and vegetables are tender, about 30 minutes. Uncover, and if there is a lot of liquid left, boil to evaporate it a bit, about 8 minutes, then reduce the heat to low and cook until it becomes a thick stew, about 40 minutes. Serve hot.

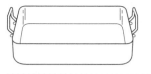

Creole Meat Loaf and Roast Potatoes

This meat loaf is a meal in itself, as the "trinity" of Creole cooking—bell peppers, onion, and celery—is included in the meat mixture. It's best to cook the meat loaf slowly so that the vegetables get cooked well. Leftover meat loaf makes a very nice po'boy sandwich with a little mayonnaise, lettuce, and tomato slices. I usually serve this with a bottle of Red Rooster Louisiana hot sauce on the table.

1 cup ketchup

1 tablespoon Worcestershire sauce

1 tablespoon Creole mustard

1 tablespoon bourbon or rye whiskey

1 tablespoon brown sugar

¾ pound ground beef

¾ pound ground pork

¾ pound ground veal

½ pound white part of French bread, soaked in milk for 5 minutes, excess squeezed out

1 large egg

1 medium red onion

½ red bell pepper, seeded and chopped

½ green bell pepper, seeded and chopped

1 celery stalk, chopped

4 large garlic cloves, finely chopped

¼ cup finely chopped fresh flat-leaf parsley

1 tablespoon hot paprika

1 teaspoon dried oregano

1 tablespoon salt

2 teaspoons freshly ground black pepper, or to taste

2 tablespoons unsalted butter, slivered

1 pound russet potatoes, peeled and quartered

Cayenne pepper, for sprinkling (optional)

1. Preheat the oven to 300°F.

2. In a large measuring cup, mix together the ketchup, Worcestershire sauce, Creole mustard, whiskey, and brown sugar.

3. In a bowl, mix together the beef, pork, veal, bread, egg, onion, bell peppers, celery, garlic, parsley, paprika, oregano, salt, and black pepper. If you have time, the meat loaf will be even better if you can blend it in a food processor until almost pasty. Transfer the meat to a lightly buttered large roasting pan and form into a log, slightly flattened on top. Spread the sauce over the meat loaf, covering the top and sides. Dot with some of the slivered butter. Place the potatoes around the meat loaf and dot them with the remaining slivered butter; sprinkle with cayenne, if desired. Bake until the top is glazed, about 3 hours. Serve hot.

Stuffed Meat Loaf with Spinach and Ricotta

This preparation is inspired by the several variations of a dish from Naples called *polpettone alla napoletana*, which basically means "big meatball in the style of Naples." The meat is seasoned as you would meatballs and stuffed with a mixture of fresh ricotta and baby spinach leaves. It's braised in a tomato sauce with red wine, and all you need to accompany it is some warm, crusty Italian bread.

2 cups small cubes of white part of French bread
1 cup whole milk
¾ pound ground beef
¾ pound ground veal or turkey
¾ pound ground pork
2 large eggs, beaten separately
2 ounces Parmesan cheese (preferably Parmigiano-Reggiano), freshly grated
2 ounces pecorino cheese, freshly grated
1 small onion, finely chopped
2 tablespoons finely chopped fresh flat-leaf parsley
Salt and freshly ground black pepper, to taste
½ pound fresh ricotta cheese
6 ounces baby spinach leaves, chopped
2 tablespoons extra-virgin olive oil
2 tablespoons unsalted butter
2 large garlic cloves, finely chopped
1 cup dry red wine
One 28-ounce can tomatoes, chopped, with their liquid
2 tablespoons tomato paste
2 teaspoons sugar
3 tablespoons finely chopped fresh basil

1. Soak the bread in the milk for a few minutes and then squeeze out and place in a bowl with the ground beef, veal, pork, one of the eggs, Parmesan and pecorino cheeses, onion, and parsley, and season with salt and pepper. Knead with both hands until well blended. Using wet hands so the meat doesn't stick, spread it out flat on a large platter.

2. In a bowl, mix together the ricotta cheese, the remaining beaten egg, and spinach. Season with salt and pepper. Spread this mixture in the center of the meat. Fold up the two sides of the flattened meat toward the center: Fold up the left long side toward the center and then the right long side and shape the meat with your hands into a log. Form the meat with wet hands to seal any cracks or openings. Seal the two ends by forming with your hands. Cover with plastic wrap and refrigerate for at least 1 hour.

3. In a large oval (preferably) flameproof baking casserole, heat the olive oil and butter over medium heat, then carefully place the meat loaf in the casserole and brown the bottom, about 4 minutes. Add the garlic and cook for 30 seconds. Add the wine and let it reduce by half, then add the tomatoes, tomato paste, and sugar and simmer covered on low for 1 hour.

4. Stir in the basil, season with salt and pepper, and cook for another 30 minutes. Lift the meat loaf with a long offset spatula (or use two spatulas) and place on a serving platter. Spoon the tomato sauce over and serve.

Pot-au-Feu

There are a number of versions of this classic French one-pot meal; this version is from Carcassonne in the Aude department of the Languedoc in southwestern France, a town that is a very well preserved medieval village. It is an old town where even the "New City" dates from the thirteenth century. To make pot-au-feu, assemble everything in the morning and let it cook all day unattended. You can even leave the house, go about your business, and return to a house perfumed with the aromas of what you will think is your farm kitchen. The Toulouse sausage can be ordered from www.gourmetfoodstore.com, or you can use mild Italian sausage.

1 head cabbage (about 1½ pounds)
¾ pound Toulouse sausage or mild Italian sausage
4½ pounds beef short ribs
1½ pounds lamb neck or shoulder, cut up
1 pound veal marrow or soup bones
6 ounces slab bacon, coarsely chopped
1 large onion, chopped
¾ pound ripe tomatoes, chopped
2 celery stalks, sliced
2 carrots, scraped and sliced
3 shallots, chopped
6 large garlic cloves, crushed
1½ cups (about ¾ pound) dried white beans
1 tablespoon dried summer savory or thyme
Salt and freshly ground black pepper, to taste
Bouquet garni, tied in cheesecloth, consisting of 15 fresh flat-leaf parsley sprigs,
    10 fresh tarragon sprigs, 3 fresh sage sprigs, 2 bay leaves
6 cups water

1. In a large flameproof enameled cast-iron baking casserole, bring several quarts of water to a boil and cook the whole cabbage until the leaves can be peeled off easily, about 10 minutes. Drain and, when cool enough to handle, core the cabbage and separate the leaves. Stuff each leaf with a heaping tablespoon or more of sausage meat squeezed out from its casing, placing it at the core end of the leaf and rolling up the leaf, tucking in the sides. Set aside.

2. Preheat the oven to 270°F.

3. Arrange the beef ribs, lamb, marrow bones, and bacon on the bottom of the casserole. Toss the onion, tomatoes, celery, carrots, shallots, garlic, and white beans around the casserole on top of and in between the meat pieces. Season with the savory, salt, and pepper and place the bouquet garni in the center. Pour in the water. Arrange the stuffed cabbage leaves on top with the remaining sausage meat and press down with anything that is heavy and ovenproof, such as a small heavy, ovenproof lid, pie pan, or small baking stone (if it fits). Place in the oven and slowly bake until the meat is falling off the bones and the beans are tender, about 8 hours. Remove and discard the bouquet garni.

Braised Beef Short Ribs and Pork Butt in Ragoût

This one-pot braise simmers all day, until the meat falls off the bones. This will result in an extraordinary flavor and enticing aromas. This braise is perfect for a blustery, cold day when you don't want to work in the kitchen but you do want the aromas of delicious food. You'll need very low heat, which some cooktops provide with simmer controls. If your cooktop does not have a simmer control, you must use a heat diffuser over the lowest BTU burner you have. Alternatively, at the lowest setting your regular cooktop has, the braise will be done in 3½ to 4 hours. The simmer method will take about 10 hours and result in a richer, thicker ragoût and more tender braised meat. I usually serve a very simple salad on the side, such as butter lettuce dressed only with salt and olive oil.

3 tablespoons unsalted butter
3 tablespoons extra-virgin olive oil
2¾ pounds beef short ribs (about 5 ribs)
One 2-pound pork butt
1 medium onion, chopped
8 large garlic cloves, chopped
One 6-ounce can tomato paste
1 cup sparkling red wine or rosé
1 cup dry white wine
Bouquet garni, tied in cheesecloth, consisting of 6 fresh flat-leaf parsley sprigs,
    1 fresh tarragon sprig, 1 fresh sage sprig, 5 fresh thyme sprigs, 5 fresh marjoram
    sprigs, 1 fresh basil sprig, and 2 bay leaves
1 pound Yukon gold potatoes, peeled and quartered
10 ounces black kale, sliced
Salt and freshly ground black pepper, to taste

1. In a large flameproof baking casserole, melt the butter with the olive oil over medium-high heat, then add the short ribs and pork butt and cook, turning once, until crispy golden on both sides, about 8 minutes. Add the onion and garlic and cook, turning and stirring, until softened, for 3 minutes. Blend the tomato paste with the wines, pour into the casserole, and stir. Add the bouquet garni, bring to a boil, reduce the heat to very low, using a heat diffuser if possible, and simmer, partially covered and turning every hour or so, until more tender, about 2 hours with a low burner setting, or 5 hours with a simmer-control setting.

2. Add the potatoes and kale, season with salt and pepper, push the kale down into the casserole as it wilts, and continue cooking until the meat falls off the bone, about 2 hours on a low setting and 5 hours on a simmer-control setting. Remove and discard the bouquet garni. Serve hot.

Polish Hunter's Stew

Bigos is a famous—the most famous—Polish stew, known as a hunter's stew, which seems to have everything in it. It is quite a production, and you'll feel obligated if you try to make it to invite any Poles you know over for dinner. I have an authentic and traditional recipe in my book *Real Stew*. This recipe I developed when I wanted a bigos without all the shopping rigmarole. That being said, I am also fortunate to have a Polish grocery near where I live, and I can get things like Cracow sausage and whatnot.

20 small pitted prunes
¾ cup Madeira
3 tablespoons pork lard (preferably) or butter
¼ pound smoked bacon slab, chopped
1 very large onion, coarsely chopped
1 duck, cut into 8 pieces
2½ pounds boneless pork shoulder, cut into chunks
2 pounds Cracow sausage or Polish kielbasa, cut into thick rounds
2 Granny Smith apples, peeled, cored, and chopped
1 cup water
½ cup dried split peas
½ cup pearl barley
1 teaspoon ground caraway seeds
1 teaspoon sugar
1 bay leaf
4 allspice berries, ground
Salt and freshly ground black pepper, to taste

1. Soak the prunes in the Madeira until needed.

2. In a large flameproof baking casserole, melt the lard with the chopped bacon over medium-high heat, then add the onion and cook, stirring, until softened, about 8 minutes. Remove the onion with a slotted spoon and reserve.

3. Add the duck and cook, turning, until browned, about 8 minutes. Remove the duck from the pan and cook the pork shoulder, turning, until browned, about another 8 minutes. Return the duck and onion to the casserole with the pork, then add the sausage, apples, soaked prunes and Madeira, water, split peas, barley, caraway seeds, sugar, bay leaf, and allspice berries, and season with salt and pepper. Bring to a boil over high heat, then reduce to very low, using a heat diffuser if necessary, and cook until very tender, about 6 hours. Remove and discard the bay leaf.

Pork, Duck, and Shrimp Pot Roast with Coca-Cola

If you have never thought of using Coca-Cola for cooking, then this is a wonderful recipe to give it a try. The resulting sauce has a dark caramel, full-bodied flavor that is very enticing. If you taste the sauce as you first start cooking, it will taste off. Slowly, however, the braise takes on the flavors of its manifold ingredients and your pot roast will metamorphose into a delicious and complex dish. A simple side salad of lettuce or coleslaw using a prepackaged bag of coleslaw mix, a little mayonnaise, and vinegar is an ideal accompaniment, along with warm soft dinner rolls or corn bread.

2 tablespoons vegetable oil

1 pound pork loin sirloin chops, cut into 1-inch cubes

4 duck legs (about 1¾ pounds)

1 medium onion, chopped

½ red or green bell pepper, seeded and chopped

1 celery stalk, chopped

Salt, to taste

1 tablespoon Creole seasoning such as Tony Chachere or Paul Prudhomme brand

1 teaspoon freshly ground black pepper

½ teaspoon freshly ground white pepper

½ teaspoon cayenne pepper

3 tablespoons all-purpose flour

1 Yukon gold potato (¾ pound), peeled and quartered

2 carrots (½ pound), scraped and cut in half

2 cups Coca-Cola

1 cup water

¾ pound jumbo shrimp (about 12), shelled (shells saved for making Quick Seafood Stock, see box page 380, if desired)

1. In a large flameproof baking casserole, heat 1 tablespoon of the vegetable oil over high heat, then add the pork and duck and cook until golden brown on all sides, about 6 minutes. Remove the meat from the casserole and reserve. Reduce the heat to medium-high.

2. Add the remaining 1 tablespoon of oil to the casserole, add the onion, bell pepper, celery, and salt and cook, stirring, until softened, about 4 minutes. Add the Creole seasoning, black pepper, white pepper, and cayenne and stir. Add the flour and stir to form a roux. Cook, stirring constantly, until mushy, 1 to 2 minutes. Return the duck and pork to the casserole along with the potato and carrots. Stir, reduce the heat to low, add the Coca-Cola and water, and cook, turning occasionally, partially covered, until tender, about 1½ hours.

3. Increase the heat to high, add the shrimp and season with salt, and cook, stirring, until orange-pink, about 2 minutes. Remove from the heat and serve.

Potpourri Pie

This utterly delicious, and admittedly unusual, meat pie is made with four kinds of meat (lamb, beef, chicken, and ham), seasoned with a little cinnamon, and then covered with an omelet and puff pastry before going into the oven. It's nicely accompanied by a tomato, endive, red onion, watercress, and arugula salad dressed with olive oil and balsamic vinegar.

½ pound boneless leg of lamb, cut into ¾-inch cubes

½ pound boneless beef chuck or London broil, cut into ¾-inch cubes

½ pound boneless, skinless chicken thighs, cut into ¾-inch cubes

1 medium onion, chopped

½ teaspoon salt, plus more as needed

½ teaspoon freshly ground black pepper, plus more as needed

½ teaspoon ground cinnamon, plus more as needed

4 tablespoons (½ stick) unsalted butter

2 cups water

½ pound cooked ham, cubed

1 cup frozen edamame soybeans or lima beans

¾ cup frozen peas

4 large eggs

½ pound frozen puff pastry, defrosted according to package instructions

1. Preheat the oven to 385°F.

2. Put the lamb, beef, and chicken thighs in a large cast-iron skillet with the onion, salt, pepper, and cinnamon and mix well. Add the butter, turn the heat to medium, and cook, stirring, until the liquid evaporates, about 15 minutes. Add 1 cup of the water and cook until a bit evaporated and saucy, about 7 minutes. Add the remaining 1 cup water and cook again until a bit evaporated and saucy, about 7 minutes. Add the ham, edamame, and peas and continue cooking, stirring, for 10 minutes.

3. Meanwhile, beat the eggs with some pepper, a pinch of cinnamon, and some salt. Pour the eggs into the skillet with the other food, cover, and cook until the eggs set but the top is still a bit runny, about 2 minutes. Turn off the heat.

4. Roll out the puff pastry large enough to cover the skillet. Lay the sheet of puff pastry over the skillet, pinching and crimping it to the edge of the skillet so that the pastry doesn't contract. Cut out heart-shaped pieces with the excess dough and arrange them attractively on top of the pie. Bake the pie until golden brown, about 30 minutes. Remove, let rest for 5 minutes, and then serve.

Santa Monica Fatboy

After a week in New Orleans eating some spectacular po'boys, I thought, we should have something like that. I mean, I know we Californians have fantastic burritos and tacos and Korean-Mexican fusion tacos (see Pork Belly and Kimchi Tacos page 158), but I thought, how about a sandwich for my duck-crazy family? A nice big, fat sandwich piled high and a little over the top. Well, bacon can't hurt, and spicy hot chorizo or even andouille sausages, some tomatoes, red onion, lettuce—what they call "dressing" in the Big Easy—on a light brioche roll for sandwiches (not a breakfast brioche). When I first made this I thought I'd need to make something else to accompany it, but no way, because this fatboy is an all-in-one sandwich!

4 brioche sandwich buns

1 tablespoon unsalted butter, at room temperature

4 boneless duck breast halves (1 pound)

4 slices thick-cut bacon, cut in half widthwise

1 fully cooked hot Louisiana-style sausage, Mexican chorizo sausage, or
    andouille sausage (about 3 ounces), quartered lengthwise

1 recipe Remoulade (see box page 264)

8 leaves lettuce

1 avocado, cut in half, pitted, flesh scooped out and sliced

1 medium heirloom tomato, cut into 4 slices

1 red onion, thinly sliced

1. Split the brioche buns and butter each half. In a cast-iron skillet, cook the buttered side of the brioche buns over medium heat until golden and crispy, about 3 minutes. Remove and set aside.

2. Lay the duck breasts skin side down in the skillet and cook over medium heat until the skin is golden brown, about 5 minutes. Turn and cook until medium-rare, about another 4 minutes; if it's splattering too much, cover with a lid. Remove and set aside. Pour off all but 3 tablespoons of the fat. Add the bacon to the skillet and cook until crisp, about 5 minutes. Remove from the skillet and pour off all but 3 tablespoons of the fat. Thinly slice the duck and return it and the bacon to the skillet along with the sausage and heat over low heat.

3. Assemble the sandwiches by spreading the remoulade on each cut side of the brioche bun. Lay a lettuce leaf on top of a bun half, then 2 slices of avocado, the duck, a slice of tomato, more remoulade, the bacon, the onion, the sausage, more remoulade, and another lettuce leaf. Place the top half of the bun on top to make a sandwich. Continue making the other sandwiches and then serve.

Remoulade

A remoulade is nothing but a French tartar sauce, and in Louisiana it is often pink from the addition of paprika.

1 large egg yolk
2 tablespoons vegetable oil
2 tablespoons finely chopped celery
2 tablespoons finely chopped scallions
2 tablespoons finely chopped fresh flat-leaf parsley
2 tablespoons finely grated fresh horseradish
1 tablespoon fresh lemon juice
1 small bay leaf, crumbled
1 tablespoon Creole mustard
1½ teaspoons mustard powder mixed with 1 teaspoon water
1 tablespoon ketchup
1 tablespoon Worcestershire sauce
1½ teaspoons white wine vinegar
1½ teaspoons Tabasco sauce
2 large garlic cloves, finely chopped
1 teaspoon sweet paprika
½ teaspoon salt

Place the egg yolk in a food processor and run for 2 minutes. While the machine is running, pour in the oil in a thin stream. Add all of the remaining ingredients and blend. Refrigerate for 2 hours before using.

Makes ¾ cup

Skillet-Fried Potatoes with Duck, Beef, and Pork

In this preparation, you'll need a large cast-iron skillet that can go into the oven for the final broiling of the tomato and pecorino cheese topping. If you use more duck than I call for, there might be too much fat, so remove a few tablespoons if you do. This dish may be prepared ahead of time, in which case bake it at 450°F for 15 minutes rather than broiling it.

¾ pound boneless duck breasts
2 pounds Yukon gold potatoes, peeled and cut into ½-inch cubes, and
    dried with paper towels
5 ounces beef, chopped
5 ounces pork, chopped
Salt and freshly ground black pepper, to taste
1½ pounds tomatoes, sliced
3 ounces pecorino cheese, freshly grated

1. Preheat a large cast-iron skillet over medium heat. Add the duck, skin side down, and cook, using a lid to control splatter, until the skin is dark golden brown, about 6 minutes. Turn and cook for another 3 minutes. Remove the duck and let rest.

2. Add the potatoes in one layer to the skillet and cook, without stirring or turning, until crispy golden brown on the bottom, about 10 minutes. Turn the potatoes with a metal spatula, making sure you scrape and lift the crusty bottom, and continue cooking for another 10 minutes. Add the chopped beef and pork, season with salt and pepper, and cook, pushing the meat into the skillet but without stirring, until it loses its pink color, about 5 minutes. Continue cooking, stirring occasionally, for another 5 minutes.

3. Preheat the broiler with the rack about 5 inches from the broiling element.

4. Slice the duck thinly and layer the pieces over the meat and potatoes. Layer the sliced tomatoes over the potatoes and meat. Sprinkle the cheese over the tomatoes and place under the broiler until bubbling vigorously, 6 minutes. Serve hot from the skillet.

Shellfish and Pork Chowder

This rich, filling, and delicious meal-in-a-pot chowder is done in a New England style with milk and no tomatoes. The lobster is optional; I use the lobster when the market has them for cheap. You will, though, have to cut it up while alive, which I realize not everyone feels comfortable doing.

2 tablespoons unsalted butter

2½ ounces salt pork, diced small

1 small onion, chopped

1 celery stalk, chopped

4 garlic cloves, slivered

6 ounces Portuguese linguiça sausage or kielbasa, sliced or diced

1 pound Yukon gold potatoes, peeled and diced

½ pound cooked ham, diced

½ pound green beans, cut into ½-inch lengths

3 cups water

2 cups whole milk

1 tablespoon fresh thyme

2 teaspoons celery salt, or to taste

1 teaspoon freshly ground black pepper

One 1¾-pound live lobster, cut up into 2-inch segments to expose the flesh (optional)

1 pound shrimp, shelled (shells saved for making Quick Seafood Stock, see box page 380, if desired)

¼ cup chopped fresh flat-leaf parsley

1. In a stewpot or flameproof baking casserole, melt the butter over medium-high heat, add the salt pork, and cook, stirring, until slightly crisp, about 3 minutes. Add the onion, celery, and garlic and cook, stirring, until softened, about 4 minutes. Add the sausages, potatoes, ham, green beans, water, milk, thyme, celery salt, and pepper, and when it is barely bubbling around the edges, reduce the heat to low and simmer until tender, about 25 minutes, making sure it doesn't ever come to a boil; otherwise it will curdle.

2. Add the lobster, if using, and cook for 8 minutes, then add the shrimp and cook, stirring, until the shrimp are orange-pink and the lobster is red, about 6 minutes. Serve with the parsley sprinkled on top.

Stir-Fried Green Beans with Ground Pork and Shrimp

This is a wonderful recipe if you want to get more vegetables into your diet. It's mostly green beans flavored with pork and shrimp. Everything cooks fast and easy. The chile-garlic sauce is sold in jars in your supermarket's Asian food aisle. A common brand is one by Lee Kum Kee. Don't be tempted to cook all the green beans at once to speed things up, or your dinner will be greasy and unappetizing: You must cook them in batches.

4 cups vegetable oil

3 pounds green beans, trimmed

2 large garlic cloves, finely chopped

¾ pound ground pork

½ pound medium shrimp (about 14), shelled and chopped (shells saved for making Quick Seafood Stock, see box page 380, if desired)

¼ cup chicken broth

1 tablespoon chile-garlic sauce

¼ cup water

1 tablespoon soy sauce

2 teaspoons salt

1½ teaspoons sugar

2 teaspoons rice vinegar

1 teaspoon sesame oil

2 scallions, trimmed and chopped

1. In a wok, heat the vegetable oil over high heat until it starts to smoke, then cook the green beans in 4 batches until slightly crispy looking, 2 minutes per batch. Remove the green beans with a slotted spoon or skimmer and reserve on a paper towel–lined platter to drain. After every batch let the oil reheat for a minute before putting in the next batch. Carefully (because it's hot) pour off all but 4 tablespoons of oil. (You may want to wait until the oil has cooled a bit before pouring off. Let the oil cool completely and save for future frying if desired.)

2. Let the remaining oil heat over high heat, then add the garlic and cook, stirring, for 10 seconds. Add the pork, shrimp, broth, and chile-garlic sauce and cook, stir-frying, for 2 minutes. Add the water, soy sauce, salt, and sugar and toss for 30 seconds. Return all the green beans to the wok and cook, stir-frying, until the liquid has nearly evaporated, about 4 minutes. Stir in the rice vinegar, sesame oil, and scallions. Toss once or twice and serve.

Stir-Fried Salmon, Ham, and Eggs with Vegetables

This recipe is not only delicious but also beautiful. There's a couple of tricky spots, though: You must be careful not to overcook the salmon and you want the eggs to look like the strings of egg in an egg drop soup and not like mush. Once finished, the food is arranged on top of shredded iceberg lettuce for a colorful and light meal.

5 teaspoons soy sauce
3 teaspoons rice wine (mirin) or dry sherry
2 teaspoons peeled and finely chopped fresh ginger
2 teaspoons finely chopped scallion
½ teaspoon salt
1 pound snow peas
½ pound cooked ham, diced
3 tablespoons water
2 teaspoons rice vinegar
2 tablespoons cornstarch
2½ tablespoons vegetable oil
1 pound fresh salmon fillet, diced
4 large eggs
1 small head iceberg lettuce, cored and shredded

1. In a large bowl, combine 3 teaspoons of the soy sauce, 2 teaspoons of the rice wine, 1 teaspoon of the ginger, 1 teaspoon of the scallions, and the salt. Add the snow peas and ham, toss, and let marinate for 15 minutes, turning occasionally.

2. In another bowl, combine the remaining 2 teaspoons soy sauce, the remaining 1 teaspoon rice wine, 1 teaspoon ginger, and 1 teaspoon scallions with the water, rice vinegar, and cornstarch.

3. In a wok, heat 2 tablespoons of the oil over high heat, add the ham and snow pea mixture, and toss several times. Add the salmon and the soy-ginger mixture and cook, stir-frying, for 2 minutes. Push the food up the sides of the wok to clear a space in the center of the wok. Add the remaining ½ tablespoon oil to the cleared space in the center of the wok, crack the eggs into the center, and slowly and carefully break the yolks and mix with the whites with a wooden spoon as they cook and become congealed and firm, about 2 minutes. Don't mix with the other food until they do. Once the eggs have congealed and are no longer gooey, toss with all the other food and cook until the salmon is still medium-rare and the eggs are no longer wet, about 1 minute.

4. Place the shredded lettuce on individual serving plates. Top with the stir-fried mixture and serve immediately.

Stir-Fried Chicken, Pork, Eggplant, and Napa Cabbage

This chicken stir-fry is substantial enough to serve on its own, but if time and a more-than-one-pot inclination allows, a bowl of steamed rice is a nice accompaniment. Everything cooks quickly, however, so it's important that all the elements be previously prepared and cut or sliced to specification.

10 ounces boneless, skinless chicken breasts, cut into thin slices

½ pound boneless pork loin, cut into thin slices

¼ cup soy sauce

3 teaspoons cornstarch

1 large egg white

¼ cup vegetable or peanut oil

5 slices (about 1 × ¼ inch thick) peeled fresh ginger

1 long Japanese eggplant (about 10 ounces), cut in quarters widthwise, then cut into sixths lengthwise

10 ounces button (white) mushrooms, sliced

½ pound napa cabbage, cored and cut into thin strips

4 large garlic cloves, finely chopped

6 fresh green Thai chiles, cut in half lengthwise and seeded

½ cup chicken broth

2 tablespoons cold water

1. Sprinkle the chicken and pork with 3 tablespoons of the soy sauce, toss, and let stand for 30 minutes, turning occasionally. Drain the meat, reserving the soy sauce. Blend the soy sauce with 1 teaspoon of the cornstarch and the egg white and beat until frothy. Add the chicken and pork to the egg white mixture and toss gently.

2. In a wok, heat 2 tablespoons of the oil over high heat. Add the chicken, pork, and ginger and cook, tossing, until they turn color, about 2 minutes. Remove from the wok and reserve.

3. Add the remaining 2 tablespoons oil to the wok and let it heat up. Add the eggplant, mushrooms, cabbage, garlic, and chiles and cook, stir-frying, for 3 minutes. Return the chicken and pork and the remaining 1 tablespoon soy sauce to the wok and cook only long enough to reheat. Stir in the broth and cook, covered, for 2 minutes.

4. Meanwhile, blend the remaining 2 teaspoons cornstarch and the cold water into a paste, then stir into the wok to thicken. Cook for 1 minute, tossing. Serve hot.

Stir-Fried Rice Noodles with Shrimp and Pork

This stir-fry packs a lot of flavor considering that it doesn't really have any spices in it. For success, the rice noodles should be soaked in hot water for 10 minutes to soften and then cut into 5-inch lengths to make stir-frying them manageable. Have all your ingredients ready to go because everything happens quickly. Set out three bowls—a large one, a medium one, and a small one—to soak the noodles, beans sprouts, and mushrooms, respectively.

5 tablespoons vegetable oil

5 scallions, trimmed and cut into ½-inch lengths

½ pound pork loin, cut into slivers

¼ cup soy sauce

8 dried black mushrooms (dried shiitake mushrooms), soaked in
    ¾ cup hot water for 15 minutes, then drained, soaking liquid reserved,
    mushrooms sliced

½ pound shrimp, shelled and diced (shells saved for making
    Quick Seafood Stock, see box page 380, if desired)

½ pound bean sprouts, soaked in hot water for 10 minutes, then drained

¾ pound thin rice noodles, soaked in hot water for 10 minutes,
    then drained and cut into 5-inch lengths

1 tablespoon chile oil or your favorite Asian-style hot sauce

½ teaspoon freshly ground black pepper

1. In a large wok, heat 3 tablespoons of the oil over high heat and stir-fry the scallions for 1 minute. Add the pork and cook, stir-frying, until it turns color, about 2 minutes. Add the soy sauce, toss, then add the mushrooms and their soaking liquid and cook, stir-frying, for 2 minutes. Add the shrimp and cook, stir-frying, until orange-pink, about 1½ minutes. Add the drained bean sprouts and cook, stir-frying, for 2 minutes. Remove the food from the wok and reserve.

2. Heat the remaining 2 tablespoons oil in the wok, add the drained and cut-up rice noodles, and cook, stir-frying gently, to brown lightly. Return the reserved food to the wok and toss to blend and reheat, about 2 minutes. Toss again with the chile oil and freshly ground black pepper, and serve.

Stir-Fried Bean Noodles with Chicken, Pork, and Shrimp

When my family wants to eat Chinese, we don't do takeout but make this dish instead. It's a rich and varied dish with so many tastes and things going on. It's easy to make even though it has a long list of ingredients. The bean noodles called for do not need to be boiled as it describes on the package directions but only soaked in hot water to become malleable before stir-frying. Both the chile oil and hot bean sauce can be found in the international foods aisle of your supermarket. In step 5, you may also add a handful of snow peas and quartered tomatoes, if you like.

For the marinade
1 teaspoon rice wine (mirin)
1 teaspoon soy sauce
1 teaspoon cornstarch
½ pound boneless, skinless chicken thighs, diced
1 pound boneless pork loin sirloin chops, diced

For the bean noodles
¾ pound bean noodles

For the sauce
½ cup chicken broth
1 tablespoon chile oil
2 teaspoons cornstarch
1 teaspoon soy sauce
1 teaspoon sugar
1 teaspoon sesame oil

For the stir-fry
5 tablespoons vegetable oil
2 large garlic cloves, finely chopped
¼ pound large shrimp, shelled and diced (shells saved for making Quick Seafood Stock, see box page 380, if desired)
1 medium onion, cut in half and then thinly sliced

1 baby bok choy, cut into bite-size pieces

1 large carrot, scraped and thinly sliced on the diagonal

5 ounces small broccoli florets

2 tablespoons soy sauce

2 tablespoons yellow bean sauce or any Asian-style bean sauce

1. For the marinade, in a medium bowl, stir together the rice wine, soy sauce, and cornstarch. Toss with the chicken and pork and set aside for 20 to 30 minutes.

2. Place the bean noodles in a bowl, cover with very hot water, and let rest until softened, about 30 minutes. Loosen the noodles with a fork or chopsticks. Cut into 4-inch lengths by picking them up from the water and snipping with scissors. Drain well.

3. Meanwhile, for the sauce, in a bowl, stir together the chicken broth, chile oil, cornstarch, soy sauce, sugar, and sesame oil. Set aside.

4. For the stir-fry, in a large wok, heat 1 tablespoon of the oil over high heat. Add the marinated chicken and pork, and the garlic and cook, stir-frying, until crispy golden brown, about 3 minutes. Push the chicken and pork up the side of the wok, add the shrimp to the middle of the wok and cook, stirring, until orange-pink, about 2 minutes. Toss the chicken, pork, and shrimp together, remove from the wok, and set aside on a platter.

5. Pour 1 tablespoon of the oil into the wok and let it heat. Add the onion, bok choy, carrot, and broccoli and cook, stirring and tossing until tender and crisp, about 4 minutes. Add 1 tablespoon of the soy sauce and toss. Transfer the vegetables to the platter with the meat.

6. Wipe the wok with a paper towel, then heat the remaining 3 tablespoons oil over high heat. Add the noodles and cook for a minute, tossing constantly, then add the bean sauce and the remaining 1 tablespoon soy sauce. Cook, stir-frying, until the noodles are heated through, about 2 minutes. Return the reserved chicken, pork, shrimp, vegetables, and sauce mixture and cook, stir-frying and tossing so everything is combined well, for 3 minutes. Transfer to the platter and serve immediately.

Spicy Shrimp and Ham Spring Roll Wraps

Once you've assembled the stuffed wrappers attractively on a platter for serving, they'll look so appetizing that you'll be hard-pressed to have leftovers. This easy dish occurred to me on a hot summer day when I didn't want to cook (much). I had originally thought of doing this with tortillas but figured that it would be too heavy. Then I remembered the leftover spring roll wrappers in my pantry. In the dry state they are stiff, but once soaked in hot water they become malleable and quite strong and resistant to tearing. Don't use egg roll wrappers, which are made of wheat and taste cornstarchy when eaten raw; make sure you use rice flour spring roll wrappers.

1 pound medium shrimp, shelled and cut in half or thirds (shells saved for making Quick Seafood Stock, see box page 380, if desired)

¾ pound cooked ham, diced

1 large garlic clove, finely chopped

1 tablespoon soy sauce

1 teaspoon peeled and finely chopped fresh ginger

½ teaspoon red chile flakes

Freshly ground black pepper, to taste

¼ cup peanut oil

Salt, to taste (optional)

½ pound bean sprouts

½ pound coleslaw mix (from a package)

½ cup whole fresh cilantro leaves (coriander leaf)

One 12-ounce package rice flour spring roll wrappers (you will have some left over)

For the dips

1 jar Chinese chile-garlic sauce

2 tablespoons dry mustard powder

1 tablespoon honey mustard

¼ cup soy sauce

1 teaspoon wasabi paste

1. Toss the shrimp, ham, garlic, soy sauce, ginger, chile flakes, and pepper together.

2. In a sauté pan, heat the peanut oil over medium-high heat, then add the shrimp and ham mixture and cook, stirring, until the shrimp turn orange-red, about 3 minutes. Season with salt, if necessary. Toss the bean sprouts, coleslaw, and cilantro together in a bowl.

3. Fill a wide bowl or deep platter with hot water and soak a rice spring roll wrapper for about 20 seconds or until softened. Lay the wrapper out on a kitchen towel to absorb excess water. Spoon a 3-inch long row of the shrimp and ham mixture along the bottom third of the wrapper. Top with the coleslaw mixture. Roll the bottom portion of the wrapper over the stuffing, doing so tightly, then fold the left and right sides inward over the first roll, tightly, and continue rolling into a cylinder as tightly as you can. Cut in half diagonally, if desired, and arrange attractively on a platter. Continue filling spring roll wrappers until you run out of stuffing.

4. Prepare the three dipping sauces. Empty the chile-garlic sauce into a shallow bowl. Stir the dry mustard together with enough water in another shallow bowl to achieve the consistency of prepared mustard, then stir in the honey mustard. Stir the soy sauce with the wasabi paste in a third shallow bowl until blended. Serve the dips with the spring rolls.

Rice

It was only after assembling this chapter on one-pot recipes featuring rice that I realized all the recipes were from Spain. Although that was an accident, the fact that Spain offers an amazing array of spectacular rice dishes that can all be cooked in a casserole or paella pan is not. Spain was one of the first places in Europe that received rice from the Arabs around 900 A.D. and an entire culture of rice cookery sprung up; the most famous preparation being paella. However, the variety of dishes is much greater, and here you'll get an opportunity to try some of the best recipes; from the rustic Rice in the Style of Andalusia on page 294 to the festive Sea and Mountain Rice Casserole on page 292.

Rice Casserole with Shrimp, Ham, and Chicken

This Spanish-style rice casserole is cooked on top of the stove and then finished in the oven and has a wonderful blend of flavors. It feeds a good group of people and has an intriguing mix of tastes that meld perfectly. For the shrimp broth called for in the recipe ingredient list, remember to save the shells from the shrimp so you can make it.

2 tablespoons extra-virgin olive oil

1 small onion, finely chopped

3 scallions, white and light green parts only, trimmed and thinly sliced

4 large garlic cloves, finely chopped

½ pound cooked kielbasa, sliced

¼ pound cooked ham, diced

¼ pound Canadian bacon, diced

¼ pound boneless, skinless chicken breasts, diced

1 cup medium-grain rice such as Calrose or short-grain rice such as Arborio

1 pound large shrimp, shelled (shells reserved)

2 cups shrimp broth (see note below)

½ cup frozen or fresh peas

2 teaspoons salt

1 teaspoon freshly ground black pepper

1 teaspoon sweet paprika or mild Spanish paprika (*pimentón*)

½ teaspoon saffron

1. Preheat the oven to 475°F.

2. In a large earthenware casserole (preferably) or a large flameproof baking casserole, heat the olive oil over high heat, then add the onion, scallions, and garlic and cook, stirring, until softened, about 10 minutes. (If using earthenware and it is not flameproof, you will need to use a heat diffuser. Earthenware heats up slower but retains its heat longer than other casseroles. When using earthenware, food may cook slower at first and then cook very quickly while retaining its heat.) Add the sausage, ham, Canadian bacon, and chicken and cook, stirring, until they change in color, about 5 minutes. Remove with a slotted spoon and reserve. Add the rice and cook, stirring, until the grains are shiny, about 2 minutes.

3. Return all the meats to the casserole, add the shrimp, shrimp broth, peas, salt, pepper, paprika, and saffron, and continue to cook on high heat until the broth begins to bubble around the edges, pushing all the shrimp down under the broth, about 5 minutes. (This will happen sooner if not using earthenware.) Reduce the heat to low and cook without stirring until the broth is absorbed, about 30 minutes. Place the casserole in the oven and bake for 5 minutes. Remove and let rest, covered, for 10 minutes before serving.

Note: To make shrimp broth, place the shells and 3 cups of water in a saucepan and bring to a boil, then simmer until needed. Strain before using.

Rice Casserole with Quail and Sausage

Many Spanish rice dishes are known simply as *arroz*, "rice," when they are cooked in a casserole on top of the stove or in the oven. If they are cooked in a steel pan they are called paella, of which there are many variations, although the classic one is from Valencia. This recipe is a flavorful, fragrant, and quite colorful dish. The Spanish *longaniza* sausage can be ordered from www.tienda.com, or you could use any sausage your supermarket offers. Serve with a simple salad.

3 tablespoons extra-virgin olive oil

6 quail, cut in half

6 Spanish *longaniza* sausages (about 1 pound)

6 ounces Canadian bacon, cut into small cubes

1½ teaspoons salt, plus more as needed

½ cup dry white wine

½ cup cooked lupine beans (from a jar is fine)

1 roasted red bell pepper or pimiento from a jar, cut into strips

1 medium tomato, peeled, seeded, and chopped (see box page 47)

1 small onion, chopped

3 large garlic cloves, finely chopped

2 cups medium-grain rice such as Calrose or short-grain rice such as Arborio

Pinch of saffron, crumbled

4 cups chicken broth

½ cup canned black beans, rinsed and drained

1. In a large earthenware casserole (preferably) or a flameproof baking casserole, heat the olive oil over medium heat, then add the quail, sausage, and bacon and cook, turning occasionally, until golden brown, about 35 minutes, adding salt as they cook. (If using earthenware and it is not flameproof, you will need to use a heat diffuser. Earthenware heats up slower but retains its heat longer than other casseroles. When using earthenware, food may cook slower at first and then cook very quickly while retaining its heat.) Add the white wine and scrape the bottom of the casserole with a wooden spoon as you stir. Once the wine has almost evaporated, about 10 minutes, remove the meat with a slotted spoon and reserve.

2. Add the lupine beans, roasted pepper, tomato, onion, and garlic to the casserole and cook, stirring, until the onion is softened, about 15 minutes. Add the rice and stir to coat with the sauce. Add the saffron to the broth, pour in the broth, and 1½ teaspoons of the salt. Bring to a boil, then reduce the heat to medium and cook, uncovered, without stirring, until just a little liquid remains, about 12 minutes. Return the quail, sausage, and bacon to the casserole along with the black beans, pushing them down into the rice.

3. Meanwhile, preheat the oven to 325°F.

4. Place the casserole in the oven and bake, uncovered, until the liquid is absorbed and the rice is almost tender. Remove from the oven, cover loosely with foil, and let sit for 10 minutes before serving.

Rice with Duck and Sausage

I can't think of a more luscious combination than duck and sausage, and baked with rice in a casserole it's a delightful one-pot meal. This preparation was inspired by many similar dishes I encountered when renting an apartment in Barcelona some years ago. Every day, I would shop at the fabulous Boqueria market in Raval or the Santa Caterina market in Sant Pere and bring everything home to my kitchen to cook. Chorizo bilbao is a kind of paprika-spiced Spanish sausage that can be found at www.donajuana.com. It could be replaced with andouille sausage, kielbasa, or hot Italian sausage. The duck can be replaced with turkey or chicken thighs.

1 teaspoon extra-virgin olive oil

4 duck legs and thighs (about 1¾ pounds)

1 teaspoon salt, plus more as needed

2 chorizo bilbao sausages (6 ounces in all), casing removed and
    cut into ½-inch slices (see note above for alternatives)

3 ounces pancetta or Canadian bacon, cut into small cubes

1 green bell pepper, seeded and cut into strips

1 ripe tomato, peeled, seeded, and chopped (see box page 47)

3 large garlic cloves, finely chopped

1 small onion, chopped

One 15-ounce can butter beans (large lima beans), rinsed and drained

1 cup medium-grain rice such as Calrose or short-grain rice such as Arborio

2 teaspoons sweet paprika

2 cups chicken broth

3 tablespoons finely chopped fresh flat-leaf parsley

1. In a large, earthenware casserole (preferably) or any round flameproof baking casserole, preferably with low sides, heat the olive oil over medium heat, then add the duck, season with salt, and cook, turning occasionally, for about 30 minutes. (If using earthenware and it is not flameproof, you will need to use a heat diffuser. Earthenware heats up slower but retains its heat longer than other casseroles. When using earthenware, food may cook slower at first and then cook very quickly while retaining its heat.) Remove the duck and set aside. Pour off all but 1 tablespoon of the duck fat. Add the sausage and pancetta and continue cooking, stirring, until crispy looking, about 4 minutes. Remove the sausage and pancetta and set aside.

2. Preheat the oven to 325°F.

3. Add the bell pepper, tomato, garlic, and onion to the casserole and cook, stirring, until the onion is softened, about 12 minutes. Stir in the butter beans, rice, paprika, and reserved sausage and pancetta and stir until the rice grains are coated with sauce. Pour in the broth and add the 1 teaspoon salt. Place the duck pieces on top and push down a little into the rice. Cook uncovered, never stirring, until just a little liquid remains, about 12 minutes.

4. Transfer the casserole to the oven and bake, uncovered, until the liquid is absorbed and the rice al dente, about 20 minutes. Remove from the oven, sprinkle with the parsley, cover loosely with foil, and let sit for 10 minutes before serving.

Rice with Chicken, Veal, Rabbit, and Pork

This magnificent preparation, called *arroz cordobés* ("Córdoba-style rice") in Spanish, is a rice preparation from the mountainous region around Córdoba that is traditionally made in a large copper kettle called a *peroles*. The variety of meat, shellfish, and spices makes it a very exciting and satisfying dish for a one-pot family meal. If you can't find rabbit, you can replace it with Italian sausage.

1 cup plus 2 tablespoons extra-virgin olive oil

1 large onion, chopped

4 large garlic cloves, chopped

¾ pound boneless veal shoulder, trimmed of fat and cut into small pieces

¾ pound boneless, skinless chicken thighs, cut into small pieces

¾ pound boneless rabbit (preferably) or mild Italian sausage, cut into small pieces

¾ pound boneless pork butt or shoulder, cut into small pieces

2 pounds ripe tomatoes, peeled, seeded, and chopped (see box page 47)

1 large green bell pepper, seeded and chopped

½ pound button (white) mushrooms, quartered

1 cup water

Juice of 1 lemon

Pinch of saffron, crumbled

1 tablespoon hot paprika

2 teaspoons salt

Freshly ground black pepper, to taste

1 cup dry white wine

12 littleneck clams, soaked in cold water with 1 teaspoon of baking soda for 30 minutes, rinsed, and scrubbed well

4 cups medium-grain rice such as Calrose or short-grain rice such as Arborio

10 ounces fresh or frozen peas

1. In a large flameproof baking casserole, heat the 1 cup of olive oil over medium heat, then add the onion and garlic and cook, stirring frequently so the garlic doesn't burn, until golden, about 10 minutes. Add the veal, chicken, rabbit, and pork and cook, tossing or stirring, until golden brown on all sides, about 12 minutes. Remove from the casserole with a slotted spoon and reserve.

2. Add the remaining 2 tablespoons olive oil to the casserole and heat over medium heat, then add the tomatoes and bell pepper and cook, stirring occasionally, until the pepper is limp, about 15 minutes. Add the reserved meat and the mushrooms to the pepper and tomatoes. Pour in the water, increase the heat to high, season with the lemon juice, saffron, paprika, salt, and pepper, and cook, stirring occasionally, for 1 minute. Reduce the heat to medium and cook, stirring occasionally, until the meat is tender, about 45 minutes.

3. Once the meat is cooked and soft, increase the heat to high, add the wine and clams, and cook for 10 minutes. Add the rice, distribute it around the casserole, and cook for 5 minutes. Reduce the heat to low, add the peas, cover, and cook, never stirring, until the water is absorbed and the rice cooked, 45 to 50 minutes. Serve hot.

Rice with Ham, Pork, and Sausage

Traditionally, this rustic dish from Andalusia is cooked in an earthenware casserole called an *olla* or *cazuela* in Spanish. This preparation is pure home cooking and you are unlikely to come across it in a restaurant. The sausage suggestions in the ingredient list are listed in order of ease of finding them in a supermarket, but also look on Internet sites such as www.arnolds-sausage.com.

¼ cup extra-virgin olive oil

½ pound cooked ham, cut into ½-inch cubes

½ pound pork stew meat, cut into ½-inch cubes

½ pound mild Italian sausage, Polish kielbasa, chicken sausage, turkey sausage, Portuguese chouriço sausage, Spanish chorizo sausage, or Spanish *longaniza* sausage

1 small onion, finely chopped

6 large garlic cloves, finely chopped

3 tablespoons finely chopped fresh flat-leaf parsley

1 tablespoon tomato paste

4 cups water

½ teaspoon saffron, crumbled

2 turnips (about ¾ pound), peeled and diced

1 teaspoon sweet paprika or mild Spanish paprika (*pimentón*)

½ teaspoon dried thyme

1 bay leaf

Freshly ground black pepper, to taste

2 cups medium-grain rice such as Calrose or short-grain rice such as Arborio

2 teaspoons salt

6 ounces snow peas

1. Preheat the oven to 425°F.

2. In a large earthenware casserole (preferably) or a flameproof baking casserole, heat the olive oil over medium heat, then add the ham, pork, sausage, onion, garlic, and parsley and cook, stirring, until the onion is softened and the pork turns color, about 8 minutes. (If using earthenware and it is not flameproof, you will need to use a heat diffuser. Earthenware heats up slower but retains its heat longer than other casseroles. When using earthenware, food may cook slower at first and then cook very quickly while retaining its heat.)

3. Meanwhile, dissolve the tomato paste in the water, then add the saffron. Add the tomato paste and water mixture, the turnips, paprika, thyme, bay leaf, and pepper to the casserole and cook until the turnips are al dente, about 12 minutes. Add the rice and salt, pushing the rice down into the liquid. Scatter the snow peas around on top and push them slightly into the liquid.

4. Cover the casserole and place in the oven to bake until the liquid is absorbed, about 20 minutes. Remove from the oven, remove and discard the bay leaf, let rest for 20 minutes, covered, and then serve.

Sea and Mountain Rice Casserole

This stove-top rice casserole with sausage, shrimp, and clams makes for a festive and complete surf and turf dinner favorite for everyone. Ideally, you would want to use a Spanish-style fresh chorizo sausage, but Italian sausage will probably prove easier to find.

⅓ cup extra-virgin olive oil

1 medium onion, finely chopped

8 large garlic cloves, lightly crushed

1 ounce pancetta, chopped

1½ pounds mild Italian sausage, fresh Spanish chorizo, or fresh Polish kielbasa, cut into ½-inch pieces

6 ounces cooked ham, diced

2 large bell peppers (any color), seeded and cut into rings

1 tablespoon hot paprika

1 teaspoon dried thyme

1 bay leaf

¼ cup dry red wine

2½ cups medium-grain rice such as Calrose or short-grain rice such as Arborio

3½ cups water

2 teaspoons salt

1 teaspoon freshly ground black pepper

¼ pound small shrimp, shelled (shells saved for making Quick Seafood Stock, see box page 380, if desired)

12 littleneck clams, soaked in cold water with 1 teaspoon baking soda for 30 minutes, rinsed, and scrubbed well

1. In a large earthenware casserole (preferably) or a large flameproof baking casserole, heat the olive oil over high heat, then add the onion, garlic, and pancetta and cook until sizzling, about 1 minute. (If using earthenware and it is not flameproof, you will need to use a heat diffuser. Earthenware heats up slower but retains its heat longer than other casseroles. When using earthenware, food may cook slower at first and then cook very quickly while retaining its heat.) Add the sausage, ham, and bell peppers and cook, stirring occasionally, for 5 minutes. Add the paprika, thyme, and bay leaf, stir, add the wine, and cook, stirring occasionally, until the sausage turns color and the wine is almost evaporated, about 15 minutes.

2. Add the rice, water, salt, and pepper and bring to a boil over high heat, then reduce the heat to low. Add the shrimp and clams, cover the casserole, and cook, without stirring, until the liquid is absorbed, the clams have opened, and the shrimp is orange-red, about 20 minutes. Turn off the heat, remove and discard the bay leaf, and let rest for 10 minutes before serving.

Rice in the Style of Andalusia

This rice preparation is not only a dish from Andalusia made with small birds, sausage, chicken, ham, and bacon, but it also is, because of those ingredients, a magnificent celebratory meal to share with an appreciative crowd. Ideally, it is cooked in a large earthenware casserole, but an enameled cast-iron casserole will work perfectly in its place. The hardest ingredient to find will be the small birds. The only one I'm familiar with that can be readily found in some specialty markets or online is quail. For others, you'll have to have a hunter in the family.

5 tablespoons extra-virgin olive oil

8 large garlic cloves, crushed

2 Cornish game hens (about 2½ pounds in all), each quartered

6 small birds (about 1¼ pounds in all) such as quail or blackbirds,
 cut in half (turkey thighs on the bone, cut in half, may also be used)

½ pound cooked ham, chopped

6 ounces Canadian bacon, chopped

½ pound fresh Spanish chorizo or hot Italian sausage, chopped

24 to 26 small cipollini onions (about ¾ pound) or pearl onions, peeled

1 bay leaf

1 tablespoon hot Spanish paprika

1 teaspoon salt

Freshly ground white pepper, to taste

5½ cups water

2¾ cups medium-grain rice such as Calrose or short-grain rice such as Arborio

1. In a very large earthenware casserole or flameproof baking casserole (about 14 inches in diameter), heat the olive oil over high heat, then add the garlic and cook until sizzling, about 1 minute. (If using earthenware and it is not flameproof, you will need to use a heat diffuser. Earthenware heats up slower but retains its heat longer than other casseroles. When using earthenware, food may cook slower at first and then cook very quickly while retaining its heat.) Add the game hens, small birds, ham, bacon, and chorizo and cook in the oil, stirring and turning, until golden brown, 15 to 20 minutes. Add the onions and bay leaf and cook until the fowl is tender (the quail leg can almost be pulled off with a good little tug), about 50 minutes, sprinkling on the paprika and seasoning with salt and pepper at some point during the cooking and adding about ½ cup water about every 10 minutes around the perimeter of the pan so it does not dry out, using about 2 cups of water in all.

2. Add the remaining water, rice, and salt, push all the rice under the water, and cook without stirring until the water is absorbed, about 25 minutes. The rice closest to the surface might be al dente at this point, so also taste the rice further down. If it is also al dente, add some boiling water and continue cooking for another 5 minutes, until it is tender. Remove and discard the bay leaf and serve.

Fowl and Game

|||||||||||||||||||||||||||||||||||||||||||||||||||||||||||||||||||||||||||||||||||||||||||||||||||||||||||||||||

Many years ago when my three children were little, we would take them to a local Chinese restaurant that happened to have spectacular Peking duck, and from that time on it became their favorite fowl, much more than chicken. Duck remains our family's favorite fowl, and I offer you two terrific duck recipes in this chapter. That being said, the Chicken Phyllo Pie in a Skillet (page 300) is one of my favorite recipes in this chapter not only because it's delicious but also because it's easy, too, and will give you a great appreciation for your cast-iron skillet. For something a little more extravagant, try the Three Birds Biryani (page 314) or the Chicken Balls in Gravy with Pistachios and Apricots (page 316) for the experience of a royal Moghul dish right in your own home. You can also try a Chinese classic made with chicken, Moo Shu Chicken (page 334), and although you may have ordered it in a restaurant and never thought of making it at home, it's actually quite easy. Too often cooks forget about turkey in months other than November, and that's a shame because it's a versatile bird, often with more flavor than chicken; there's a bunch of great turkey recipes at the end of the chapter, including one that will give you a great idea for the Thanksgiving turkey carcass. One piece of advice I'd like to give about fowl, especially chicken: Buy organic chickens that were fed a natural diet and stay away from industrially produced chicken and you will have a truly fantastic-tasting fowl that tastes like chicken and not some bland, water-injected unidentifiable white meat.

Chicken Ratatouille

This preparation should look familiar to you, as it's nothing but ratatouille made with chicken. The big difference is that the chicken gets cooked first and all the vegetables are cooked together. All it needs is some crusty warm French bread for dipping into the flavorful juices. It seems like the recipe calls for a lot of olive oil, but you serve this dish with a slotted spoon and leave most of the olive oil behind.

1 cup extra-virgin olive oil
2 chicken breast halves with ribs and skin (about 1½ pounds),
   each half cut in two
1 pound onions, coarsely chopped
2 pounds eggplant, peeled and cubed
1½ pounds tomatoes, peeled and cut into large chunks
1½ pounds zucchini, cut in half lengthwise, then sliced in 1-inch chunks
1 large green bell pepper, seeded and cut into thin strips
3 large garlic cloves, crushed
¼ cup loosely packed small fresh basil leaves
2 tablespoons herbes de Provence
8 fresh thyme sprigs
1 tablespoon salt
Freshly ground black pepper, to taste

1. In a large flameproof baking casserole, heat 3 tablespoons of the olive oil over medium heat, then add the chicken, skin side down, and the onions and cook, stirring and turning occasionally, until the chicken is golden brown and the onions are golden brown on the edges, about 15 minutes. Remove the chicken and set aside.

2. Add the remaining oil to the casserole and let it heat over medium heat. Add the eggplant, tomatoes, zucchini, bell pepper, and garlic and shake or stir gently. Add the basil, herbes de Provence, and thyme, season with the salt and pepper, and stir to mix. Partially cover and simmer over medium-low heat, stirring occasionally to prevent sticking, for 30 minutes.

3. Reduce the heat to low, place the chicken pieces on top of the vegetables, and continue cooking, stirring occasionally, until more liquid has evaporated and the vegetables are tender, about 30 minutes more. Serve with a slotted spoon to leave excess oil behind, placing the chicken pieces on top of the vegetables.

Chicken Phyllo Pie in a Skillet

This recipe uses ground chicken, which is easy to find in the supermarket, but I sometimes will take a boneless and skinless chicken breast and thigh meat and pulse it briefly in a food processor, as I like the texture better. The taste will be the same no matter what you do. You can prepare the entire pie and refrigerate it to bake later. It's hard to believe that this is all made in one skillet, but it's a pie with a top crust only.

¼ cup extra-virgin olive oil
1 pound Yukon gold, white, or red potatoes, peeled if large and diced small
1¼ pounds ground chicken
1 pound zucchini, diced small
1 medium onion, chopped
¼ cup finely chopped fresh flat-leaf parsley
2 tablespoons finely chopped fresh mint
1 teaspoon ground cumin
1 teaspoon sweet paprika
1¼ teaspoon salt
1 teaspoon freshly ground black pepper
3 large eggs, beaten
¼ teaspoon ground cinnamon
6 sheets phyllo pastry (about ¼ pound), defrosted and handled
   according to package instructions
4 tablespoons (½ stick) butter, melted

1. Preheat a 12-inch cast-iron skillet over medium-high heat and preheat the oven to 400°F.

2. Add the oil to the skillet and let it heat for a minute or two. Add the potatoes and cook, without stirring in the first 3 minutes, until crispy golden on the bottom. Scrape the potatoes up with a metal spatula, making sure you scrape up the crispy bottoms, turn, and continue cooking, stirring occasionally, for 3 minutes.

3. Add the chicken, zucchini, onion, parsley, mint, cumin, paprika, salt, and pepper and cook, stirring to mix all the ingredients well, until the chicken turns color and the zucchini is softer, 7 to 8 minutes.

4. Remove from the heat, stir in the eggs, and sprinkle with the cinnamon. Lay the sheets of phyllo over the contents of the skillet, brushing each sheet with some of the melted butter and tucking the overlapping edges into the skillet. Bake until the top is golden brown, about 20 minutes. Serve hot.

Picante de Pollo

When I was writing my book *Some Like It Hot*, my editor took a bunch of her authors out for dinner, where I met Maria Baez Kijac, who had just published her wonderful book *The South American Table*. Through Maria I was introduced to a Bolivian specialty called *sajta*, a kind of stew known as hot chicken (*picante de pollo*), and a chile paste called *ají panca en pasta* that I started using like a crazy person because I so loved its taste. You can buy the chile paste at the grocery andf gourmet foods section of www.amazon.com, although I provide a recipe for homemade (page 303). The dish is meant to be spicy-hot, but you can adjust the amount of chile used to your taste.

2 tablespoons extra-virgin olive oil

1 large onion, finely chopped

1 teaspoon salt

½ pound tomato, peeled, seeded, and chopped (see box page 47)

½ green bell pepper, seeded and finely chopped

¼ cup finely chopped fresh flat-leaf parsley

2 scallions, white and light green parts only, finely chopped

2 large garlic cloves, finely chopped

4 dried red chiles, soaked in water for 1 hour, seeded, and puréed in a
    mini food processor or grinder with 1 tablespoon water

¼ cup *ají panca en pasta* (see box page 303)

1 teaspoon dried oregano

1 teaspoon ground cumin

½ teaspoon freshly ground black pepper

One 3-pound chicken, cut into 6 pieces, skin removed

¾ pound Yukon gold potatoes, peeled and diced

1 cup chicken broth

1 cup frozen or fresh peas

1. In a large flameproof baking casserole, heat the oil over medium heat, then add the onion and cook, stirring, until translucent, about 6 minutes. Season with the salt and add the tomato, bell pepper, parsley, scallions, garlic, chile purée, ají panca en pasta, oregano, cumin, and pepper. Cover and cook, stirring occasionally, until thick, about 6 minutes.

2. Add the chicken, potatoes, and chicken broth and bring to a near boil over high heat. Before the broth starts boiling, reduce the heat to low and simmer, partially covered and turning occasionally, until the chicken is tender, 50 to 60 minutes.

3. Add the peas and cook for 5 minutes. Transfer to a serving platter and serve hot.

Ají Panca en Pasta

Ají panca is the name of a particular Peruvian chile that, when it is ripe, is nearly purple in color; at that time it is picked and sun-dried. This chile paste is made by soaking the dried chiles in water and then blending them into a paste. Dried *ají panca* chiles are available by searching the grocery and gourmet foods section of www.amazon.com, although I make some suggestions for substitutes.

10 dried *ají panca* chiles or a combination of 6 dried guajillo chiles and
    8 dried red árbol chiles
2 fresh *ají panca* chiles or fresh red jalapeño chiles
1 tablespoon safflower oil
½ teaspoon freshly ground cumin seeds
½ teaspoon salt

In a bowl, soak the dried chiles in warm water to cover until very soft, 3 to 5 hours. Remove and place in a food processor with the fresh chiles, oil, cumin seeds, and salt. Purée until smooth, about 2 minutes. Transfer to a jar or container and refrigerate until needed.

Makes about 1¼ cups

Chicken with Queso Fundido

This simple dish is made in a 9-inch cast-iron skillet to feed four people, but you can double the recipe and use a 12-inch cast-iron skillet to feed more people should you decide a dinner party is in order. The chicken and chiles are cooked first, and then the cheese is melted and the chicken goes on top. Spoon the dish into warm flour tortillas and roll up for a delicious dinner. An avocado and tomato salad is all you need to accompany it.

2 fresh poblano chiles
1 large fresh jalapeño chile
1 tablespoon vegetable oil
½ small onion, thinly sliced
½ pound boneless, skinless chicken breasts, cut into strips
¼ pound Monterey Jack cheese, cut into ½-inch cubes
¼ pound mild orange cheddar cheese, cut into ½-inch cubes
Flour tortillas, warmed, for serving

1. Preheat the oven to 375°F.

2. Place the poblano and jalapeño chiles on a wire rack set over a burner on high heat and roast, turning occasionally with tongs, until their skins blister black on all sides. Remove the chiles and place in a paper or heavy plastic bag to steam for 20 minutes, which will make peeling them easier. When cool enough to handle, rub off as much blackened peel as you can and remove the seeds by rubbing with a paper towel (to avoid washing away flavorful juices) or by rinsing under running water (to remove more easily). Slice into thin strips and reserve.

3. In a 9-inch cast-iron skillet, heat the vegetable oil over medium heat, then add the onion and cook, stirring occasionally, until translucent, about 2 minutes. Add the chile strips and chicken and cook until the chicken turns color, about 4 minutes. Remove from the skillet and reserve.

4. Scatter the Jack and cheddar cheese cubes on the bottom of the skillet and place in the oven until the cheeses have melted but are not bubbling, about 10 minutes. Sprinkle the chicken and chile mixture on top, return to the oven, and bake until bubbling, about 5 minutes. Serve with warm tortillas.

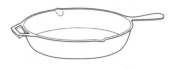

Chicken and Chayote in Roasted Poblano Chile Sauce with Walnuts

Chayote, called *mirliton* in Louisiana and also known as pear squash or christophene, is a mild-tasting kind of soft-fleshed squash that is best handled like zucchini. It's a popular vegetable in Mexico and is readily available in most U.S. markets. In this preparation it's the perfect accompaniment to the equally mild chicken; both are seasoned with slightly piquant poblano chiles. It's all cooked in a large cast-iron skillet and finished under the broiler.

1½ pounds fresh poblano chiles
½ cup walnut halves
4 boneless, skinless chicken breast halves (about 1¼ pounds), each cut in half
Salt, to taste
All-purpose flour, for dredging
1 tablespoon unsalted butter
2 tablespoons vegetable oil
1 medium onion, thinly sliced
1 pound (about 2) chayote, peeled and diced
2 large garlic cloves, finely chopped
1 cup crème fraîche, sour cream, or Mexican crema
¼ pound queso Chihuahua or Monterey Jack cheese, shredded

1. Place the chiles on a wire rack set over a burner on high heat and roast until their skins blister black on all sides, turning occasionally with tongs. Remove the chiles and place in a paper or heavy plastic bag to steam for 20 minutes, which will make peeling them easier. When cool enough to handle, rub off as much blackened peel as you can and remove the seeds by rubbing with a paper towel (to avoid washing away flavorful juices) or by rinsing under running water (to remove more easily). Cut into strips and set aside.

2. Preheat a large cast-iron skillet over medium-high heat, then cook the walnuts in the dry skillet, stirring, for 1 minute. Remove the walnuts and set aside.

3. Season the chicken with salt. Dredge the chicken in flour, patting off any excess flour.

4. Melt the butter with 1 tablespoon of the oil in the skillet and once the butter stops sizzling, add the chicken and cook on both sides, turning once, until light golden brown, about 4 minutes. Remove and set aside. Reduce the heat to medium.

5. After about 2 minutes, add the remaining 1 tablespoon oil to the skillet and let it heat. Add the onion and chayote and cook, stirring, until softened and golden, about 15 minutes. Add the garlic and poblano chile strips, cover, and cook, stirring once, for 2 minutes. Add the crème fraîche, stir well to mix it into the vegetables, and cook for 6 minutes more.

6. Meanwhile, set the oven rack 5 to 6 inches below the heating element and preheat the broiler.

7. Arrange the chicken breasts in the skillet, pushing them down and covering them a little with the poblano chile sauce. Sprinkle with the cheese and the reserved toasted walnuts and place under the broiler just until the cheese is well melted, about 2 minutes.

Chicken and Leek Quesadillas

You'll love the multifunctionality of your cast-iron skillet with this recipe, as it cooks perfectly and can be cleaned easily. You cook everything in it, one after the other, and then serve. The chicken gets cooked first with a golden brown and juicy finish before you cut it up and shred it. Once everything is cooked it's tossed together, stuffed into tortillas, and pan-fried until done. I like to use the mix of cheeses, but you can use one cheese if you like.

2 fresh poblano chiles

3 tablespoons extra-virgin olive oil

1 pound boneless, skinless chicken thighs

Salt and freshly ground black pepper, to taste

2 leeks, white and light green parts only, split lengthwise, washed well, and sliced

⅓ cup chopped fresh cilantro (coriander leaf)

1 teaspoon chili powder

1 teaspoon ground cumin

Eight 12-inch flour tortillas

2½ ounces queso Oaxaca or hard mozzarella cheese, shredded

2½ ounces mild cheddar cheese, shredded

2½ ounces Monterey Jack cheese, shredded

1 lime, quartered

Sour cream, for garnish

1 avocado, cut in half, pitted, flesh scooped out, and sliced

1. Place the chiles on a wire rack set over a burner on high heat and roast until their skins blister black on all sides, turning occasionally with tongs. Remove the chiles and place in a paper or heavy plastic bag to steam for 20 minutes, which will make peeling them easier. When cool enough to handle, rub off as much blackened peel as you can and remove the seeds by rubbing with a paper towel (to avoid washing away flavorful juices) or by rinsing under running water (to remove more easily). Cut into strips and place in a bowl.

2. Grease a large cast-iron skillet with 1 tablespoon of the olive oil and heat over medium-low heat. Season the chicken thighs with salt and pepper, add to the skillet, and cook, turning occasionally, until golden brown, about 20 minutes. Remove the thighs and shred or pull apart with a fork. Place in the bowl with the poblano chiles.

3. Pour 1 tablespoon of the olive oil into the skillet, add the leeks, and cook, stirring, until softened, about 10 minutes. Transfer the leeks to the bowl with the chicken and toss with the cilantro, chili powder, and cumin. Scrape up any bits in the skillet with a metal spatula and give the skillet a wipe with a paper towel. It does not have to be thoroughly clean, just enough to wipe up any bits. Grease the skillet with the remaining tablespoon olive oil and lay a tortilla in the skillet. Top with a quarter of the chicken mixture and a quarter of the shredded cheeses. Place another tortilla on top and cook, turning once with a spatula, until both sides are golden brown and the cheese has melted, about 3 minutes in all. Keep them warm as you cook the remaining tortillas. Serve with lime wedges, sour cream, and avocado.

Pan-Cooked Chicken and Orzo

This Greek-inflected dish is cooked entirely in the pan. You'll first pan-sear the chicken until golden, then remove it and cook the orzo. The key part is making sure the orzo is cooked before you return the seared chicken to the skillet so that the chicken doesn't overcook. I like to serve this with a salad of chopped tomato, green bell peppers, scallions, onion, garlic, olives, feta cheese, and a tiny amount of fresh green chile all dressed with olive oil and lemon juice.

3 tablespoons extra-virgin olive oil
1 pound boneless, skinless chicken breasts, cut into 1-inch pieces
½ cup orzo pasta
½ small onion, finely chopped
1 large garlic clove, finely chopped
2 cups water or chicken broth
1 cup diced carrots
1 cup fresh or frozen peas
1 teaspoon salt
¼ teaspoon ground cinnamon
Freshly ground black pepper, to taste
One 2-ounce piece feta cheese, crumbled into large chunks
2 tablespoons fresh lemon juice
2 tablespoons chopped fresh dill

1. In a large sauté pan, heat 1 tablespoon of the olive oil over high heat, then cook the chicken pieces until golden brown on both sides, about 4 minutes in all. Remove and reserve. Reduce the heat to medium.

2. After 5 minutes, add the remaining 2 tablespoons oil to the pan and add the orzo, onion, and garlic and cook, stirring occasionally, until slightly golden, about 2 minutes. Add the water and scrape the bottom of the pan to lift any food particles while you stir. Add the carrots, peas, salt, cinnamon, and pepper and cook, uncovered, stirring a few times, until the broth is almost absorbed, about 15 minutes. Return the reserved chicken to the pan, pushing it down into the orzo, stir in the feta cheese, lemon juice, and dill, and cook until the cheese is hot and the chicken cooked through, about 3 minutes. Serve hot.

Chicken and Sweet Potato Curry

This chicken curry is a spicy dish, not spicy-hot but rather spicy-spicy from a variety of enticing ingredients. It has a hint of sweetness from the brown sugar, which creates an interesting foil for the spices. Serve the dish very hot (temperature-wise) with some griddled store-bought naan.

2 medium onions, cut into several large pieces

2 large garlic cloves

One 1-inch cube fresh ginger, peeled

3 tablespoons white wine vinegar

2 teaspoons freshly ground cumin seeds

1 teaspoon ground turmeric

1 teaspoon paprika

¼ cup vegetable oil

One 3-pound fryer chicken, cut up into serving pieces

4 whole cloves

One 2-inch cinnamon stick

1½ cups water

2 teaspoons brown sugar

1½ teaspoons salt

3 sweet potatoes (about 2 pounds), peeled and quartered

1. Put the onions, garlic, ginger, vinegar, cumin seeds, turmeric, and paprika in a food processor and blend until a smooth paste.

2. In a large flameproof baking casserole, heat the vegetable oil over medium-high heat, then brown the chicken pieces on all sides, about 6 minutes. Remove from the casserole and set aside.

3. Add the onion paste to the casserole and cook, stirring, for 1 to 2 minutes. Add the cloves and cinnamon stick and cook for another minute.

4. Return the chicken to the casserole along with the water, brown sugar, and salt. Cover, reduce the heat to low, and simmer for 30 minutes.

5. Add the sweet potatoes and continue to simmer over low heat, covered, until the sweet potatoes are tender and the chicken falls off the bone with a little tug from a fork, about 1 hour. If there is a lot of liquid left in the casserole, remove the chicken and sweet potatoes and reduce over high heat for a few minutes. Remove and discard the cinnamon stick. Return the chicken and sweet potatoes and heat for a minute or two before serving.

Three Birds Biryani

In Indian cooking, *biryanis* are grand and festive rice dishes cooked in layers in a casserole and highly seasoned with spices, especially saffron. Biryani is a beautiful yellow color when done and a meal in itself. There are several steps, some waiting time, and a long list of ingredients, but don't let any of that deter you. It's not that hard to make, and the result is spectacular and will please everyone. You can also use one of the fowl called for in the recipe if you like rather than all three.

1½ cups whole-milk plain yogurt

3 tablespoons fresh lime juice (from 1 or 2 limes)

4 large garlic cloves, crushed

2 teaspoons very finely chopped peeled fresh ginger

1 tablespoon ground coriander

1 teaspoon ground cumin

¼ teaspoon cayenne pepper

¼ teaspoon freshly ground black pepper

¼ teaspoon ground cloves

¼ teaspoon ground cinnamon

¼ teaspoon ground cardamom

10 ounces boneless, skinless turkey breast, cut into 1½-inch pieces

10 ounces boneless, skinless chicken breasts, cut into 1½-inch pieces

10 ounces boneless duck breasts (skin removed if desired), cut into 1½-inch pieces

5 tablespoons clarified butter (preferably) or unsalted butter, melted

1¼ cups long-grain rice such as basmati, soaked in water for 30 minutes, then rinsed and drained

1 cup water

1 teaspoon salt, plus more as needed

3 large onions, sliced

¼ teaspoon ground saffron, dissolved in 3 tablespoons milk

¼ cup cashews

2 large hard-boiled eggs, shelled and quartered

1. In a bowl, combine the yogurt with the lime juice, garlic, ginger, coriander, cumin, cayenne, black pepper, ground cloves, cinnamon, and cardamom and mix well. Toss this mixture with the turkey, chicken, and duck and set aside in the refrigerator to marinate for 2 to 4 hours.

2. In a large flameproof baking casserole, melt 1 tablespoon of the butter over medium-high heat, then add the rice and cook, stirring, until it begins to stick, about 1 minute. Add the water and salt, reduce the heat to low, cover, and cook until half-cooked, 4 to 5 minutes. If there is any liquid left, drain the rice. Transfer from the casserole to a bowl with a rubber spatula and set the rice aside.

3. Scrape any remaining rice from the casserole if necessary. Add the remaining 4 tablespoons butter to the casserole and melt over medium heat. Add the onions and cook, stirring frequently, until golden, 30 to 35 minutes. Add the birds and their marinade, season lightly with salt, reduce the heat to very low, cover, and cook, stirring occasionally, until the birds are tender, making sure the liquid never boils, about 50 minutes.

4. Meanwhile, preheat the oven to 300°F.

5. Remove half the birds and onions and spread what remains over the bottom of the casserole. Spoon half the rice over the remaining birds in the casserole. Add the other half of the birds (that you removed) and layer the remaining rice over them. Sprinkle with the saffron dissolved in the milk. Cover tightly and bake until fully cooked, about 35 minutes. Serve topped with the cashews and eggs.

Chicken Balls in Gravy with Pistachios and Apricots

This rich Moghul dish from northern India is extravagant in flavor, which the term *Moghul* has come to mean in culinary circles. The Moghuls, whose ancestors were Tartars from Persia, founded an empire in northern India and dominated in the sixteenth and seventeenth centuries. Moghul influence can be seen in the architecture as well as the food of India. Moghul cooking is synonymous with a rich, lavish, princely style of cookery. Delightfully, this dish can be prepared up to a day ahead and is, in fact, even tastier that way. Serve with skillet-warmed naan or pita bread and a green salad.

2½ cups chopped onions

2 large garlic cloves, 1 chopped, 1 mashed in a mortar with a pestle

One 1-inch piece fresh ginger, peeled, half of it chopped, half of it mashed with a mortar and pestle

¼ cup fresh cilantro (coriander leaf)

10 whole blanched almonds, ground in a spice mill

1 large egg

2 thick slices French or Italian bread (about 2½ ounces), crust removed, broken up

2 teaspoons salt

½ teaspoon freshly ground black pepper

1 pound ground chicken

¼ cup vegetable oil

½ teaspoon cumin seeds

1 cup chopped fresh or canned tomatoes

2 tablespoons sour cream or whole-milk plain yogurt

1 teaspoon ground coriander

1 teaspoon garam masala

1 teaspoon ground fenugreek (optional)

½ teaspoon ground turmeric

½ teaspoon ground cumin

¼ teaspoon cayenne pepper
1½ cups water
10 dried apricots, finely chopped
1 tablespoon pistachios
1 cup fresh or frozen peas

1. Place 1¼ cups of the onion, the chopped garlic clove, and the chopped ginger in a food processor and pulse until very fine. Add the cilantro, almonds, egg, bread, 1 teaspoon of the salt, and ¼ teaspoon of black pepper and process again until very fine. Add the chicken and process until everything is well blended. Make 25 chicken balls about the size of a small lime, using wet hands so the mixture does not stick.

2. In a large nonstick pan, heat 2 tablespoons of the oil over medium heat, then cook the chicken balls in one layer, shaking the pan and turning occasionally, until they turn color on all sides, 4 to 5 minutes. Remove and reserve.

3. Add the remaining 2 tablespoons oil to the pan and heat over medium-high heat. Add the cumin seeds and shake the pan, then add the mashed garlic and grated ginger and cook for about 15 seconds. Add the remaining 1¼ cups onion and cook, stirring, until softened, about 4 minutes. Reduce the heat to medium, stir in the tomatoes, and cook, stirring, for 5 minutes. Stir in the sour cream and cook, stirring, for 3 minutes. Season with the remaining 1 teaspoon salt, the remaining ¼ teaspoon pepper, the coriander, garam masala, fenugreek, turmeric, ground cumin, and cayenne. Add the water, apricots, and pistachios and bring to a boil over high heat. Add the chicken balls, reduce the heat to low, and cook until the chicken balls are firm and cooked through, about 15 minutes. Add the peas and cook, stirring carefully, for 10 minutes. Serve hot.

Chicken and Rice in Lemon Zest Yogurt

The key to this dish is stabilizing the yogurt so it can be used to braise the chicken and cook the rice and not otherwise curdle and separate. There's nothing hard about that when you follow the directions, which will result in a warm and comforting meal for a cold night. Make sure you use chicken thighs and not chicken breasts in this dish, as the longish cooking time would otherwise overcook the breast. Also, don't use more turmeric than is called for. Serve with a simple salad.

2 tablespoons extra-virgin olive oil

1 medium onion, thinly sliced

1 large garlic clove, finely chopped

1 pound boneless, skinless chicken thighs, cut into smaller portions

¼ cup slivered almonds

¼ teaspoon ground turmeric

½ cup water

⅓ cup medium-grain rice such as Calrose or long-grain rice such as basmati

3 cups whole-milk plain yogurt

1 egg white, beaten

2 teaspoons cornstarch

¾ teaspoon salt

1 cup fresh or frozen peas

2 tablespoons grated lemon zest

1. In a flameproof baking casserole, heat the olive oil over medium-high heat, then add the onion and garlic and cook, stirring frequently so the garlic doesn't burn, until translucent, about 5 minutes. Add the chicken thighs, almonds, and turmeric and cook until the chicken thighs turn color, about 12 minutes. Remove the chicken from the casserole and reserve.

2. Add the water and rice to the casserole and bring to a boil, stirring, then cook until the water evaporates. Add the yogurt to the casserole and stir in until smooth. Beat in the egg white, cornstarch, and salt. Stir in one direction over high heat until it starts to bubble, about 3 minutes. Return the chicken to the casserole, reduce the heat to medium, and cook, stirring, until it is thick, about 5 minutes. Add the peas and lemon zest and cook until tender, about 10 minutes. Taste and correct the seasoning, and serve in a bowl.

Steamed Moroccan Chicken

This Moroccan style of cooking chicken is usually done in a *couscousière*, but a colander or steamer basket set on top of large pot will work just as well, as long as the seal is tight and even. *Dajaj mu-fawwar* (steamed chicken) is a typical family-style meal and although delicious, it is nothing fancy. This method of one-pot cooking chicken through steaming is very simple, and there will be a lot of unexpected flavor that belies the simple method. There is no turning, no stirring, and, please, no looking: Try not to lift the lid for at least 1 hour. The chicken will become silky and its texture very delicate. It's done when a skewer stuck into the thigh portion of the chicken runs with clear juice and when the vegetables are very tender. This could take from 1½ to 2¼ hours, so check as needed after the 1-hour mark. Remember to start the preparation early enough because you will want the chicken to marinate. At the end of cooking there is some work involved, of dividing the chicken, spooning the vegetables into soup bowls, and mixing the stuffing with some of the steaming broth, so factor that time in, too, when serving. In Morocco, this dish might be known by its French name, *poulet à la vapeur*, steamed chicken.

4 tablespoons (½ stick) unsalted butter, at room temperature

Juice and zest from 2 lemons

2 teaspoons salt

1 teaspoon ground ginger

¼ teaspoon powdered saffron

One 4-pound chicken

½ cup finely chopped fresh cilantro (coriander leaf), stems reserved

½ cup finely chopped fresh flat-leaf parsley, stems reserved

½ cup finely chopped fresh mint, stems reserved

1 large fresh jalapeño chile, finely chopped

5 large garlic cloves, finely chopped

1 tablespoon coriander seeds

1 tablespoon sweet paprika

½ teaspoon ground cumin, plus more for garnish

½ teaspoon freshly ground black pepper

1 medium onion, studded with 4 cloves

2 bay leaves

1 pound small Yukon gold potatoes, peeled

1 pound carrots, scraped and cut into 2½-inch lengths

1 pound green beans, trimmed and cut into 2½-inch lengths

1 red bell pepper, seeded and coarsely chopped

1. In a bowl, mix together the butter, lemon juice, 1 teaspoon of the salt, the ginger, and saffron. Rub this mixture over the chicken, including inside the body cavity. Refrigerate for at least 2 hours and preferably 4 hours.

2. In a bowl, stir together the lemon zest, cilantro, parsley, mint, jalapeño chile, garlic, coriander seeds, 2 teaspoons of the paprika, the cumin, the remaining 1 teaspoon salt, and the pepper. Stuff this mixture into the cavity and rub the remaining 1 teaspoon paprika over the outside of the bird.

3. Fill the bottom portion of a couscousière with water, making sure the top of the water does not touch the perforated bottom of the top part when it is put on. Alternatively, fill a large pot that can snugly fit your colander, strainer, or steamer basket on top. Add the onion with cloves, bay leaves, and the reserved herb stems to the pot and bring to a boil over high heat.

4. Place some of the potatoes, carrots, green beans, and bell pepper on the bottom of the top part of the couscousière, in a colander, or a steamer basket. Set the chicken on top of the vegetables, surrounding the chicken with excess vegetables, pushing them down into the spaces available. Place the colander, steamer basket, or top part of the couscousière on top of the larger pot. If the edge where the pot and colander join has a space for steam to escape, wrap a wet kitchen towel around to seal them. Cover the colander or steamer with a lid. Reduce the heat to medium or medium-low.

(continued)

5. Steam until the chicken is tender and the juices run clear, about 2 hours, but check after 1½ hours; the steaming could take as long as 2¼ hours depending on your pot and heat. Transfer the chicken to a platter and the vegetables to a bowl, and strain the broth. Season the broth with salt and pepper. Remove the stuffing from the chicken with a spoon and mix it with 4 cups of the broth in a big bowl. Carve the chicken into 6 equal portions.

6. Spoon the steamed vegetables into 6 soup bowls and add a portion of chicken to each. Spoon the reserved stuffing-broth mixture over the chicken and vegetables and serve. Remaining broth can be frozen for soup.

Braised Chicken, Leeks, and Yogurt

This dish gives a wonderfully mild taste that is improved with the addition of a little lemon juice at the end. Serve with some sliced tomatoes dressed with olive oil, parsley, and salt and some heated flatbread.

5 tablespoons extra-virgin olive oil

1 pound boneless, skin-on chicken breasts, cut into 1-inch cubes

Salt and freshly ground black pepper, to taste

1¾ pounds leeks, white and light green parts only, split lengthwise, washed well, and sliced

¾ pound turnips, peeled and diced

2 large garlic cloves, finely chopped

1 teaspoon ground coriander

½ teaspoon ground sumac (optional)

½ teaspoon hot or sweet paprika

¼ teaspoon ground allspice

½ cup whole-milk plain yogurt

Juice from ½ lemon

1. In a flameproof baking casserole, heat 2 tablespoons of the olive oil over high heat, then sear the chicken, skin side down, until golden, about 3 minutes. Season with salt and pepper, turn, cook on the other side for 2 minutes, and then remove the chicken and reserve.

2. Add the remaining 3 tablespoons olive oil to the casserole, reduce the heat to low, add the leeks, turnips, and garlic, and cook, stirring, until caramelized and tender, about 40 minutes; keep the casserole covered for the first 20 minutes and uncovered for the next 20 minutes. Stir in the coriander, sumac (if using), paprika, allspice, and salt to taste. Cook, stirring, for 5 minutes. Return the chicken to the casserole along with the yogurt and cook until saucy and hot, about 5 minutes. Add the lemon juice, stir, and serve.

Chicken Hunter's Style

This is a variation of the Italian-American chicken cacciatore, made here with a varied set of ingredients including more vegetables. Peperoncini chiles are sometimes called Italian frying peppers; they are long yellowish green chiles with almost no heat.

2 tablespoons extra-virgin olive oil
1½ pounds chicken thighs
1 medium onion, cut in half and then sliced
2 large garlic cloves, finely chopped
½ cup dry white wine
1 pound Yukon gold potatoes, peeled and cubed
½ pound small brown mushrooms
One 14-ounce can chopped tomatoes
1 small green bell pepper, seeded and cut into strips
1 small red bell pepper, seeded and cut into strips
4 peperoncini chiles (Italian frying peppers), seeded and cut into strips
1 fresh rosemary sprig
Salt and freshly ground black pepper, to taste

1. In a flameproof baking casserole, heat the olive oil over medium heat, then cook the chicken thighs, skin side down, until golden brown, about 8 minutes. Turn the chicken thighs, add the onion and garlic, and cook, stirring, until softened, about 4 minutes. Pour in the white wine and cook until it has nearly all evaporated, about 8 minutes.

2. Add the potatoes, mushrooms, tomatoes, green and red bell peppers, chiles, and rosemary sprig. Place the chicken thighs on top of the vegetables. Season with salt and pepper, cover, and cook until bubbling, about 30 minutes. Uncover and continue cooking until the potatoes are tender, about 1 hour. Taste and correct the seasoning and then serve.

Chicken and Pepper Stew

Countless Italian-American families will talk about their nonna's *spezzatino* made with beef, pork, lamb, or chicken. It's usually an all-in-one meal, a *piatto unico* as they say in Italian, and only needs some warm crusty bread and perhaps a salad on the side. In this stew, it's really about a colorful variety of mild and slightly hot peppers and chiles.

½ cup extra-virgin olive oil
5 green bell peppers, seeded and sliced
1 red bell pepper, seeded and sliced
1 small onion, sliced or chopped
5 peperoncini chiles (Italian frying peppers) or fresh New Mexico/Anaheim chiles, seeded and sliced
2 garlic cloves, chopped
3 tablespoons chopped fresh flat-leaf parsley
3 teaspoons chopped fresh rosemary
Salt and freshly ground black pepper, to taste
1½ pounds boneless, skinless chicken breasts, cut into 1-inch pieces
½ cup dry white wine

1. In a large flameproof baking casserole, heat the olive oil over high heat, then add the bell peppers, onion, chiles, garlic, parsley, rosemary, salt, and pepper and cook, stirring frequently, until softer, 6 to 7 minutes.

2. Add the chicken and cook, stirring, for 3 to 4 minutes. Pour in the white wine and cook until it evaporates, about 10 minutes. If there is still a good amount of liquid left in the casserole, you can either remove the chicken and peppers with a slotted spoon, reduce the chicken and wine broth for 5 minutes over high heat, then return the chicken and peppers for 1 minute to reheat (for a richer taste); or simply remove and serve the chicken and peppers with a slotted spoon.

Chicken and Spinach

When my children were little they ate everything and were never finicky eaters; in fact, there was a "you snooze, you lose" principle at work with most food. However, they had two approaches to the food sitting before them: gobble or pick. This one-pot meal I used to serve them got gobbled. It's also easy on the cook, tastes great, and is quick to prepare. You can use prepackaged shredded carrots and spinach leaves to make it even easier.

3 tablespoons extra-virgin olive oil
2 garlic cloves, finely chopped
1 cup shredded carrots (from a bag)
2 red bell peppers, seeded and chopped
1½ pounds boneless, skinless chicken breasts, fat removed, cubed
¼ teaspoon ground cinnamon
Salt and freshly ground black pepper, to taste
10 ounces baby spinach leaves (from a bag), cut into thin strips if desired
¼ cup dry white wine

1. In a large flameproof baking casserole, heat the olive oil over medium-high heat, then add the garlic and cook, stirring, for less than 1 minute. Add the carrots and bell peppers and cook, stirring, for 2 to 3 minutes.

2. Add the chicken, cinnamon, salt, and pepper and cook for 1 minute, then add the spinach and wine. Cook until the wine has evaporated and the spinach wilted, 5 to 6 minutes, continuing to fold the spinach into the casserole as it wilts. Serve immediately.

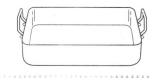

Roast Chicken Stuffed with Spinach with Roast Potatoes

In this preparation you will be using only a roasting pan, so keep in mind that your potatoes will be as important as the chicken when you're cooking. I like to use a young chicken weighing 2¾ to 3 pounds, which is enough to feed four people. I tested this recipe once using a unique-looking potato cultivar sold at my farmers' market here in southern California called Lakers Bakers, a two-tone potato that had a lot of flavor, but you can use any baking potato.

½ pound baby spinach leaves
1 small garlic clove, finely chopped
¼ pound fresh ricotta cheese
1 large egg
Salt and freshly ground black pepper, as needed
1 young chicken (about 3 pounds)
3 russet baking potatoes (1 pound), cut into eighths
3 tablespoons extra-virgin olive oil

1. Preheat the oven to 375°F.

2. Place the spinach, by handfuls or batches, along with the garlic in a food processor and process until a very fine paste (or chop with a knife). Transfer to a bowl and stir in the ricotta, egg, salt, and pepper with a fork until blended. Season the inside of the chicken with salt and pepper and stuff with the spinach mixture.

3. Truss the chicken and place in a roasting pan. Surround with the potatoes, drizzle the olive oil over both, and bake until the potatoes are tender and the chicken is golden brown and the juices run clear when skewered in the thigh, about 1¾ hours. Remove from the oven, let rest for 10 minutes, then carve and serve.

Summer Vegetables with Cornish Game Hens

In this slow-cooked Turkish stew the vegetables slowly release their flavors, creating a highly tasty dish. The freshest vegetables are what you want to use here for the best result. The only liquid is the liquid they give up as they cook. As you will see, the stars here are the vegetables more than the chicken, and that's why I list them first in the title.

8 tablespoons (1 stick) unsalted butter

¾ pound green beans, trimmed and cut into 2-inch lengths

2 medium zucchini, peeled lengthwise in zebra stripes, then cut into 1-inch-thick pieces

4 green bell peppers, seeded and quartered

2 small long eggplants, peeled lengthwise in zebra stripes, then cut into 1-inch-thick pieces

2 small onions, quartered

¼ pound small okra, trimmed

2 Cornish game hens (about 3 pounds), each cut into 4 pieces

Salt and freshly ground black pepper, to taste

2 large ripe tomatoes, halved, seeds squeezed out, and grated against the largest holes of a grater

1. In an earthenware casserole (preferably) or flameproof baking casserole, melt the butter over medium-high heat, and once it stops bubbling add the green beans, zucchini, bell peppers, eggplants, onions, and okra and stir to mix well. Lay the game hen pieces on top, season with salt and pepper, pour the tomatoes on top, reduce the heat to low, cover, and simmer until the game hen is tender, about 2 hours. (If using earthenware and it is not flameproof, you will need to use a heat diffuser. Earthenware heats up slower but retains its heat longer than other casseroles. When using earthenware, food may cook slower at first and then cook very quickly while retaining its heat.)

2. Uncover and cook for another 30 minutes. Serve immediately with a slotted spoon.

Stir-Fried Chile Chicken with Eggplant

Some years ago I had a wonderful chicken and eggplant stir-fry in a restaurant in San Francisco's Chinatown. Although it was a ridiculously piquant dish, we couldn't stop eating it, and I have often thought how one could re-create it, as I was unsuccessful in getting the recipe from the restaurant. The original dish was covered with about a hundred, dried red 1-inch-long chiles and it was quite intimidating, beautiful to behold, and ultimately delicious.

¾ pound boneless, skinless chicken thighs, shredded or cut into 1-inch pieces
½ pound green beans, chopped into ½-inch pieces
2 tablespoons rice wine (mirin) or vermouth
4 teaspoons soy sauce
6 tablespoons peanut oil
2 large garlic cloves, thinly sliced
One ½-inch cube fresh ginger, peeled and thinly sliced
25 fresh Thai chiles, halved lengthwise
1 tablespoon Sichuan peppercorns (optional)
1½ pounds eggplant, peeled and diced
3 scallions, cut into thirds
1 teaspoon salt
½ teaspoon sugar
¼ cup water
2 teaspoons sesame oil

1. Toss the chicken and green beans in a large glass or ceramic bowl with the rice wine and soy sauce and marinate for 30 minutes.

2. In a large wok, heat 2 tablespoons of the peanut oil over high heat. Add the chicken and green beans and cook, stir-frying, until golden brown, about 5 minutes. Remove with a skimmer and set aside.

3. Add 1 tablespoon of the peanut oil to the wok, add the garlic and ginger, and cook, stirring, until they start to turn color, about 20 seconds. Add the chiles and Sichuan peppercorns (if using), and cook, stirring, for another 20 seconds; remove the wok from the heat if the chiles look like they are turning black.

4. Add the remaining 3 tablespoons peanut oil, let it heat for a minute, then add the eggplant and cook, stir-frying, to coat the eggplant and make it a bit softer, about 2 minutes. Return the chicken to the wok, add the scallions, and stir. Season with the salt, add the sugar, and stir. Add the water and toss until the chicken is well coated, about 4 minutes. Remove from the heat and stir in the sesame oil. Serve immediately.

Diced Chicken with Peppers and Cashews

This is a quite simple preparation that is enhanced by the delicious and piquant taste of shishito chiles, also called padrón chiles, which are cooked whole. They're not always easily found, so you have three alternatives: a very hot dish with serrano chiles; a milder one with slivers of New Mexico/Anaheim chiles; and a sweet one with green bell peppers.

1 pound boneless, skinless chicken breasts, cut into ½-inch dice

5 teaspoons soy sauce

2½ teaspoons cornstarch

2 tablespoons water

3 tablespoons vegetable oil

½ pound fresh shishito/padrón chiles (preferably; kept whole) or

    2 fresh New Mexico/Anaheim chiles, seeded and slivered, or

    2 green bell peppers, seeded and cut into squares

2 red bell peppers, seeded and diced

¾ pound onion, diced (2 cups)

5 scallions, trimmed and cut into 1½-inch lengths

¼ pound diced eggplant (1 cup)

Six ⅛-inch-wide slices peeled fresh ginger

1½ teaspoons rice wine (mirin)

1 teaspoon sesame oil

Freshly ground black pepper, to taste

1 cup unsalted cashews

1. Marinate the chicken pieces in a glass or ceramic bowl with 2 teaspoons of the soy sauce, 1 teaspoon of the cornstarch, and 1 tablespoon of the water for 30 minutes.

2. In a wok, heat 1½ tablespoons of the oil over high heat, add the chicken pieces, and cook, stir-frying, until golden, about 2 minutes. Remove and reserve. Add the chiles and cook, tossing constantly, until crinkly-skinned and slightly blackened, about 4 minutes. Remove and reserve with the chicken.

3. Add the remaining 1½ tablespoons oil to the wok and let it heat. Add the bell peppers, onion, scallions, eggplant, and ginger and cook, tossing, until glistening and softened, about 4 minutes. Return the chicken and chiles to the wok with the remaining 3 teaspoons soy sauce, the remaining 1½ teaspoons cornstarch, the remaining 1 tablespoon water, the rice wine, sesame oil, and pepper and cook, tossing, until well mixed, about 2 minutes. Add the cashews, toss, and serve.

Moo Shu Chicken

This is a much-simplified and very easy take on the Chinese dish moo shu pork. Here you can use a bag of supermarket-bought coleslaw mix instead of shredded Chinese vegetables. It makes the most sense to use flour tortillas to make this preparation, but spring roll wrappers are quite nice and can be eaten after a short soak without cooking.

For the marinade
2 tablespoons soy sauce
2 tablespoons water
1 tablespoon sesame oil
3 garlic cloves, crushed
2 teaspoons peeled and grated fresh ginger
2 teaspoons sugar

For the chicken
1 pound boneless, skinless chicken breasts, cut into ¼-inch-thick strips
1 tablespoon peanut oil
One 1-pound package coleslaw mix
⅔ cup chopped scallions
2 teaspoons peeled and grated or finely chopped fresh ginger
1 tablespoon cornstarch, dissolved in ¼ cup water
20 rice spring roll wrappers, soaked in tepid water for 10 minutes, or
    eight 12-inch flour tortillas,
    warmed in the oven
⅓ cup hoisin sauce

1. In a bowl, combine the marinade ingredients. Toss with the chicken with the marinade. Cover and let rest in the refrigerator until needed.

2. In a wok, heat the peanut oil over high heat. Add the chicken and cook, stir-frying, until it turns white, 2 to 3 minutes. Add the coleslaw, scallions, ginger, and cornstarch mixture and cook, stirring and tossing, until the coleslaw is softened, about 4 minutes.

3. If using rice spring roll wrappers, pat them dry with paper towels first. Spread one side of a spring roll wrapper with 2 teaspoons hoisin sauce, then spoon ½ cup of the chicken mixture into the center. Fold the bottom edge over the filling, then fold the right and left sides inward and continue to roll up. Set aside as you make the remaining wrappers. Serve immediately.

Chinese Boiled Chicken Dinner

In China, this dish would be made with a freshly killed chicken and it would be boiled quickly in a short time, then left to cool and eaten cold as an appetizer. I've changed the idea only slightly, as our processed chickens require a slightly different method of cooking, taking a bit longer; plus I serve the boiled dinner hot. The results are delicious and truly a "chicken-in-a-pot" dish. If you decide to use English pea pods remember to pull off their "string" when trimming them so that when they are cooked the pods will pop open to reveal their peas. The chile-garlic sauce is sold in jars in supermarkets along with other products in the Asian food aisle.

> 4 thick slices peeled fresh ginger
> 5 dried red chiles
> One 4-pound chicken
> 6 turnips (1½ pounds), peeled and quartered
> 1½ pounds English pea pods or snow peas

> **For dip #1**
> 1 tablespoon peeled and very finely chopped fresh ginger
> 1 tablespoon very finely chopped fresh scallions
> 1 tablespoon peanut oil
> ½ teaspoon sesame oil
> Salt, to taste

> **For dip # 2**
> 2 tablespoons soy sauce
> 1 tablespoon chile-garlic sauce (from a jar)

> **For dip #3**
> 2 tablespoons coarse sea salt
> 1 tablespoon coarsely crushed fresh black pepper

1. In a pot large enough to hold the chicken and vegetables snugly, bring about 6 cups of water to a boil over high heat with the ginger and chiles. Add the chicken and turnips, cover, and boil for 10 minutes over high heat. Reduce the heat to very low, add the pea pods, cover, and simmer for 20 minutes. Turn off the heat and let the chicken cool in the pot, covered, for 30 minutes.

2. Meanwhile, make the dipping sauces. In one bowl, mix together the ginger, scallion, oils, and salt. In a second bowl, combine the soy sauce and chile-garlic sauce. In a third bowl, combine the salt and pepper.

3. Remove the chicken from the broth and split in half lengthwise. Cut into smaller pieces through the skin and bone with a cleaver or large, heavy chef's knife. Arrange on a platter and surround with the quartered turnips and the pea pods. Serve with the dips.

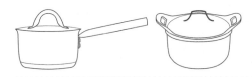

Curried Chicken Noodles

This Thai-inspired dish will be all the easier when you set up all your preparations beforehand, keeping everything covered with plastic wrap and then cooking the dish in only 15 to 20 minutes. Many of the more exotic-sounding ingredients are often found in the international aisle of your supermarket, excepting perhaps the Thai shrimp paste, the yellow bean sauce, and the black Chinese vinegar, all of which you may need to order online from sites such as www.templeofthai.com or by searching at the grocery and gourmet foods section of www.amazon.com.

For the chile paste

8 dried red chiles

2 tablespoons chopped shallots

1 tablespoon finely chopped garlic

1 teaspoon peeled and chopped fresh ginger or fresh galangal

1 tablespoon chopped fresh cilantro (coriander leaf) root or stem

1 tablespoon ground turmeric

1 teaspoon Thai shrimp paste

For the noodles

1 cup sliced napa cabbage

½ cup black Chinese vinegar or rice vinegar

¼ cup vegetable oil

2 tablespoons sliced garlic

1 pound ground chicken

½ pound cherry tomatoes

1½ cups water

1 pound bean sprouts

2 tablespoons Thai or Vietnamese fish sauce

1 tablespoon Thai yellow bean sauce or fermented black bean sauce

½ pound thin bean thread noodles

¼ cup chopped fresh cilantro (coriander leaf)

2 scallions, trimmed and sliced diagonally into 1-inch pieces

2 limes, cut into wedges, for serving

2 tablespoons red chile flakes

1. Place the chile paste ingredients in a mini food processor, or use a mortar and pestle, and blend until a paste forms.

2. Place the napa cabbage in a bowl, cover with the vinegar, and let stand for 2 hours. Drain.

3. In a saucepan or flameproof baking casserole, heat the oil over medium heat, then add the garlic and cook, stirring, until light golden, about 1 minute. Remove the garlic with a slotted spoon and set aside.

4. Add the chile paste mixture to the oil and cook, stirring, until you can smell it, about 30 seconds. Add the chicken and cook, stirring and breaking it up with a wooden spoon. Add the tomatoes, water, bean sprouts, drained napa cabbage, fish sauce, and bean sauce. Stir, reduce the heat to low, and simmer until cooked through and soft, about 15 minutes.

5. While the chicken cooks, soak the noodles in hot water for 15 minutes. Remove, drain well, and divide the noodles equally among 4 bowls. Spoon the curry over the noodles. Garnish the tops with the fried garlic, cilantro, and scallions. Serve with the lime wedges and chile flakes.

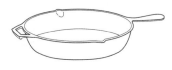

Chicken Banh Mi Sandwiches

In southern California, the banh mi sandwich was introduced by Vietnamese immigrants. Originally invented in French Indochina, the sandwich combined elements from both French and Vietnamese cuisines. The French part is seen in the baguette, mayonnaise, and pâté, and the Vietnamese contribution is found in the fish sauce, pickled vegetables, chiles, and cilantro. The most popular versions besides chicken are those made with pork belly, crushed pork meatballs, grilled pork, or scrambled egg. The banh mi's popularity is traveling quickly across America, where it is now known as a Vietnamese po'boy in New Orleans, a Vietnamese sub in New York, and a Vietnamese hoagie in Philadelphia.

For the chicken marinade

2 tablespoons Thai or Vietnamese fish sauce

2 tablespoons fresh lime juice

1 tablespoon sugar

1 fresh red Thai chile, thinly sliced

1 garlic clove, finely chopped

2 boneless, skinless chicken breast halves (1 pound)

For the pickled vegetables

½ pound daikon, peeled and grated

1 large carrot, scraped and grated

½ cup rice vinegar

1 tablespoon sugar

Salt, to taste

For the sandwich

2 tablespoons vegetable oil

1 tablespoon Thai or Vietnamese fish sauce

½ teaspoon soy sauce

One 24-inch-long soft-crust baguette, split lengthwise

¼ pound truffle-flavored duck or pork pâté, thinly sliced

½ medium red onion, cut in half, then cut into ¼-inch slices

2 fresh jalapeño chiles, thinly sliced
¾ cup packed fresh cilantro (coriander leaf) sprigs
2 tablespoons mayonnaise
Lettuce leaves

1. For the marinade, in a bowl, stir together the fish sauce, lime juice, sugar, chile, and garlic. Toss the chicken with the marinade and marinate in the refrigerator for 1 hour.

2. Meanwhile, toss the daikon and carrot with the rice vinegar, sugar, and salt and let rest until needed. Drain before using.

3. Preheat a cast-iron skillet over high heat for 10 minutes. Wipe the chicken pieces dry with paper towels. Place in the skillet and sear, turning once, until golden brown on both sides, about 4 minutes in all. Remove from the skillet, let rest for 5 minutes, then cut into 1-inch-long thin slices.

4. For the sandwich, in a small bowl, mix together the oil, fish sauce, and soy sauce and brush the bottom half of the baguette with the sauce. Layer the bottom with the pâté slices and arrange the onion, jalapeños, and cilantro on top. Spread mayonnaise on the other half of the bread. Layer the sliced chicken, lettuce, and drained daikon and carrot slaw on top, close the sandwich, and cut into quarters. Serve.

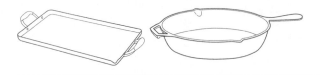

Griddled Chicken and Tzatziki Wraps

Tzatziki is the famous Greek yogurt and garlic sauce that goes with so many foods from gyros to kebabs. For this wrap, you'll marinate the chicken first, which you can do overnight or during the day, and then everything is assembled.

For the chicken marinade
- 1 small onion, thinly sliced
- 2 large garlic cloves, finely chopped
- 2 tablespoons extra-virgin olive oil
- 1 tablespoon fresh lemon juice
- 1 bay leaf, finely crumbled
- ¼ teaspoon sweet paprika
- ¾ pound boneless, skinless chicken breasts, cut in half horizontally into 2 thinner pieces
- Salt and freshly ground black pepper, to taste

For the tzatziki sauce
- 2 large garlic cloves
- ½ teaspoon salt
- 1 cup whole-milk plain yogurt
- 1 teaspoon dried mint
- 1 teaspoon fresh lemon juice

For the wrap
- 2 teaspoons extra-virgin olive oil
- 1 medium zucchini, peeled and thinly sliced lengthwise
- 1 medium onion, thinly sliced
- 2 sheets lavash bread or sandwich wraps (½ pound)
- 2 ounces mixed baby greens (from a bag)
- 2 ripe tomatoes (about ¼ pound), sliced

1. For the marinade, in a ceramic or glass bowl or casserole, mix together the onion, garlic, olive oil, lemon juice, bay leaf, and paprika. Toss the chicken with the marinade and marinate in the refrigerator for 4 to 6 hours. Remove the chicken, pat dry with paper towels, and season with salt and pepper. Discard the marinade.

2. Meanwhile, make the tzatziki sauce. Using a mortar and pestle, pound the garlic with the salt until mushy. Whisk into the yogurt along with the mint and lemon juice and set aside in the refrigerator until needed.

3. Preheat a cast-iron griddle or skillet over high heat. Add 1 teaspoon of the oil to the skillet, add the zucchini slices, and cook, turning once, until golden brown, 3 to 4 minutes. Remove and set aside. Add the remaining 1 teaspoon oil to the skillet, add the onion, and cook, stirring, until beginning to get soft, 2 to 3 minutes. Remove and set aside.

4. Add the chicken to the pan and cook until golden brown and crispy on both sides, about 6 minutes. Remove and let rest on a cutting board for a couple of minutes, then slice thinly or chop.

5. Meanwhile, arrange 1 sheet of lavash bread on the work surface in front of you with a short side toward you. Spread half the greens on the lower portion, then half the onion, half the tomato, half the zucchini, and half the chicken. Drizzle or spoon the yogurt sauce on top and roll up tightly. Set aside as you continue with the remaining sandwich. Cut each wrap into quarters on the diagonal and serve.

Satay Chicken Wraps

For the best wrap, you'll want to marinate the chicken in the marinade suggested below and you'll also want to make your own peanut butter from fresh peanuts in your food processor or buy freshly made peanut butter in supermarkets that offer a grinder. You could dispense with both marinade and fresh peanut butter, but then you'll just have an unremarkable chicken sandwich with peanut butter and not a magnificent satay chicken wrap. The "sweet chili sauce" called for in the ingredient list is usually found in the international aisle of your supermarket along with other Asian food products.

For the marinade

3 tablespoons brown sugar

2 tablespoons soy sauce

2 tablespoons Thai or Vietnamese fish sauce

1 lemongrass stalk, inedible outer portions removed, inner portion
　finely chopped

1 shallot, thinly sliced

3 large garlic cloves, chopped

1 small fresh red jalapeño chile, sliced, or ¼ teaspoon cayenne pepper

One 1-inch square piece fresh ginger, peeled and thinly sliced

2 teaspoons finely chopped fresh turmeric or ¼ teaspoon ground turmeric

1 tablespoon ground coriander

1 teaspoon ground cumin

For the chicken

1½ pounds boneless, skinless chicken breasts

1 tablespoon vegetable oil

For the sauce and garnishes

  1 cup smooth fresh peanut butter

  ½ cup sweet chili sauce

  1 tablespoon soy sauce

  Eight 12-inch flour tortillas

  1 fresh red jalapeño chile, seeded or not, cut into thin strips

  ½ head iceberg lettuce, shredded

  1 medium onion, thinly sliced

  2 carrots, scraped and shredded

1. In a ceramic or glass bowl, mix together the marinade ingredients. Toss the chicken breasts with the marinade and marinate in the refrigerator for 6 to 12 hours. Remove the chicken and discard the marinade.

2. In a large cast-iron skillet, heat the vegetable oil over medium heat, then cook the chicken, turning once, until golden and crispy on both sides, 7 to 8 minutes. Remove, let rest on a cutting board for a few minutes, then thinly slice.

3. For the sauce, in a bowl, stir together the peanut butter, sweet chili sauce, and soy sauce. Lay a tortilla in front of you and spread some of the peanut butter mixture on the lower portion. Top with some of the jalapeño, chicken, lettuce, onion, and carrots. Tightly roll up the tortilla and continue with the others. Cut each roll-up in half diagonally, arrange on a platter, and serve.

Hoisin Duck Wraps

This delicious sandwich wrap is thought to have been invented in Great Britain, perhaps around Brighton, where a duck wrap is also a vulgar expression denoting a particular sex act. There's nothing vulgar here; rather it's pure ecstasy when you sink your teeth into this perfect and intriguing blend of duck, hoisin, and watercress. This all-in-one sandwich means you don't really need to accompany it with anything, although serving it with some dips might be nice, such as soy sauce or prepared mustard or store-bought duck sauce, or all three.

1½ pounds boneless duck breasts
Eight 12-inch flour tortillas
¾ cup hoisin sauce, plus more as needed
2 large cucumbers, peeled, split lengthwise, seeded, and cut into bâtons
14 scallions, chopped
1 to 2 bunches watercress, chopped

1. Preheat a large cast-iron skillet over medium heat. Add the duck breasts, skin side down, and cook, turning once, until golden brown and crispy on both sides, 8 to 10 minutes. Cover the skillet if it is splattering too much. Remove and let rest for 5 minutes. Thinly slice the duck breasts.

2. Lay a tortilla in front of you on a work surface. Spread 1 to 2 tablespoons of hoisin sauce over the tortilla. Arrange some of the cucumber, scallions, and watercress over the bottom portion of the tortilla. Arrange a portion of the duck on top and tightly roll up the tortilla. Set aside while you roll the others. Cut each in half diagonally and arrange on a platter for serving. Any remaining vegetables can be used to garnish the platter.

Ragoût of Duck and Okra

This Tunisian ragoût is made with the piquant spices loved by Tunisians, including paprika and chile. Ideally, the okra used should be small fresh ones kept whole. Typically, this tagine is served with couscous, but here, following the one-pot concept, I suggest warm Arabic bread to accompany the ragoût. Ask the butcher to cut up the duck for you if it's not sold frozen, or even if it is.

¼ cup extra-virgin olive oil
One 4½-pound duck, cut up into 10 pieces
1 large onion, finely chopped
5 large garlic cloves, finely chopped
1 tablespoon tomato paste, dissolved in 1 tablespoon water
1 teaspoon freshly ground caraway seeds
1 teaspoon freshly ground coriander seeds
1 teaspoon hot paprika
1 teaspoon harīsa (see box page 140), plus more for garnish
1 teaspoon salt
1 teaspoon freshly ground black pepper
½ teaspoon cayenne pepper (optional)
1 cup water
1 pound okra, trimmed
Flatbread, for serving

1. In a tagine or large flameproof baking casserole, heat the oil over medium heat, then add the duck along with the onion, garlic, dissolved tomato paste, caraway, coriander, paprika, harīsa, salt, black pepper, and cayenne, if using, and cook, turning frequently, until lightly browned, about 10 minutes. Add the water and bring to a boil. Immediately reduce the heat to low, cover, and simmer until the duck is tender, about 1 hour.

2. Remove the duck with a slotted spoon and place in a deep serving platter, keeping it warm. Increase the heat to high, add the okra, cover, and reduce the sauce until it is thick and the okra is cooked, about 15 minutes, adding a little water if the liquid evaporates too quickly. Pour the okra and sauce over the duck and serve with flatbread and harīsa on the side.

Stir-Fried Duck with Green Pepper

The success of this preparation lies in you being able to cut up a duck. If the legs and thighs are sold separately, then buy four of them, otherwise cut up the whole duck into 6 pieces and remove the meat from the legs, thighs, and one breast with a paring and boning knife. Save the remaining breast, wings, and carcass for another purpose. Alternatively, you can use boneless turkey thighs, although the taste will be different, of course. If using duck, you can place the bones in a saucepan, cover with 2 cups water, and simmer for an hour to create a light duck stock that you could use in place of the chicken broth called for, but that does mean using two pots instead of one. You will also want to use the very thin bean thread noodles that can sit in very hot water to become soft and not the kind you boil. The sweetened red bean sauce and the black bean paste might be available in the international foods aisle of better supermarkets, or you could order them online at www.koamart.com.

2 tablespoons rice wine (mirin)

1 tablespoon black bean paste, mixed with ⅛ teaspoon cayenne pepper

2 teaspoons sweetened red bean sauce

2 teaspoons soy sauce

1 teaspoon finely chopped garlic

2 tablespoons vegetable or peanut oil

1¼ pounds boneless duck thigh and leg, cut into 1-inch pieces

One 2 × 1-inch piece fresh ginger, peeled and sliced

4 fresh red Thai chiles, seeded and cut into thin shreds

4 green bell peppers, seeded and cut into 1-inch pieces

1 cup chicken or duck broth

6 ounces thin bean thread noodles, soaked in very hot water for 5 minutes, then drained well

6 scallions, trimmed and cut into 1-inch pieces

1 tablespoon chile oil

1 teaspoon sesame oil

1 teaspoon sugar

1 cup unsalted cashews

1. In a small bowl, stir together the rice wine, black bean paste, sweetened red bean sauce, soy sauce, and garlic.

2. In a wok, heat the oil over high heat. Add the duck and cook, stir-frying, until it turns golden brown, 6 to 7 minutes. Remove with a slotted spoon and reserve. Discard all but 3 tablespoons of the remaining fat.

3. Add the ginger and Thai chile shreds and cook, tossing, for 10 seconds. Add the reserved duck, bell peppers, and seasoning mix from step 1 and stir. Add the chicken broth, reduce the heat to medium, and simmer for 5 minutes. Increase the heat to high and add the bean thread noodles, scallions, chile oil, sesame oil, and sugar. Cook, stir-frying, until very well mixed, about 3 minutes. Add the cashews, toss gently, then serve.

Turkey Jambalaya

Jambalaya is a rice dish famous in the Creole cooking of Louisiana, a kind of Louisiana version of the Spanish paella. Besides the rice, jambalaya usually contains ham, chicken, sausage, shrimp, and oysters seasoned with herbs. Apparently this word *jambalaya* comes from an old Provençal word *jambalaia*, which referred to a dish made of chicken and rice. But the famous Provençal poet, Nobel Prize winner, and gastronome Frédéric Mistral (1830–1914) claimed that the original jambalaya was an Arab dish. In this recipe, turkey is used in place of chicken and the spicing and finish veer away from the Louisiana version.

2 tablespoons rendered duck fat, chicken fat, bacon fat, or canola oil
1 ounce salt pork, chopped
3 tablespoons all-purpose flour
1 red bell pepper, seeded and finely chopped
1 green bell pepper, seeded and finely chopped
1 small onion, finely chopped
1 celery stalk, finely chopped
1 teaspoon garlic powder
½ teaspoon dried oregano
½ teaspoon dried thyme
½ teaspoon ground cumin
½ teaspoon cayenne pepper
¼ teaspoon fennel seeds
1 teaspoon freshly ground black pepper
Salt, to taste
1 bay leaf
1 cup white wine
3 cups chicken broth
½ cup medium-grain rice such as Calrose or short-grain rice such as Arborio
1 pound boneless turkey breast, diced

1. In a large flameproof baking casserole, melt or heat your fat of choice over high heat with the salt pork until the salt pork is crispy, about 5 minutes.

2. Add the flour to form a roux and cook, stirring constantly, until caramel colored, about 3 minutes. Add the bell peppers, onion, and celery to the casserole and cook, stirring, for 5 minutes. Add the garlic powder, oregano, thyme, cumin, cayenne, fennel seeds, black pepper, salt, and bay leaf, stir, and cook for 1 minute. Add the wine and cook for 1 minute more. Add the broth, bring to a boil, add the rice, reduce the heat to low, and then add the turkey and cook until the turkey is firm and cooked through and the rice is tender, about another 20 minutes. Remove and discard the bay leaf. Serve hot.

Turkey Vindaloo

This spicy-hot dish from Goa on India's west coast is typical fare in most Indian restaurants. In this recipe it's made with turkey rather than chicken and is served with warmed naan or other flatbread.

1 tablespoon ground coriander
1 teaspoon ground turmeric
1 teaspoon ground cumin
½ teaspoon ground cloves
3 fresh green chiles
One 1-inch piece ginger, peeled
4 large garlic cloves
½ cup white wine vinegar
3 tablespoons vegetable oil
2 large onions, cut in half, then thinly sliced
3 pounds turkey parts such as thigh, breast, wings, cut up into
    smaller serving pieces
3 Yukon gold, white, or red potatoes (1¼ pounds), peeled and cut into
    ¾-inch cubes
1½ cups water
1 cinnamon stick
2 teaspoons salt
1 cup fresh or frozen peas

1. In a small bowl, mix the coriander, turmeric, cumin, and cloves together. In a blender, blend together the spice mixture, chiles, ginger, garlic, and vinegar until smooth.

2. In a large sauté pan, heat the oil over medium heat, then add the onions and cook, stirring, until golden, about 20 minutes. Add the turkey, potatoes, water, cinnamon stick, salt, and the vinegar mixture from the blender, cover, reduce the heat to low, and simmer, stirring occasionally, until the turkey and potatoes are tender, about 1 hour. Add the peas 5 minutes before the turkey is done. Remove and discard the cinnamon stick. Serve hot.

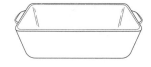

Makes 2 servings

Southwest Turkey Bake

This is just a very quick way to assemble a meal for two people with leftover Thanksgiving turkey.

1 teaspoon extra-virgin olive oil
½ pound cooked turkey breast, cut into bite-size pieces
1 ripe tomato, chopped
3 tablespoons chopped onion
3 tablespoons chopped green bell pepper
⅛ teaspoon ground cumin
⅛ teaspoon cayenne pepper
Salt and freshly ground black pepper, to taste
4 slices Colby or Monterey Jack cheese
¼ cup dry red wine

1. Preheat the oven to 425°F.

2. Grease a small baking casserole with the olive oil. In a bowl, toss the turkey, tomato, onion, bell pepper, cumin, cayenne, salt, and black pepper together. Transfer to the casserole, cover with the cheese, sprinkle with the wine, and bake until bubbling, about 20 minutes. Serve hot.

Post-Thanksgiving Turkey Risotto

Although you can make this risotto throughout the year, it's perfect as a weekend-after-Thanksgiving one-pot dinner when you're tired and just want something delicious using leftover turkey. Remove the meat from your roast turkey and place the carcass in a large pot with cut-up onion, carrot, and celery, bring to a boil, then reduce the heat to low and simmer for 4 hours. Strain, and you have your turkey broth for the risotto. (You don't have to do this, but if it's the weekend, why not, and it'll be better.) If you want to make this at any other time of the year and you don't have turkey broth, use chicken broth.

2 tablespoons extra-virgin olive oil (if using raw turkey)

1¼ pounds boneless, skinless turkey breast, cooked or not (diced if cooked)

2 teaspoons salt, plus more as needed

Freshly ground black pepper, to taste

½ small onion, finely chopped

½ carrot, finely chopped

1 ounce pancetta, chopped

1 large garlic clove, finely chopped

2 cups short-grain rice such as Arborio

¾ pound winter squash flesh, diced

½ cup dry white wine

8 cups turkey or chicken broth

1 cup frozen peas

1 cup freshly grated Parmesan cheese (3 ounces)

2 tablespoons finely chopped fresh flat-leaf parsley

2 tablespoons chopped fresh chives

1. If using raw turkey, heat the olive oil in a medium flameproof baking casserole over high heat, then add the turkey breast and cook, turning once, until golden on all sides, about 4 minutes in all. Season with a little salt and pepper, remove, and dice the turkey breast.

2. Add the onion, carrot, pancetta, and garlic to the casserole over medium heat and cook, stirring, until softened, about 4 minutes. Add the rice, squash, and the 2 teaspoons salt and cook, stirring, for 1 minute. Stir in the wine and cook until it is mostly evaporated. Reduce the heat to low, add 1 cup of broth, and cook, stirring frequently, until the liquid is absorbed. Add another cup of broth and continue adding smaller and smaller amounts of broth, cooking and stirring and letting it absorb, until the rice and squash are almost tender, about 45 minutes.

3. Stir in the reserved turkey you just cooked or the leftover cooked turkey along with the peas, cheese, parsley, and chives and cook until the cheese melts and the turkey is heated through, about 10 minutes. Serve immediately.

Seared Turkey Breast with Squash and Cabbage

Some years ago I began to notice that supermarkets sold turkey breast halves for a very good price. I began to buy these half breasts, cut the meat off the bone, divide it into serving portions, freeze them, and save the carcass for stock. Occasionally, I'd find a smaller half breast, and thus this recipe came to be. Here's a great one-pot meal for turkey lovers.

One 2-pound bone-in turkey breast
2 tablespoons extra-virgin olive oil
One 1¼-pound butternut or acorn squash, peeled, seeded, and cut
   into ½-inch-thick pieces
2 fresh jalapeño chiles, sliced (optional)
1¼ pounds green cabbage, cut in half, cored, and thinly sliced
Salt and freshly ground black pepper, to taste

1. Preheat a cast-iron skillet over medium-high heat for 10 minutes.

2. Cook the turkey breast, skin side down, until golden brown and crispy, about 8 minutes. Turn the turkey, reduce the heat to low, and cook until golden and firm, about 40 minutes. Remove the turkey and keep warm.

3. Add the olive oil to the skillet and let it heat. Add the squash and chiles (if using) and cook, stirring occasionally, until softened, about 15 minutes. Add the cabbage and cook, stirring, until wilted, about 10 minutes. Season with salt and pepper.

4. Transfer the vegetables to a serving platter. Cut the turkey breast into 4 equal pieces with a cleaver or large heavy chef's knife. Place the turkey pieces on top of the vegetables and serve.

Makes 6 servings

Braised Rabbit and Mushrooms

Most rabbits sold today are frozen, but even so a braised rabbit with mushrooms is some fine eating. The rabbit cooks long and slow, and it needs only a salad and some crusty French baguette to accompany it. I call for cipollini onions; these small, flat onions look like they've been squashed a bit, but you can use yellow onions in their place. Demi-glace is another name for a flavored broth that has been boiled down to a syrupy state. It is sold in the frozen foods sections of better supermarkets and also in vacuum-sealed foil packets. In its place you may use 1 teaspoon of beef base paste.

One 2¾-pound rabbit, cut into 6 pieces
All-purpose flour, for dredging
Salt and freshly ground black pepper, to taste
3 tablespoons unsalted butter
3 slices bacon or pancetta, chopped
1 medium onion, finely chopped
2 large garlic cloves, finely chopped
1 pound cipollini onions (about ¾ pound)
1 pound brown mushrooms
1½ cups dry red wine
¼ cup demi-glace or 1 teaspoon beef base paste
Bouquet garni, tied in cheesecloth, consisting of 5 fresh flat-leaf parsley sprigs,
    5 fresh tarragon sprigs, 5 large leaves fresh sorrel (optional), 5 fresh thyme sprigs,
    and 1 bay leaf

1. Dredge the rabbit in flour, season with salt and pepper, and tap off any excess flour. In an earthenware casserole (preferably) or a flameproof baking casserole, melt the butter with the bacon over high heat, then add the rabbit and brown on one side, about 5 minutes. Add the chopped onion and garlic and cook, mixing well and turning the rabbit, for 1 minute. (If using earthenware and it is not flameproof, you will need to use a heat diffuser. Earthenware heats up slower but
(continued)

retains its heat longer than other casseroles. When using earthenware, food may cook slower at first and then cook very quickly while retaining its heat.)

2. Add the cipollini onions and whole mushrooms and cook for 10 minutes. Pour in the wine and demi-glace and add the bouquet garni. Bring to a boil, then reduce the heat to low and cook until the rabbit is tender and the sauce syrupy, 2¼ to 2½ hours. Taste and correct the seasoning. Discard the bouquet garni and serve immediately.

Fish

||||||||||||||||||||||||||||||||||||||||||||||||||||||||||||||||||||||||||||||||||||||||||||||||||||||||||||||||||||||||||||||||||

Fish and shellfish are ideal in one-pot cookery because they're generally delicate and cook quicker than beef or pork. You'll find yourself using a stewpot often, especially if you decide to make the surprisingly delicious Baja Seafood Stew (page 370), from a place we don't usually associate with our favorite dishes. Simple all-in-one fish dishes are very appealing because of their short cooking times and straightforward preparation, such as the Finnish-inspired Salmon and Potato Stew (page 374), which is flavored with fresh dill. Once again the Chinese come through for us with excellent one-pot cookery, in a wok of course, in dishes like the Stir-Fried Shrimp with Snow Peas and Black Bean Sauce (page 408), which is difficult to stop eating. Sometimes it's nice to go over the top, and the Seafood Phyllo Pie (page 416) with its shrimp, mussels, oysters, mushrooms, and cream is certainly that. It's hard to believe you make it all in one pot, since it seems so complex at first glance.

Moqueca

This traditional Brazilian fish stew is found on the coast of northern Brazil and typically uses red palm oil, called dende oil in Brazil, as a flavoring agent. One can sometimes find it in Whole Foods markets, but in any case I call for it optionally and usually buy it from the grocery and gourmet foods section of www.amazon.com. The key to the preparation is very fresh fish. The stew is filling and luscious; serve crusty bread to soak up the sauce.

2 pounds firm-fleshed white fish fillets or steaks such as halibut,
    shark, onagi, or swordfish, cut into large portions

6 large garlic cloves, finely chopped

½ cup fresh lime juice

2 teaspoons salt

2 teaspoons freshly ground black pepper

3 tablespoons extra-virgin olive oil

1 medium onion, chopped

1 yellow bell pepper, seeded and chopped

1 red bell pepper, seeded and chopped

1 tablespoon sweet paprika

¼ teaspoon red chile flakes

2 cups chopped tomatoes

¼ cup chopped scallions, green part only

1 large bunch fresh cilantro (coriander leaf), chopped,
    with some set aside for garnish

One 14-ounce can unsweetened coconut milk

1 tablespoon red palm oil (optional)

Crusty French or Italian bread, for serving

1. Put the fish in a ceramic or glass bowl and toss with the garlic, lime juice, ½ teaspoon of the salt, and ½ teaspoon of the black pepper. Cover with plastic wrap and refrigerate until needed, but at least 2 hours.

2. In a large flameproof baking casserole, heat the oil over medium heat, then add the onion and cook, stirring, until softened, about 5 minutes. Add the bell peppers, paprika, and red chile flakes and cook, stirring occasionally, until the bell peppers soften, 5 minutes. Add the tomatoes and scallions, season with ½ teaspoon salt and ½ teaspoon black pepper, and cook, stirring occasionally, for 5 minutes. Stir in the chopped cilantro.

3. Remove half of the vegetables from the casserole and reserve. Shake the casserole to spread out the remaining vegetables to form a bed for the fish and arrange the fish and its marinade on top of the vegetables. Season with salt and pepper. Return the vegetables you removed to the casserole and cover the fish with them. Pour the coconut milk and red palm oil, if using, over the fish and vegetables. Season with the remaining salt and pepper.

4. Increase the heat to medium-high and once the liquid starts to bubble on the edges, reduce the heat to medium-low, cover, and simmer until the fish is cooked through, 12 minutes. Taste and correct the seasoning, if necessary, and serve garnished with the reserved cilantro and with crusty bread on the side.

Baked Cod with Carrots and Cream Sauce

This recipe is inspired by the cooking of Provence, where cooks enjoy using a variety of fresh and dried herbs in fish dishes. A fish similar to cod, hake, is also a favorite fish from Spain to Provence, although it needs to be cooked carefully since it is fragile and flakes easily. Serve with warm crusty bread or a salad.

2 tablespoons unsalted butter
4 cod steaks (about 1¼ pounds), about ¾ inch thick at the center
10 thin carrots (about ½ inch diameter, measured in the middle), trimmed, scraped, and cut lengthwise into very thin sticks
½ cup finely chopped onions
2 small garlic cloves, finely chopped
1 tablespoon finely chopped fresh summer savory leaves or ½ teaspoon dried savory
2 teaspoons finely chopped fresh basil leaves
Salt and freshly ground white pepper, to taste
1 cup heavy cream

1. Preheat the oven to 400°F.

2. Grease a rectangular or oval baking casserole that can accommodate the fish and carrots in one layer along with 1 tablespoon of the butter. Lay the fish in the middle and surround with the carrots. Mix the onions, garlic, savory, and basil together and then spoon over the fish. Season with salt and pepper and pour the cream over the fish. Very thinly slice the remaining butter and dot the top with it. Bake until the fish begins to flake, 20 to 25 minutes. Serve hot.

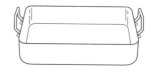

Baked Whole Fish with Potatoes

The only difficulty in preparing this delicious—and easy—dish is in finding the whole fish, which seems so hard these days. You'll need a pretty big fish, about 3 pounds, to make this recipe called *orata alla pugliese*, a popular preparation in the region of southern Italy called Apulia. It's made in its homeland with a kind of sea bream, called *orata* in Italian and *daurade* in French. Serve with a tomato and olive salad.

½ cup finely chopped fresh flat-leaf parsley
3 large garlic cloves, finely chopped
½ cup extra-virgin olive oil
4 russet baking potatoes (about 2 pounds), peeled and sliced ¼ inch thick
Salt, to taste
2 ounces pecorino cheese, freshly grated
One 3-pound striped bass, rock cod, black cod, or red snapper, scaled,
    gutted, lateral fins snipped off, head and tail left on, washed well

1. Preheat the oven to 350°F.

2. In a bowl, toss the parsley and garlic together. In a large roasting pan, spread half of the oil over the bottom, then sprinkle half of the garlic and parsley on the bottom. Lay half of the potatoes in the roasting pan, season with salt, and sprinkle half the cheese on top. Lay the fish on top of the potatoes, season with salt, and cover with the remaining garlic and parsley, potatoes, and cheese, in that order, layering the potato slices so they resemble fish scales. Season the top with salt. Drizzle the remaining ¼ cup olive oil over the fish. Bake until the dorsal fin can be pulled off with a tug, or 10 minutes per inch of fish measured at the thickest part of the fish, about 40 minutes for a 3-pound fish.

3. Serve hot from the roasting pan: Make an incision along the spine. Push or cut the meat and potatoes off the top side of the fish, separate the spine from the head, and lift it out in one piece; discard the spine. Serve the remaining portions of fish, using a spatula.

Griddled Stuffed Sea Bass

This recipe is very simple to prepare and cook, and fun, too, as you eat communally using pieces of warm flatbread to pick off the meat of the fish along with its aromatic stuffing. You can use any fish that weighs 1 to 1¼ pounds. Ask the fishmonger, if you want to save some time, to scale and gut the fish, but leave the head and tail on. Some fish stores will get fancy on you and label this fish *branzino*, but that's only Italian for "sea bass."

Two 1- to 1¼-pound sea bass, scaled, gutted, dorsal and lateral fins
    removed, head and tail left on, washed well
Sea salt, to taste
2 bunches fresh flat-leaf parsley, 8 sprigs left whole, the remaining
    leaves finely chopped
10 fresh mixed green and red chiles, sliced and seeded
20 cherry tomatoes, cut in half
¼ cup extra-virgin olive oil
1 lemon, thinly sliced
4 large loaves whole wheat flatbread, warmed

1. Place a cast-iron griddle over 1 or 2 burners depending on the shape and size of your griddle, turn the heat to low, and let it heat up while you prepare the fish. Alternatively, prepare a hot charcoal fire and let it die down significantly or preheat a gas grill on low and lay your cast-iron griddle on the grilling grate.

2. Season the fish with salt inside and out. Stuff the cavity with 4 sprigs of the parsley in each fish, three-quarters of the chiles, and three-quarters of the tomatoes. Use 4 toothpicks to skewer the belly cavity closed. Cover the fish with the olive oil and roll the fish in some of the chopped parsley. Place on the griddle and cook, without turning or moving, until the bottom is nearly black and crispy, about 20 minutes. Turn and cook the other side for 20 minutes.

3. Cover a large platter from which you can eat communally with the remaining chopped parsley, remaining tomatoes, remaining chiles, and the lemon slices. Transfer the fish to the platter and set on top of the vegetables. Serve with whole wheat flatbread, taking a small piece of bread and using it to pull off some meat and the various garnishes. When you have eaten all the meat above the spine, carefully remove the spine and its bones and discard and continue eating the bottom portion.

Swordfish, Soft-Shell Clams, and Fennel

This is a dish that will be easier to prepare in New England, where soft-shell clams (sometimes labeled as "steamer clams") are more common than elsewhere. About once a year, though, here on the West Coast we get soft-shell clams and I serve this beautiful dish to both family and guests, as it can all be prepared in advance and then cooked at the last minute. Soft-shell clams are not always available, so you may use littleneck clams in their place. I sometimes add a second fish to the pot to create more flavor. I particularly like halibut cheeks, but they're hard to find, so any flaky white-fleshed fish is okay. If swordfish is not available or prohibitively expensive, you can replace it with shark, mahimahi, or yellowtail.

¼ cup extra-virgin olive oil

1¼ pounds swordfish, cut into 4 pieces

1 fennel bulb, bulb sliced and cut in half, leaves and stalks chopped

¾ pound tomatoes

12 green olives, pitted and halved

2 large garlic cloves, finely chopped

2 salted anchovy fillets, rinsed

3 tablespoons capers

2 tablespoons chopped fresh oregano

Salt and freshly ground black pepper, to taste

1 pound soft-shell clams or 2 pounds littleneck clams, soaked in cold water to cover for 30 minutes

6 ounces halibut cheeks or red snapper fillet (optional)

Juice from ½ lemon

1. In a flameproof baking casserole, heat a film of olive oil over high heat until smoking, add the swordfish pieces, and cook, turning only once, until golden brown on both sides, about 3 minutes in all. Remove and reserve.

2. Add the remaining olive oil, then add the slices of fennel bulb and cook, stirring, until they develop crispy brown edges, about 4 minutes. Add the fennel leaves and stalks, tomatoes, olives, garlic, anchovy fillets, capers, oregano, salt, and pepper, reduce the heat to medium-low, and cook, stirring occasionally, until softer, about 6 minutes. Add the clams and stir. Lay the flaky fish, if using, and partially cooked swordfish on top of the clams. Cover and cook until the clams open, about 8 minutes. Discard any clams that have not opened. Pour the lemon juice over the fish and serve.

Albacore Tuna with Baby Carrots, Fresh Peas, and Dill

This springtime recipe can be made with albacore tuna or opah, a firm-fleshed fish popular in Iceland, where they call it *guðlax* (pronounced GUTH-lax). It can be found in both Atlantic and Pacific fish stores. Both fish have pink flesh that makes for a very attractive presentation when cooked with the colorful vegetables.

2 tablespoons unsalted butter
¾ pound fresh albacore tuna or opah
½ pound fresh peas
6 ounces young carrots
Water
Salt and freshly ground black pepper, as needed
1 tablespoon chopped fresh dill

In a sauté pan, melt the butter over medium heat, then sear the fish on both sides until it turns color. Remove from the pan and reserve, keeping the fish warm. Add the peas, carrots, water, salt, and pepper and cook until half cooked, about 6 minutes. Return the fish to the pan along with the dill and cook for 3 to 4 minutes per side. Season with more salt and pepper and serve.

Tuna and Shrimp with Bell Peppers

This colorful dish is an appetizing summer recipe in which the natural sweetness of bell peppers flavors the seafood. You could serve this on top of linguine, but I prefer the one-pot concept of just topping some chewy toasted bread with the mixture. You could use scallops in place of the shrimp and swordfish in place of the tuna.

¼ cup extra-virgin olive oil
1 medium onion, thinly sliced
1 yellow bell pepper, seeded and thinly sliced
1 red bell pepper, seeded and thinly sliced
1 fresh green chile, seeded and chopped
4 large garlic cloves, finely chopped
1½ pounds large shrimp, shelled (shells saved for making
    Quick Seafood Stock, see box page 380, if desired)
1 pound tuna steak, cut into 1-inch strips
Salt, to taste
6 tablespoons dry white wine
4 slices round French or Italian country bread (about ¼ pound), toasted

1. In a large sauté pan, heat 3 tablespoons of the olive oil over medium heat, then add the onion, bell peppers, chile, and garlic and cook, stirring occasionally, until softened, about 25 minutes. Remove with a slotted spoon and reserve.

2. Increase the heat to medium-high, pour in the remaining 1 tablespoon olive oil, and let it heat for a minute or two. Add the shrimp, tuna, and salt. Cook, tossing, for 1 minute. Pour in the wine and cook until the liquid is reduced by three-quarters, about 5 minutes. Return the vegetables to the pan and cook until they are heated. Place the toasted bread on a serving platter or individual plates and top with the seafood and vegetables. Serve immediately.

Baja Seafood Stew

Baja California is that Mexican peninsula that resembles a tail swinging south of California. The cooking of the region is hot and spicy, and a favorite fish is mahimahi. This seafood stew is excellent; the shrimp, clams, crab, and fish are given an intriguing twist from the palpable taste of fresh orange juice and hot chiles. Serve with corn tortillas.

¼ cup extra-virgin olive oil
1 small onion, finely chopped
2 fresh green jalapeño chiles, seeded and finely chopped
2 large garlic cloves, finely chopped
2 pounds ripe tomatoes, peeled, seeded, and chopped (see box page 47)
1½ cups fresh orange juice
2 cups dry white wine
1 tablespoon finely chopped fresh basil leaves
1 tablespoon finely chopped fresh cilantro (coriander leaf)
1 tablespoon orange zest
1 tablespoon sugar
1 teaspoon salt
½ teaspoon dried oregano
½ teaspoon freshly ground black pepper
24 littleneck clams, washed well and soaked in cold water to cover with
    1 tablespoon baking soda for 1 hour, then drained
6 ounces crabmeat, picked over for shell pieces
1½ pounds large shrimp, shelled (shells saved for making
    Quick Seafood Stock, see box page 380, if desired)
1 pound mahimahi, yellowtail, cod, or sea bass fillets, cut into 1-inch pieces
Corn tortillas, for serving

1. In a large flameproof baking casserole, heat the olive oil over medium-high heat, then add the onion, chiles, and garlic and cook, stirring, until translucent, 3 to 5 minutes. Add the tomatoes, orange juice, white wine, basil, cilantro, orange zest, sugar, salt, oregano, and pepper. Bring to a boil over high heat, reduce the heat to low, and simmer, uncovered, for 15 minutes.

2. Add the clams, cover, and cook until they open, 5 to 10 minutes. Discard any clams that have not opened and remain firmly shut. Add the crab, shrimp, and fish, carefully folding them into the broth. Bring to a boil, then reduce the heat, cover, and cook until the shrimp are pink and the fish flakes easily with a fork, about 5 minutes, shaking the casserole rather than stirring. Serve hot with corn tortillas.

Portuguese Kale Soup

Contrary to the name, this is actually a stew popular on Cape Cod and in southeastern Massachusetts and first made by Portuguese immigrants, who have a long, historic, and strong presence there. A good number of traditional, and old, Cape Cod dishes are called Portuguese-style, such as this luscious stew with fish, clams, linguiça sausage, and kale. Many of the local clam shacks on Cape Cod will offer a Portuguese kale soup or a variation on this recipe. The Portuguese-style linguiça sausage is rather easily found in supermarkets in New England, but elsewhere you can use Spanish-style (not Mexican-style) chorizo, hot Italian sausage, Cajun andouille sausage, or Polish kielbasa.

2 tablespoons extra-virgin olive oil

½ cup diced salt pork

1 large onion, chopped

2 garlic cloves, crushed

2 pounds fingerling or red potatoes, cut into 1-inch cubes

1 pound ripe tomatoes, cut in half, seeds squeezed out, and grated
against the largest holes of a grater

1 pound linguiça or kielbasa, cut up

1 pound kale, trimmed of heaviest stems and sliced

6 cups water

5 teaspoons salt

1 tablespoon dry white wine or sherry vinegar

1 teaspoon dried thyme

1 teaspoon freshly ground black pepper

¼ teaspoon red chile flakes

Pinch of saffron, crumbled (optional)

2 pounds striped bass, sea bass, or other firm-fleshed fish fillets,
cut into large chunks

24 littleneck clams, washed well and soaked in cold water to cover for
30 minutes with 1 tablespoon baking soda, then drained

1. To a large soup pot or flameproof baking casserole over medium heat, add the olive oil and then the salt pork and cook, stirring occasionally, until crispy, about 10 minutes. Add the onion and garlic and cook, stirring, until softened, about 5 minutes. Add the potatoes, tomatoes, linguiça sausage, kale, water, salt, vinegar, thyme, pepper, red chile flakes, and saffron, if using, bring to a boil, then reduce the heat to low, cover, and simmer until the potatoes are nearly cooked, 40 to 45 minutes.

2. Turn the heat to high and bring to a furious boil. Add the fish and clams, and cook until the clams open, 8 to 10 minutes. Discard any clams that have not opened. Check the seasoning. Let sit for 5 to 10 minutes before serving.

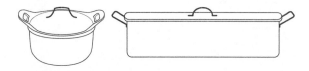

Salmon and Potato Stew

Ideally, you will make this Scandinavian stew with a whole, freshly caught salmon weighing about 3 pounds. Since finding a whole salmon in a fish store is less and less likely these days, I've adapted this recipe to accommodate two fillets. Serve with rye or pumpernickel bread. If you have a fish poacher—and whether you have secured a whole salmon or not—this is a fine time to use it; otherwise a large flameproof baking casserole will work. Serve with crusty French bread.

1 large bunch fresh dill

One 3-pound salmon, cleaned and gutted, dorsal and lateral fins removed, head and tail left on, washed well, or 2½ pounds salmon fillets

2½ quarts water

1 medium onion, thinly sliced and separated into rings

3 tablespoons white wine vinegar

20 whole allspice berries

10 whole white peppercorns

1 tablespoon sea salt

1 bay leaf

2 pounds new potatoes such as Yukon gold or fingerling, cut into 1-inch cubes or left whole

2 cups whole milk (optional)

1 cup heavy cream

Rye, pumpernickel, or crusty bread, for serving

1. Set aside 10 sprigs of the dill and chop enough of the remainder to get ½ cup. If there is any dill left, save it for another use.

2. Put the salmon in a large flameproof baking casserole or fish poacher. Cover with the water, onion, vinegar, allspice, peppercorns, salt, bay leaf, and the 10 dill sprigs and bring the water to just below a boil over high heat. As soon as the first little bubble starts in the water, 10 to 15 minutes, turn the heat off and remove the salmon from the water. Strain the liquid and return it to the casserole. Season the salmon with salt and refrigerate if you are not going to prepare the stew immediately.

3. Put the potatoes in the salmon-poaching broth, bring to a boil over medium heat, about 20 minutes, then cook until tender, about another 15 minutes. Pour in the milk, if using, then add the cream and the chopped dill. Place the salmon in the broth and cook until it is beginning to flake, about 5 minutes. Taste and correct the seasoning and serve immediately.

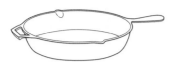

Salmon with Leeks and Potatoes

This is an amazing dish partly because you'll wonder how something so simple can taste so good. Of course, the key is using the freshest salmon and drying the potatoes with paper towels before cooking. I really enjoy the extravagance of the once-a-year availability of wild Copper River salmon from Alaska; however farm-raised salmon is about the only thing one can get these days. There were once some problems with farm-raised salmon, but many of them have been addressed by modern fish farms. This dish can also be made with Arctic char, an orange-fleshed fish with a salmon-trout taste. Because you are cooking everything in one skillet, it's important to pay attention to the sequence and the steps of this recipe.

> 5 tablespoons extra-virgin olive oil
> 3½ pounds leeks, white and a small portion of light green part only,
>   trimmed, split lengthwise, washed well, and sliced
> 2 tablespoons unsalted butter
> 2 pounds Yukon gold potatoes, peeled, sliced ¼ inch thick,
>   dried with paper towels
> Salt and freshly ground black pepper, to taste
> 1¾ pounds salmon fillet, skin on, cut into four pieces
> ¼ cup chopped fresh dill
> Crème fraîche or sour cream, for garnish

1. Preheat the oven to 350°F.

2. In a large cast-iron skillet, heat 2 tablespoons of the oil over medium-high heat, then add the leeks and cook until softened, about 8 minutes, stirring constantly during the last 3 minutes. Remove the leeks by scraping up all the bits with a spatula and slotted spoon and set aside. Wipe the skillet with a paper towel.

3. Add the butter and 2 tablespoons of the oil to the skillet and once the butter melts, layer the potatoes, overlapping in a concentric circle until the entire skillet is covered, making a second layer if necessary. Season with salt and pepper, drizzle with the remaining 1 tablespoon oil, and cook without stirring or turning until the bottom is crispy, 7 minutes. Transfer the skillet to the oven and bake until the top is light golden, about 30 minutes.

4. Remove the skillet from the oven and increase the oven temperature to 450°F.

5. Sprinkle both sides of the salmon with the dill, salt, and pepper. Spoon the reserved leeks on top of the potatoes and lay the salmon fillets on top of the leeks, skin side up. Return to the oven and bake until cooked through, 12 minutes. Remove from the oven, place a dollop of crème fraîche on top of the salmon, and serve hot.

Note: If you like a crispy skin, remove the skillet from the oven, turn the oven setting to broil, then return the skillet to the broiler and broil until the skin is crispy, a couple of minutes.

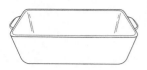

Roast Salmon, Beets, and Potatoes with Dilled Yogurt Sauce

The late-season German butterball potatoes are perfect for this dish. They are round, with smooth golden skins and yellow flesh. You can grow them yourself or find them at farmers' markets. In their place, use any potato cut into pieces of the same shape or size. All you need to accompany the roast salmon is a simple green salad made with Bibb lettuce, endive, and walnuts, if desired, and dressed with a couple of tablespoons of the yogurt dressing thinned with a bit of olive oil and vinegar.

For the yogurt dressing
- 1 large garlic clove
- ½ teaspoon salt
- 1 cup whole-milk plain yogurt
- ¼ cup finely chopped fresh dill

For the roast vegetables and fish
- Eight 1¼-inch diameter baby red beets (about 6 ounces)
- Eight 1¼-inch diameter baby orange beets (about 6 ounces)
- 16 German butterball or Yukon gold potatoes (about 1 pound), peeled and cut into 1-inch pieces
- 10 ounces parsnips, peeled and cut into 1-inch pieces
- 3 tablespoons extra-virgin olive oil
- Salt and freshly ground black pepper, to taste
- 1¼ pounds salmon fillet, cut into 4 pieces
- 3 tablespoons chopped fresh dill

1. Preheat the oven to 400°F.

2. To make the yogurt dressing, using a mortar and pestle, mash the garlic with the salt until mushy, then stir into the yogurt along with the chopped dill. Beat with a fork until smooth and set aside at room temperature.

3. In a baking casserole, toss the beets, potatoes, and parsnips with the olive oil and season with salt and pepper. Bake until the vegetables are easily pierced with a fork, about 45 minutes.

4. Season the salmon with salt and place on top of the root vegetables, skin side up, and bake until it flakes, about 12 minutes. Sprinkle with the dill. Serve with the yogurt sauce on the side.

Quick Seafood Stock

The secret to risotto cookery is a flavorful broth, ideally homemade. That's not always possible, so I often use canned bouillon, pastes, granules, and bouillon cubes. However, there is a little trick for getting a serviceable cooking stock to use for risotto cookery, and that's putting shells and other inedible pieces of various seafood into very hot water (from the tap) and letting it steep until needed. It's not as good as the real thing, but it's better than nothing and better than water. It works especially well when your recipe calls for shrimp.

Shrimp shells, lobster shells, crab shells, fish skin, and/or inedible fish parts such as fins and tails
Some onion skins and celery tips
5 cups very hot water
Salt and freshly ground black pepper, to taste

Place the seafood parts, onion skins, and celery tips in the very hot water and let sit for 1 hour. Drain through a fine-mesh strainer. Season with salt and pepper.

Makes 5 cups

Spicy Bluefish and Shrimp Stew

This spicy stew is soul-warming fare as the weather gets a bit colder. On the West Coast you can use blue mackerel or mahimahi in place of the Atlantic bluefish. You can keep the stew simmering for quite some time if you like, before cooking the seafood. In any case, once the seafood goes in, it cooks rapidly, in about 6 minutes.

¼ cup extra-virgin olive oil
¼ cup finely chopped onion
4 large garlic cloves, finely chopped
¼ cup finely chopped celery
1 fresh New Mexico/Anaheim chile, seeded and chopped
2 tablespoons finely chopped fresh flat-leaf parsley
3 large ripe tomatoes, cut in half, seeds squeezed out, and grated against
    the largest holes of a standing grater down to the peel
4 dried red chiles
1 cup dry white wine
½ cup water
½ pound bluefish, cut into bite-size pieces
½ pound medium shrimp, shelled (shells saved for making Quick Seafood Stock, see
    box page 380, if desired)
4 slices round French or Italian country bread (about ¼ pound), toasted

1. In a stewpot, heat the olive oil over medium-high heat, then add the onion, garlic, celery, fresh chile, and parsley and cook, stirring, until softened, about 8 minutes. Add the tomatoes, dried chiles, wine, and water and bring to a near boil. Reduce the heat to low and simmer for 10 minutes. The broth can be kept warm like this for a few hours or you can finish the dish right away.

2. Bring the broth to a boil over high heat, then add the bluefish and cook until it looks like it will almost fall apart, about 3 minutes. Add the shrimp and cook until they turn orange-red all over, about 3 minutes. Turn off the heat and serve hot with the bread.

Bengali Fish Stew

In this fish stew popular among Bengalis who live in eastern India and Bangladesh, the spices used stamp the fish stew in a way that is unmistakable. The recipe calls for *panch phoran*, which is a spice mix sold in Indian groceries. You can readily make it yourself, as it's made of a ground blend of equal amounts of fenugreek, nigella seeds, fennel seeds, cumin, and mustard seeds. Try to use two or more fish to make the stew all the better, as long as everything is very fresh.

One 2-inch piece fresh ginger, peeled
2 large garlic cloves
¼ cup vegetable oil
4 cardamom pods, crushed
4 whole cloves
3 small bay leaves
1 teaspoon *panch phoran* (see headnote)
1 small onion, finely chopped
4 fresh green serrano chiles, seeded or not, sliced
1 tablespoon ground coriander
2½ teaspoons salt, or more to taste
2 teaspoons ground cumin
½ teaspoon ground turmeric
¼ teaspoon cayenne pepper
⅛ teaspoon hot paprika
2 cups water
1 pound mixed fish (choose 2 or 3 fresh fish such as cod, mahimahi, yellowtail, and/or sea bass)
1 pound spinach leaves, sliced
Indian naan or any flatbread, for serving

1. Using a mortar and pestle, pound the ginger and garlic until mushy, adding about a tablespoon of water to make it mushier, if necessary.

2. In a stewpot or large saucepan, heat the oil over medium heat until smoking. Remove the pot from the heat for 30 seconds. Add the cardamom, cloves, bay leaves, and *panch phoran*, return the pot to low heat, and cook, stirring well, until the mixture starts to darken, about 30 seconds. Add the onion and cook, stirring, until softened, 3 minutes.

3. Add the ginger-garlic paste and green chiles and continue to cook, stirring well, for 1 minute. Add the coriander, salt, cumin, turmeric, cayenne, and paprika, and stir well to combine, then add the water.

4. Bring the mixture to a boil over high heat, then reduce the heat to low and simmer until the liquid is a little reduced, about 15 minutes. Add the fish and cook until it starts to flake, about 4 minutes. Remove and discard the bay leaves. Add the spinach and incorporate it by folding it into the broth once it wilts, 3 to 4 minutes. Serve immediately with naan.

Bullinada

As one follows the Mediterranean coast of France south from Provence, one passes through Languedoc and arrives in Roussillon, or French Catalonia. In the small coastal villages of the Côte Vermeille, as it's known, you will find the fish stew called *bullinada*. Traditionally, it is made in a glazed earthenware stewpot. Bullinada can be eaten as two courses. First, transfer the fish and potatoes to a platter and serve the broth; then serve the fish. Because this is originally a Mediterranean fish stew it uses local fish, so you will have to use whatever is local and fresh in your vicinity. I give many suggestions for fish, but remember you don't have to be a purist about this, so use common sense and buy what's freshest and available.

3 tablespoons pork lard (preferably) or unsalted butter

1 large onion, chopped

Leaves from 1 bunch fresh flat-leaf parsley (20 to 25 sprigs), chopped

¼ teaspoon cayenne pepper

Salt, to taste

Pinch of saffron, crumbled

Freshly ground black pepper, to taste

1 pound ripe tomatoes (optional), peeled, seeded, and sliced (see box page 47)

6 large garlic cloves, finely chopped

2 pounds Yukon gold, red, or white potatoes, peeled and sliced ⅛ to ¼ inch thick

1 pound redfish or cod fillets, cut into even-size pieces

1 pound monkfish fillets, cut into even-size pieces

1 pound sea bass, striped bass, whiting, or pollack fillets,
    cut into even-size pieces

1 pound scorpion fish, sculpin, red snapper, tilefish, or porgy fillets,
    cut into even-size pieces

Bouquet garni, tied in cheesecloth, consisting of 1 fennel stalk,
    6 fresh thyme sprigs, and 1 bay leaf

2 quarts water, salted with 2 to 3 tablespoons sea salt

2 tablespoons extra-virgin olive oil

4 to 6 tablespoons veal or beef marrow, to your taste (optional)

1. In a large earthenware casserole or stewpot (preferably) or flameproof baking casserole, melt the pork lard over medium heat, then add the onion and cook, stirring occasionally, until golden, about 12 minutes. (If using earthenware and it is not flameproof, you will need to use a heat diffuser. Earthenware heats up slower but retains its heat longer than other casseroles. When using earthenware, food may cook slower at first and then cook very quickly while retaining its heat.) Spread the onion evenly around the bottom of the casserole and sprinkle with the parsley, cayenne, salt, saffron, and black pepper.

2. Cover the onion with the tomatoes (if using), the garlic, half the potatoes, and the fish. Cover the fish with the remaining potatoes. Add the bouquet garni and barely cover with the salted water. Cover the casserole and turn the heat to high. Once it starts to boil, in about 14 minutes, add the olive oil and boil furiously until the fish is about to break apart, about 10 minutes. Remove and discard the bouquet garni.

3. Transfer the fish and potatoes to a platter. Place a tablespoon of marrow (if using) in each soup bowl, ladle the soup on top, and serve immediately.

Valencia Seafood Casserole

This dish, known as *arroz con mariscos* (rice with seafood), is cooked in an earthenware casserole known as a *cazuela* and not in a paella pan, so it's slightly different than paella. The earthenware gets very hot and retains its heat, so the dish can still be warm even an hour later, perfect if you need to hold things up. Although water will be fine for the broth, if you happen to have some previously made lobster, fish, or shrimp stock, it will improve the dish considerably. Even if you don't, you can take the shells from the shrimp in this recipe and let them soak in the hot water for an hour, and you'll have a nicely flavored stock in which to cook the rice. You can also leave the orange peel in the rice, as it falls apart and is delightful to happen upon as you eat.

For the broth
½ cup dry white wine
1 long piece of orange peel without white pith
½ teaspoon saffron, crushed slightly in a mortar and pestle
6 cups hot water or Quick Seafood Stock (see box page 380)

For the rice casserole
½ cup extra-virgin olive oil
¾ pound yellowtail, swordfish, shark, or similar fish, cut into 8 pieces
¾ pound monkfish, mahimahi, onagi, grouper, or similar fish, cut into 8 pieces
¾ pound halibut, cod, black cod, striped bass, hake, or similar fish,
    cut into 8 pieces
1 tablespoon salt, plus more as needed
12 jumbo shrimp, shelled (shells saved for making Quick Seafood Stock,
    page 380, if desired)
1 medium onion, chopped
10 large garlic cloves, finely chopped
1 roasted red bell pepper, seeded and cut into strips
3 tomatoes (about 1 pound), halved, seeds squeezed out, and
    grated against the largest holes of a standing grater down to the peel
1 tablespoon sweet Spanish paprika
3½ cups medium-grain rice such as Calrose or short-grain rice such as Arborio

1 tablespoon finely chopped fresh flat-leaf parsley
1 bay leaf, crumbled
5 ounces fresh runner beans or green beans, cut into 2-inch lengths
Allioli, for serving (see box page 388)

1. Add the white wine, orange zest, and saffron to the water. (If you are using the stock and you have used the shrimp shells to make it, remove them first.)

2. In a large earthenware casserole or low-sided flameproof baking casserole, heat the olive oil over high heat. Season the fish with the salt and add to the casserole. Cook, turning once, until the fish turns color on both sides, about 2 minutes. (If using earthenware and it is not flameproof, you will need to use a heat diffuser. Earthenware heats up slower but retains its heat longer than other casseroles. When using earthenware, food may cook slower at first and then cook very quickly while retaining its heat.) Remove the fish and reserve. Season the shrimp with salt, add to the casserole, and cook until they turn orange-red, about 1 minute. Remove and reserve with the fish.

3. Add the chopped onion, garlic, and red bell pepper to the casserole and cook, stirring constantly so they don't burn, for 1 minute. Add the tomatoes and paprika and cook, stirring, for another 1 to 2 minutes. Add the rice, parsley, and the crumbled bay leaf and stir so all the grains are coated. Pour in the broth. Add the runner beans, pushing them down into the broth. Place the fish and shrimp on top, without pushing them down into the broth, and cook, uncovered, never stirring or poking, until the broth is absorbed and the rice is sticky and tender, about 20 minutes. Remove from the heat, cover with a kitchen towel, and let sit for 10 minutes before serving. Serve with Allioli.

Allioli

In Catalonia and Valencia, *allioli* is a garlicky condiment used as frequently as Americans use ketchup. In Provence, a similar preparation is called aioli. Both words are a contraction of the words *all*, "garlic," *i*, "and," and *oli*, "oil." Traditionally, the Catalan version is made only with garlic, olive oil, and salt using a mortar and pestle. This recipe uses egg and is made in a food processor.

> 5 large garlic cloves (about 1½ ounces)
> ½ teaspoon salt, plus more as needed
> 1 large egg
> 1 cup extra-virgin olive oil
> Freshly ground white pepper, to taste

1. In a mortar, mash the garlic and ½ teaspoon salt together with a pestle until mushy. Transfer the garlic to a food processor with the egg and process for 30 seconds.

2. With the machine running, slowly drizzle in the oil in a very thin stream through the feed tube until absorbed. Season with more salt, if desired, and white pepper. Cover with plastic wrap and refrigerate for 1 hour before using to let the emulsion solidify a bit. Store in the refrigerator for up to 1 month.

Makes 1½ cups

Risotto of Crayfish, Portobello Mushroom, and Broccoli Rabe

Although crayfish (crawfish) are ideal for this preparation, they're not always available outside of the Gulf Coast, so shrimp or crab are a fine substitute. If you don't happen to have any home-made fish broth, you can try the Quick Seafood Stock recipe on page 380, or use fish bouillon cubes or canned fish bouillon.

6 tablespoons (¾ stick) unsalted butter
1 tablespoon extra-virgin olive oil
¾ pound broccoli rabe, heavy stems removed and chopped
1 portobello mushroom (about ¼ pound), chopped
2 large garlic cloves, finely chopped
1 cup short-grain rice, such as Arborio (do not rinse)
1 teaspoon salt, or more as needed
Freshly ground black pepper, to taste
4 to 6 cups fish broth or Quick Seafood Stock (see box page 380)
½ pound cooked and chopped crayfish, lobster, crab, or shrimp

1. In a flameproof baking casserole, melt 3 tablespoons of the butter with the olive oil over high heat. Once the butter has stopped bubbling, add the broccoli rabe, mushroom, and garlic and cook, stirring constantly, for 2 to 3 minutes. Add the rice, salt, and pepper and cook for 1 minute.

2. Reduce the heat to medium-low. Add 1 cup of the broth and stir. Once the liquid evaporates, pour in another ½ cup broth. Continue adding broth in smaller and smaller amounts as it evaporates and is absorbed and cook uncovered, stirring frequently, until the rice is between al dente and tender, 45 minutes to 1 hour (sometimes less and sometimes a little more depending on the rice). If you run out of broth, continue with water. Stir in the crayfish and continue cooking until heated through, stirring, about 5 minutes. Add the remaining 3 tablespoons butter and serve once it melts.

Risotto with Fish and Vegetables

Although risotto is served in northern Italy as a first course and not a main course, this version of risotto is a big, flavorful, and complex (in taste) dish that's perfect for a large dinner party when you only want to serve a one-pot meal. The two great sources of flavor, and the key to the preparation, are the mix of fish and the broth. Ideally, you should use four kinds of fish. The best way to do that is if your fishmonger sells "chowder pieces" or "soup fish," that is, leftover bits of cut-up fish to be used for soups, stews, or broths. These might include carcasses and heads, too. If your fishmonger does not sell such a thing, then you might have to resort to buying fish broth in a can, paste, or cube. Alternatively, never throw away shrimp shells or lobsters shells, which you can use to make Quick Seafood Stock (see box page 380).

¼ cup extra-virgin olive oil
4 tablespoons (½ stick) unsalted butter
1 small onion, finely chopped
2 large garlic cloves, finely chopped
1 medium zucchini, diced
3 cups short-grain rice such as Arborio
7 to 8 cups fish, shrimp, or lobster broth or a mixture of all three or
　　Quick Seafood Stock (see box page 380)
1 tablespoon salt
1 cup frozen or fresh peas
2 teaspoons freshly ground white pepper
1 pound mixed fish (your choice), cut into ¾-inch pieces
1 cup freshly grated Parmesan cheese (about 2½ ounces)
2 tablespoons finely chopped fresh flat-leaf parsley

1. In a flameproof baking casserole or a large saucepan, heat the olive oil with 2 tablespoons of the butter over medium-high heat until the butter melts, then add the onion and garlic and cook, stirring, until softened, about 4 minutes. (If using earthenware and it is not flameproof, you will need to use a heat diffuser. Earthenware heats up slower but retains its heat longer than other casseroles. When using earthenware, food may cook slower at first and then cook very quickly while retaining its heat.) Add the zucchini and rice and cook, stirring, to coat all the grains.

2. Add 2 cups of the broth and the salt and cook, stirring, until the broth starts to bubble, then reduce the heat to medium-low and cook, stirring, until the first amount of broth has almost evaporated. Add another cup of broth as you cook, stirring frequently, until it too has evaporated. Add the peas and keep adding broth in smaller amounts until the rice is soft, about 30 minutes in all. Season with the white pepper and stir.

3. Add the fish and cook, stirring, until it is cooked through, about 6 minutes. Add the remaining 2 tablespoons butter, the cheese, and parsley and stir. Serve after a minute or two, once the cheese has melted.

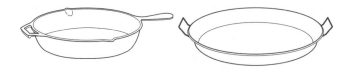

Green Rice with Salmon

Not only is this dish easy to make, but it's also startlingly attractive and you'll admire your cooking before serving. You can make it in a cast-iron skillet or a paella pan and serve it directly from the pan with a garnish of upland cress leaves. You might think "What's upland cress?" but you probably have already eaten it plenty of times; it's a milder relative of watercress and is often sold in place of watercress in many supermarkets.

2 cups medium-grain rice such as Calrose or short-grain rice such as Arborio
2¾ cups chicken broth
2 cups loosely-packed fresh flat-leaf parsley
2 cups loosely packed fresh cilantro (coriander leaf)
2 fresh green serrano chiles, seeded or not
3 tablespoons unsalted (preferably) pumpkin seeds
3 large garlic cloves, coarsely chopped
¼ cup vegetable oil
6 tablespoons finely chopped white onion
1¾ pounds salmon fillet, cut into 4 pieces
2 teaspoons salt, or more as needed
Freshly ground black pepper, to taste
5 tablespoons sour cream
3 tablespoons heavy cream
Upland cress leaves or watercress, for garnish

1. Put the rice in a strainer and let the strainer rest in a bowl of very hot water for 10 minutes. Drain and rinse under running water.

2. In a blender, purée 1 cup of the chicken broth with the parsley, cilantro, chiles, pumpkin seeds, and garlic until smooth, about 2 minutes running constantly. Set aside.

3. In a large cast-iron skillet or paella pan, heat the oil over medium-high heat. Add the rice and cook, stirring occasionally, until it begins to stick to the bottom of the skillet, 4 to 5 minutes. Add the onion and continue cooking, stirring, until the onion is soft, about 3 minutes.

4. Add the green purée to the rice and continue cooking over high heat, stirring and scraping the bottom of the pan, until the rice has absorbed all of the liquid, 2 to 3 minutes. Shake the skillet to distribute the rice evenly.

5. Lay the salmon on top of the rice. Season the salmon with a little salt and pepper. Pour in the remaining 1¾ cups broth and the remaining 2 teaspoons salt, and cook, uncovered, over medium-high heat without stirring until the liquid has been absorbed and there are air holes in the rice, 8 to 10 minutes. Remove from the heat, cover with a paper towel, and place the lid on top. Let the rice swell up, about 10 minutes.

6. Mix the sour cream and cream together and drizzle attractively over the rice and salmon (you can use a squeeze bottle to do this if you like, otherwise let it drip from a spoon). Serve from the skillet with upland cress leaves on the side.

Rice Pilaf with Octopus

This preparation is best made with the kind of cut-up octopus one can find in the salad bar of a Whole Foods Market or in Japanese markets. You can use canned octopus, too, but in that case stir it in at the end. If you just can't find octopus, use smoked mussels from a can. This dish also has some green in it, and that green can come from chiles for a spicy version or peas for a non-spicy version; it's up to you.

2 tablespoons unsalted butter
½ small onion, finely chopped
3 fresh green serrano chiles, seeded and sliced, or 1 cup fresh or frozen peas
1 small garlic clove, finely chopped
1½ cups long-grain rice such as basmati, rinsed well or soaked in
    tepid water for 30 minutes, then drained
½ pounds cooked octopus, cut into ½-inch segments
2½ cups water
1½ teaspoon salt
Freshly ground black pepper, to taste
1 tablespoon chopped fresh mint

In a heavy saucepan, melt the butter over medium heat, then add the onion, chiles, and garlic and cook, stirring, until softened, about 4 minutes. Add the rice and octopus and stir to coat all the grains. Add the water and salt, and bring to a vigorous boil over high heat. Turn off the heat, place a kitchen towel or paper towel over the saucepan, cover, and let sit until all the water is absorbed and the rice is tender, about 45 minutes. Serve with a sprinkling of black pepper and the mint.

Makes 4 servings

|||||||||||||||||||||||||||||||||||||||||||||||||||||||||||||||||||||||||||||||||||||||||||||||||||||||||||||||||||||

Rice Pilaf with Fish

This easy pilaf can stand alone with its pleasant tastes and smell of olive oil, bell pepper, and bay leaf, but I like to serve it with a salad of chopped cucumber, tomato, scallion, and olives with lemon and olive oil dressing.

¼ cup extra-virgin olive oil
½ cup finely chopped onion
1 celery stalk, finely chopped
½ green bell pepper, seeded and finely chopped
1 cup long-grain rice such as basmati, soaked in water to cover for 30 minutes
    or rinsed well under running water, then drained
½ pound medium shrimp, shelled (shells saved for making Quick Seafood Stock,
    if desired)
½ pound haddock, cod, grouper, red snapper, or similar fish,
    cut into 1-inch cubes
¼ cup finely chopped fresh flat-leaf parsley
1 bay leaf
2 cups fish broth or Quick Seafood Stock (see box page 380)
Salt and freshly ground black pepper, to taste

1. Preheat the oven to 400°F.

2. In a flameproof baking casserole, heat the olive oil over medium-high heat, then add the onion, celery, and bell pepper and cook, stirring occasionally, until softened, 5 to 6 minutes. Remove with a slotted spoon and reserve.

3. Add the drained rice to the casserole you cooked the vegetables in and cook, stirring, over medium-high heat for 1 minute. Return the reserved vegetables to the casserole along with the shrimp, fish, parsley, and bay leaf. Mix well but gently. Pour in the fish broth and season with salt and pepper. Cover and bake for 20 minutes. Remove from the oven, place paper towels under the lid to absorb moisture, and leave to rest, covered, for 12 minutes. Remove and discard the bay leaf. Serve hot.

Couscous with Fish

The traditional method of cooking couscous in its home in North Africa is by steaming the dried couscous, a process that can take 3 hours. Today, there are boxes of precooked couscous that are partially or wholly cooked then dried. Steaming the precooked couscous takes about 1½ hours. However, curiously, many couscous packages have instructions in multiple languages, and those in English, French, Italian, and Spanish stipulate that one soak the couscous in boiling water and broth for 5 to 8 minutes, yet the Arabic instructions stipulate steaming only. Well, given that couscous is an Arab-Berber food, I don't want to be a clod about the proper way to cook couscous, so I always steam it and never soak it.

Although soaking is an enormous time-saver, it results in an inferior couscous, a heavy, leaden mass of wheat that swells in your stomach instead of on the plate. On the other hand, if that's a trade you're willing to make, then go ahead and follow the package instructions. This recipe and the one on page 62 are based on the steaming method of precooked couscous. If you wish to follow the package instructions for soaking, then follow the method described in the box on page 398. There is a middle road, too: Soak the couscous as described then steam it for 20 minutes. If you do that then you'll need an extra quart of water.

Couscous is one of the staple foods of the North African country of Tunisia. Tunisia has a long coastline and an active, but local, fishing industry. The most popular fish are grouper, sea bream, and gray mullet, and when steamed as in this couscous preparation the ideal is to use more than one kind for the fullest flavor. If you have the fish mentioned above, great, otherwise choose two of the following (there are many more that would work): red snapper, sole, sea bass, cod, halibut, porgy, redfish, pomfret, drumfish, ling, John Dory, blackfish.

¼ cup extra-virgin olive oil

2 medium onions, finely chopped

2 large garlic cloves, finely chopped

1 tablespoon harīsa (see box page 140) dissolved in 3 tablespoons water, plus more for garnish

½ teaspoon freshly ground black pepper

4 cups water

One 28-ounce can whole plum tomatoes, chopped with its liquid

2 large Yukon gold potatoes (1½ pounds), peeled and quartered

2 large carrots, scraped and cut in half

1 large turnip (¾ pound), peeled and quartered

2 bay leaves

2 cups (16 to 18 ounces) precooked couscous

3 tablespoons unsalted butter, at room temperature

1 teaspoon salt

1½ pounds fish of your choice, preferably two kinds, such as red snapper, gray mullet, or other (see headnote), cut into small fist-size pieces

1. In the bottom of a *couscousière* or a large stewpot that can fit a colander on top, heat the olive oil over medium-high heat, then add the onions, garlic, harīsa, cumin, and pepper and cook, stirring frequently, until softened, 5 minutes. Add the water, tomatoes, potatoes, carrots, turnip, and bay leaves and bring to a boil.

2. Put the couscous into the top part of a couscousière or in a colander lined with cheesecloth. Place on top of the bottom part of the couscousière or on top of the large pot, if using a colander, and cover with the lid. If using a colander and there is a space between the colander and the pot, wrap with a wet kitchen towel to seal the space. Steam the couscous for 20 minutes. Once you see steam rising from the couscous, add 1 tablespoon of the butter and the salt to the couscous. Stir and fluff with a fork and continue cooking, covered, until the vegetables are nearly tender, about 15 minutes.

(continued)

3. Add the fish to the broth, replenish the broth with some water, and bring back to a boil with the top part on top. Cook until the fish begins to flake, about 8 minutes. Remove the top part with the couscous, fluff the couscous with a fork, then carefully (so they don't break apart too much) remove the vegetables and fish with a slotted spoon and reserve in a bowl. Remove and discard the bay leaves. Add some more water to the broth, replace the top part or colander, and continue steaming the couscous, covered, until soft and fluffy, fluffing occasionally, 50 to 60 minutes more. Return the reserved vegetables and fish to the broth 3 minutes before the couscous is finished cooking.

4. Transfer the couscous to a serving bowl and fold the remaining 2 tablespoons of butter into the couscous. Once the butter is melted, stir with a fork until all the grains are glistening. Mound the couscous attractively in a large serving bowl or platter. Transfer the vegetables and broth to a tureen for serving or scatter the fish and vegetables attractively on the mounded couscous and serve the broth separately. When diners serve themselves, have each person place three serving spoonfuls of couscous into a bowl. Top with vegetables and two to three ladlefuls of broth. Add a teaspoon of harīsa, if desired, and let the bowl sit to absorb some broth before eating.

Couscous with Fish: Soaking/Steaming Method

Ingredient measurements are the same as in the recipe on page 396.

In a large saucepan or stewpot, heat the olive oil over medium-high heat, then cook, stirring frequently, the onion, garlic, harīsa, cumin, and black pepper until softened, 2 to 3 minutes. Add 4 cups water, the tomatoes, potatoes, carrots, turnip, and bay leaves and bring to a boil. Cook until the vegetables are tender, about 20 minutes. Add the fish to the broth and replenish the broth with some water if it is too thick (it should be more like broth than sauce). Place the couscous in a bowl, add 2½ cups fish broth to it, and let soak, covered, for 6 to 8 minutes. Fluff the couscous and add the butter or olive oil. If desired, remove the fish and vegetables from the broth, remove and discard the bay leaves, and place the top portion with the couscous on top of the *couscousière* or pot, and steam over high heat for 20 minutes. Remove the couscous, fluff again, and mound attractively in a large serving bowl or platter. Transfer the fish, vegetables, and broth to a tureen for serving or scatter the fish and vegetables attractively on the mounded couscous and serve the broth separately.

Squid and Potato Stew

Nowadays, fish stores often sell a product labeled "squid steak," which I suspect is actually cuttlefish, a cousin of squid. Cuttlefish, because it's thicker, would be ideal in this preparation, but you can of course use large squid. What I like about this stew is how the potatoes take on the flavor of the squid in a rich tomato and olive oil ragoût. If you are unable to find cuttlefish and use squid instead, the amount of time you need to simmer will be reduced, so keep checking with a skewer, which should slide somewhat easily into the squid. Don't be alarmed by the amount of olive oil, which may seem a ridiculous quantity, but remember that you don't eat it all. Fingerling, yellow Finn, and Yukon gold are nice boiling potatoes to use in this dish.

1½ cups extra-virgin olive oil
1 medium onion, finely chopped
2 pounds cuttlefish or large squid, cleaned and cut into strips, with tentacles
4 large garlic cloves, finely chopped
⅔ cup dry white wine
1½ cups canned or fresh tomato purée
1 cup water
½ cinnamon stick
1 whole clove
½ bay leaf
Salt and freshly ground black pepper, to taste
¾ pound Yukon gold, fingerling, or yellow Finn potatoes, peeled and cut into wedges
1½ cups pitted imported green olives

1. In a flameproof baking casserole, heat the olive oil over medium heat, then add the onion and cook, stirring occasionally, until translucent, about 7 minutes. Add the cuttlefish and garlic and cook until mixed well, about 2 minutes. Pour in the wine and let it reduce by half, about 8 minutes, stirring a few times. Add the tomato purée, water, cinnamon, clove, and bay leaf, season with salt and pepper, reduce the heat to low, cover, and simmer for 3 hours, stirring once in a while.

2. Add the potatoes and olives and simmer for another 1 hour. Remove and discard the cinnamon stick, clove, and bay leaf. Serve hot with a slotted spoon to leave the olive oil behind.

Shrimp with Cliff's Orange Devil Sauce

This recipe is a quick stir-fry with a piquancy that is prodigious, frankly even thermonuclear from the roasted habanero sauce that I concocted for my book *Some Like It Hot*. It's a simple preparation, but you will want to accompany it with something bland to cut the heat, such as bread or corn tortillas. This is a preparation only for those of you who love the hottest foods possible.

1½ pounds large shrimp, shelled (shells saved for making
    Quick Seafood Stock, see box page 380, if desired)
¼ pound chanterelle or trumpet mushrooms, sliced
6 scallions, trimmed and chopped
¼ cup finely chopped fresh cilantro (coriander leaf)
2 large garlic cloves, finely chopped
1 tablespoon Cliff's Orange Devil Sauce (see box page 401) or any
    habanero-based hot sauce
½ teaspoon chili powder
Salt, to taste
¼ cup peanut oil
8 corn tortillas, warmed, for serving

1. In a bowl, toss together the shrimp, mushrooms, scallions, cilantro, garlic, hot sauce, chili powder, and salt.

2. Pour the peanut oil into the wok and heat over high heat until smoking. Add the shrimp mixture and cook, stir-frying constantly, until the shrimp are firm and orange-red, 3 to 4 minutes. Serve hot with the corn tortillas.

Cliff's Orange Devil Sauce

When I was writing my book *Some Like it Hot*, I planted a habanero plant that produced copiously. Meanwhile, I was trying dozens of hot sauces and not caring for most of them, so I decided to make my own. This hot sauce is best for the plainest foods. Roasting the habanero chiles brings out a very sweet and fruity bouquet, but don't let that fool you. This is an extremely hot sauce and a serving of half a teaspoon will be plenty. Store in the refrigerator.

40 fresh habanero chiles
10 large garlic cloves (unpeeled)
10 tablespoons apple cider vinegar
½ teaspoon sugar
¼ teaspoon salt
⅛ teaspoon freshly ground black pepper

1. Preheat the oven to 450°F.

2. Place the habanero chiles and garlic in a roasting pan and roast until black spots appear on the chiles, 15 to 17 minutes. Remove and set aside to cool.

3. Remove any remaining stems from the chiles, remove the peels from the garlic, and place both in a blender. Add the vinegar, sugar, salt, and pepper and blend until smooth. Transfer to a small bottle, using a funnel, and store in the refrigerator. The sauce will keep for up to 1 year.

Makes about 1 cup

Stir-Fried Shrimp with Bell Peppers and Bok Choy

This stir-fry will give you an enormous sense of accomplishment since it will taste better than anything you can get in a Chinese restaurant outside of Chinatown. The one item that may be difficult to find in a supermarket is the yellow bean sauce, although you should look in the international aisle of your supermarket first. It can also be found through Internet sources such as www.templeofthai.com or by searching the grocery and gourmet foods section of www.amazon.com and in Chinese and Thai markets. Serve with steamed or leftover rice if desired or a tomato, cucumber, and scallion salad.

¼ cup yellow bean sauce

3 tablespoons soy sauce

2 tablespoons cornstarch

1½ teaspoons rice wine (mirin) or dry sherry

¾ teaspoon freshly ground black pepper

¼ cup vegetable oil

¾ cup unsalted cashews

3 ounces pork belly, sliced, or Canadian bacon

5 large garlic cloves, finely chopped

1½ tablespoons peeled and finely chopped fresh ginger

1 large leek, white part only, split lengthwise, washed well, julienned, then cut into 1½-inch lengths

1 pound large shrimp, shelled and cut in half (shells saved for making Quick Seafood Stock, if desired)

½ teaspoon salt, plus more to taste

2 green bell peppers, seeded and cut into strips

¾ pound bok choy, cut into strips

2 small zucchini, peeled and julienned

3 scallions, cut on the diagonal into 1-inch lengths

½ cup shrimp broth or water

2 teaspoons sesame oil

1. In a bowl, stir together the yellow bean sauce, soy sauce, cornstarch, rice wine, and black pepper. Set aside.

2. In a large wok, heat 3 tablespoons of the oil over high heat until nearly smoking. Add the cashews and cook until they turn light brown, about 15 seconds. Remove with a slotted spoon or skimmer and set aside. Add the pork belly and cook, stir-frying, for 1 minute. Add the garlic and ginger and cook, stir-frying, for 30 seconds. Add the leek and cook, tossing, until a little softer, about 2 minutes. Remove the leek and set aside.

3. Add the remaining 1 tablespoon oil to the wok and let it heat for 1 minute. Add the shrimp and salt and stir-fry, tossing constantly, until orange-pink and firm, about 2 minutes. Remove the shrimp and reserve with the leek.

4. Add the green bell peppers, bok choy, zucchini, and half the scallions to the wok and cook, stir-frying, for 1 minute. Add the soy sauce mixture and the shrimp broth, cover, and cook for 2 minutes. Return the shrimp and leek to the wok, add the sesame oil and reserved cashews, cook for 1 minute, and then serve hot with the remaining scallions on top.

Deep-Fried Shrimp Balls on Bean Sprout Nests

This is not an everyday recipe. This recipe is for a time when you want a challenge. It is labor-intensive with lots of ingredients, but the result is worth the effort. In its preparation, the one pot you'll use is your wok, in which you will deep-fry everything. Successful deep-frying is easy and guaranteed by observing two rules. First, make sure the oil temperature does not fall below 340°F by using a candy/deep-fry thermometer available from any supermarket, and second, do not crowd the wok with too much food. You *must* cook in batches or else your food will be greasy and soggy. This preparation is popular in China and you may have had something similar in a Chinese restaurant. Preparing it at home is made even easier with a food processor to mix the shrimp balls, although it's not necessary, as you can pulverize the shrimp by beating it with a mallet.

For the shrimp balls
¾ pound ground pork
1 pound shrimp, shelled (shells saved for making Quick Seafood Stock,
    see box page 380, if desired)
1 cup cornstarch
One 1½-inch piece fresh ginger, peeled and very finely chopped
4 scallions, trimmed, white part finely chopped; green parts
    cut into 1-inch pieces, for garnish
7 fresh or canned water chestnuts, outer skin peeled off if fresh, very finely chopped
3 tablespoons soy sauce
2 tablespoons sesame oil
2 egg whites (reserve the yolks for making the nests)
1 tablespoon rice wine (mirin) or dry sherry
1½ teaspoons ground Sichuan peppercorns (optional)
2 teaspoons salt

For the bean sprout nests
½ pound fresh bean sprouts

1 bunch (½ pound) bok choy or yu choy (flowering Chinese cabbage),
   heavy stems removed and thinly shredded
½ cup cornstarch
2 large eggs, separated, whites beaten to form soft peaks, yolks reserved
1 tablespoon soy sauce
1 tablespoon red chile flakes
1 teaspoon sesame oil
1 teaspoon salt
4 cups peanut or vegetable oil

For dipping
2 tablespoons powdered mustard mixed with a little water
Soy sauce

1. To prepare the shrimp balls, place the pork and shrimp in a food processor and run until it forms a very finely pulverized mass. Transfer to a bowl and mix in the cornstarch, ginger, white part of the scallions, water chestnuts, soy sauce, sesame oil, egg whites, rice wine, Sichuan peppercorns, and salt, blending thoroughly and vigorously. Refrigerate until needed.

2. To prepare the bean sprout nests, in a bowl, stir together the bean sprouts, bok choy, cornstarch, 4 egg yolks (which includes the 2 reserved yolks from the shrimp ball ingredients), 2 beaten egg whites, soy sauce, chile flakes, sesame oil, and salt. Set aside.

3. In a wok, heat the oil over high heat until it registers 340°F on a deep-fry thermometer, then reduce the heat to maintain this temperature.

4. Using your hands and a large spoon, form the shrimp mixture into 16 balls the size of a plum, dipping your hands into a bowl of water so it doesn't stick. You will only be able to cook about six at a time, so cook in three batches. Slip the shrimp balls into the oil carefully so they don't splash. Cook, turning, until golden brown,
(continued)

about 8 minutes. Remove from the oil with a skimmer and transfer to paper towels to drain; keep warm as you cook the second and third batches.

5. Cook the bean sprout nests by forming a small nest with your hands and sliding it into the hot oil, cooking, turning once, until golden brown, about 4 minutes. Remove from the oil with a skimmer. The nests will fall apart slightly on the edges and look scraggly, and that's fine. Arrange the nests on a platter and place the fried shrimp balls on top. Serve with the green part of the scallions, the mustard mixture, and the soy sauce.

Seafood with Tomatoes

This is a sweet little recipe to make for yourself and a friend. It can be made very quickly and is an ideal recipe for a delicious meal with stuff you've picked up at the market on your way home. You don't have to use the fish called for here; buy what's fresh and appetizing looking. It's always served with little toasts, called *crostini* in Italian.

¼ cup extra-virgin olive oil
1 small onion, finely chopped
6 ounces swordfish, shark, tuna, or mahimahi
4 littleneck clams (about ½ pound)
8 mussels, debearded
1½ cups water
½ pound ripe tomatoes, peeled, seeded, and chopped (see box page 47)
2 garlic cloves, finely chopped
2 tablespoons finely chopped fresh flat-leaf parsley
1 dried red chile
Salt and freshly ground black pepper, to taste
½ pound red snapper fillet
8 to 10 little toasts, made from a French baguette

In a flameproof baking casserole, heat the olive oil over medium heat, then add the onion and cook, stirring, until translucent, about 6 minutes. Add the swordfish, clams, mussels, water, tomatoes, garlic, parsley, chile, salt, and pepper and cook for 7 to 8 minutes. Add the red snapper and cook until the clams open, the swordfish is firm to the touch, and the red snapper is about to flake, 6 to 8 minutes. Serve hot with the toasts.

Stir-Fried Shrimp with Snow Peas and Black Bean Sauce

This quick wok stir-fry only takes a handful of minutes to prepare. The black bean paste may be the only thing not available in your supermarket, although you should try the international aisle under Chinese foods to make sure. Otherwise, do as I do and buy it from the Korean online grocer www.koamart.com or search the grocery and gourmet foods section of www.amazon.com. If worse comes to worst, just leave it out.

2 tablespoons rice wine (mirin) or dry sherry

4 teaspoons soy sauce

1 tablespoon peeled and finely chopped fresh ginger

1 teaspoon sugar

¼ teaspoon freshly ground black pepper

3 tablespoons water

1 tablespoon cornstarch

2 tablespoons vegetable oil

1 large garlic clove, crushed

½ teaspoon salt

1 pound large shrimp, shelled (shells saved for making Quick Seafood Stock, see box page 380, if desired)

1 tablespoon fermented black bean paste

1 pound snow peas, trimmed

½ cup chicken or shrimp broth

1. In a bowl, combine the rice wine, 3 teaspoons of the soy sauce, ginger, sugar, and pepper. In another bowl, combine the water, cornstarch, and remaining 1 teaspoon soy sauce and blend until it forms a paste.

2. In a large wok, heat the oil over high heat until nearly smoking, then add the garlic and salt and cook, stirring, until the garlic is light brown, about 30 seconds. Add the shrimp and fermented black beans and cook, tossing, until the shrimp are firm and the paste liquid, about 2 minutes. Remove the shrimp and reserve.

3. Add the snow peas and toss several times, then add the soy-ginger mixture and cook, tossing, for 30 seconds. Reduce the heat to medium, return the shrimp to the wok, add the broth, cover, and cook for 1 to 2 minutes. Stir in the cornstarch paste and toss several times, then serve.

Asian Noodles with Shrimp and Bok Choy

The bean thread noodles, as well as the fish sauce and oyster sauce, can all be found in your supermarket's international food aisle. Bean thread noodles are thin, translucent noodles that can be softened by simply leaving them in a bowl of hot water. That's perfect for this one-pot meal with its complementary flavors inspired by Thai cookery.

½ pound thin bean thread noodles
1 teaspoon whole black peppercorns
1 tablespoon coarsely chopped fresh cilantro (coriander leaf) stems
2 tablespoons coarsely chopped garlic
2 tablespoons vegetable oil
1 pound large shrimp, shelled (shells saved for making Quick Seafood Stock, see box page 380, if desired)
1 tablespoon finely chopped fresh ginger
2 scallions, trimmed and chopped
¼ cup chicken broth
2 tablespoons Thai or Vietnamese fish sauce
1 tablespoon oyster sauce
1 tablespoon rice wine (mirin)
1 teaspoon soy sauce
1 teaspoon sesame oil
1 teaspoon sugar
¼ teaspoon salt
½ pound bok choy, chopped
1 tablespoon coarsely chopped fresh cilantro (coriander leaf) leaves

1. Place the noodles in a large bowl, cover with hot water, and let sit for 15 minutes, until they become soft.

2. Meanwhile, place the black peppercorns in a mortar and grind with a pestle. Add the cilantro stems and garlic and pound until it forms a mushy pesto.

3. In a large flameproof baking casserole or soup pot (preferably earthenware), heat the oil over medium heat, then add the cilantro pesto and cook, stirring, for 1 minute. (If using earthenware and it is not flameproof, you will need to use a heat diffuser. Earthenware heats up slower but retains its heat longer than other casseroles. When using earthenware, food may cook slower at first and then cook very quickly while retaining its heat.) Add the shrimp and ginger and cook, stirring, for 1 minute. Add the scallions and stir, then remove all the shrimp from the casserole and set aside.

4. In a bowl, stir together the chicken broth, fish sauce, oyster sauce, rice wine, soy sauce, sesame oil, sugar, and salt.

5. Place the drained noodles into the casserole. Add the shrimp mixture and bok choy and pour the chicken broth mixture over it all. Toss a little, cover tightly, and cook over medium heat until the noodles are clear, about 10 minutes. Sprinkle with the cilantro leaves and serve immediately.

Buckwheat–Beer Batter Fried Dinner

This isn't exactly an easy recipe if you're unfamiliar with deep-frying. On the other hand, if you have a home-use deep fryer, this recipe will be a cinch. From a practical point of view, it's a little too much work to make this for more than four people unless you have a large built-in deep fryer. If you have neither, for practicality, you'll need two 6-quart pots for the frying oil. This recipe is based on a tempura-like batter into which all the foods are dipped before frying. For success, make sure all your ingredients are prepared and ready to go; make sure the batter is ice-cold; and make sure the frying oil has reached its proper temperature of 360°F. Lastly, make sure you serve the food quickly. Properly prepared fried food will have very little oil on it; if it is greasy, then you've goofed. To avoid goofing, never fry too much food at once. Let the oil cool after use, and it can be used for deep-frying the next time.

For the dipping sauce
¼ cup soy sauce

3 tablespoons rice vinegar

1 tablespoon chile oil

For the beer batter
2 quarts peanut or canola oil, for frying

1½ cups buckwheat flour, rice flour, or all-purpose flour

½ cup cornstarch

1 teaspoon kosher salt, or more as needed

¼ teaspoon baking soda

2¼ cups ice-cold beer (lager)

2 large egg yolks

For the fried foods
½ pound eggplant, sliced ¼ inch thick

½ pound yam, peeled and sliced ¼ inch thick

½ pound red bell pepper, seeded and cut into ½-inch-wide slices

½ pound zucchini, sliced ¼ inch thick lengthwise

1 pound mixed fish, cut into chunks

1. Stir together the dipping sauce ingredients and set aside until ready to serve.

2. Preheat the frying oil in two 6-quart saucepans, a quart in each one, until it registers 360° to 375°F on a deep-fry/candy thermometer. Alternatively, preheat a home-use deep-fryer to 360°F. Turn the oven to the warm setting. Spread some paper towels on a large platter or tray to receive the fried food as it finishes cooking. Have a skimmer at hand ready to remove the food from the oil.

3. In a bowl, mix together the flour, cornstarch, salt, and baking soda. Whisk in the beer and egg yolks until you have a dense batter that resembles thick syrup, not a pancake batter. The batter must be ice-cold.

4. Working rapidly, fry one food at a time by dipping the vegetables first in the batter, letting the excess drip off. Deep-fry the vegetable pieces, making sure you never crowd the fryer so the oil temperature does not drop. You *must* cook in batches. Cook until golden, 2 to 4 minutes depending on the vegetable. Remove, drain on the paper towel–strewn platter, and let sit in the warm oven as you continue cooking. Continue cooking the remainder of the vegetables. Season the fish with salt and cook the fish in the same manner, 3 to 4 minutes. Serve immediately with the dipping sauce.

Cajun Oyster Stew

There are two oyster stews from Louisiana: Cajun-style and Creole. The difference is that Creole cooking is typical of the city, that is, New Orleans, and it is made with cream and milk. Cajun-style is country-style, that is, Bayou-style, made not with cream but with a dark brown roux. This recipe is adapted from one by Louisiana Chef John Folse of Lafitte's Landing Restaurant in Donaldsonville, Louisiana. Chef Folse argues that the original oyster stew was made with a brown roux and not cream or milk, which was not found in New Orleans recipes from the early 1700s after the founding of the town. This makes sense because it was later immigrants, the Germans, who brought more dairy and sausage making. You will need about 2 quarts of oyster liquid for this recipe, and your 2 to 4 dozen oysters will not provide that amount. Therefore you must buy the oyster liquid or make some by blending about 8 oysters with 6 to 7 cups of water in a blender. Louisiana oysters are *Crassostrea virginica*, the most common American oyster. In this recipe, I've used Hood Canal oysters from Washington State, *Crassostrea gigas*, a large and meaty oyster originally from Japan that's also called a Pacific oyster. They are seeded in the Pacific Northwest and often sold already shucked and jarred. The 30 Hood Canal oysters called for should give you 3½ to 4 cups of shucked oysters. However, if you can get Gulf oysters or Atlantic oysters then by all means use them over the Pacific ones. Making the dark brown roux is a bit tricky, so pay attention to the instructions and be absolutely sure to have your *mise en place* all set up and ready to go; you will not have time to chop anything once the cooking starts.

¾ cup vegetable oil
1 cup all-purpose flour
1 medium onion, chopped (about 1 cup chopped)
2 celery stalks, chopped (about 1 cup chopped)
1 green bell pepper, seeded and chopped (about 1 cup chopped)
2 large garlic cloves, finely chopped
2 teaspoons Creole seasoning such as Tony Chachere or Paul Prudhomme brand
½ teaspoon cayenne pepper

2 quarts oyster liquid or 7½ cups water blended in a blender with 8 oysters
    until liquid with no bits
8 frozen vol-au-vent puff pastry shells, defrosted according to the package
    instructions
30 Hood Canal (Pacific) shucked jarred oysters, juice saved, or 72 Gulf or
    Atlantic oysters in the shell, shucked, juice strained and saved
1 cup chopped scallions
½ cup finely chopped fresh flat-leaf parsley
2 teaspoons salt
1 teaspoon freshly ground black pepper

1. In a flameproof baking casserole, heat the oil over medium-high heat. Add the flour, whisking constantly and somewhat rapidly without stopping until a dark brown roux is achieved, 7½ minutes. At about the 5-minute mark the roux will look like caramel. During the last minute of cooking as the roux turns dark brown, like chocolate, stir faster or it will burn, then immediately add the onion, celery, bell pepper, garlic, Creole seasoning, and cayenne, which should already be pre-mixed in a bowl sitting next to the burner, and cook, stirring, until the vegetables are softened, about 4 minutes. Slowly pour in the oyster liquid and whisk until well blended, then reduce the heat to low and simmer for 45 minutes, stirring occasionally.

2. Preheat the oven to 400°F.

3. Prepare and bake the vol-au-vent puff pastry shells according to the package instructions, keeping them warm after they're baked.

4. Add the oysters to the casserole and cook until their edges have curled up, 6 to 8 minutes. Garnish with the scallions and parsley, then season with the salt and black pepper. Place a vol-au-vent shell in a bowl and ladle a generous serving of oyster stew into the center of the shell and surrounding it, and serve.

Seafood Phyllo Pie

Everything happens in the skillet in this mixed seafood pie. You start by cooking the aromatics—the onion, garlic, and mushrooms—and then in goes the raw seafood topped with buttered sheets of phyllo pastry, and in 25 minutes you've got a spectacular seafood pie. There will be some liquid in the skillet, so serve the pie with bread to absorb the delicious juices. It's a rich dish best accompanied by a simple green salad.

10 tablespoons (1 stick plus 2 tablespoons) unsalted butter, at room temperature
Six 1-inch-thick slices dense white country bread (about 6 ounces)
1 pound button mushrooms, sliced
½ small onion, finely chopped
2 large garlic cloves, finely chopped
¼ cup all-purpose flour
1 teaspoon sweet paprika
⅛ teaspoon cayenne pepper
Salt and freshly ground black pepper, to taste
1 pound mussels (about 20), shucked, juices saved (shells saved for making
    Quick Seafood Stock, page 380, if desired)
8 oysters, shucked and juices saved (shells saved for making Quick Seafood Stock,
    page 380, if desired), or one ½-pound container shucked oysters
3 tablespoons heavy cream
1 tablespoon fresh lemon juice
¾ pound rockfish or red snapper fillets, cut into 1-inch cubes
¾ pound medium shrimp (about 40), shelled (shells saved for making
    Quick Seafood Stock, page 380, if desired)
½ pound fresh crab claw meat (shells saved for making Quick Seafood Stock,
    page 380, if desired)
1 cup fresh or frozen peas
3 tablespoons finely chopped fresh flat-leaf parsley
3 tablespoons finely chopped fresh cilantro (coriander leaf)
7 sheets phyllo pastry (about 4 ounces)

1. Preheat the oven to 400°F.

2. Preheat a 12-inch cast-iron skillet over medium heat for 10 minutes. Spread 2 tablespoons of the butter on both sides of the bread slices, then cook in the skillet until golden brown on both sides. Remove and set aside.

3. Melt 4 tablespoons of the butter in the skillet and the remaining 4 tablespoons butter in a butter warmer or small saucepan. Add the mushrooms, onion, and garlic to the skillet and cook, stirring, until softened, about 15 minutes. Add the flour and stir to form a roux. Season with the paprika, cayenne, salt, and black pepper.

4. Strain the juices of the mussels and oysters through a strainer into the skillet. Set the mussels and oysters aside and stir the juice into the mushroom mixture. Add the cream and lemon juice, reduce the heat to low, and cook, stirring, until it thickens, about 8 minutes. Turn off the heat. Add the rockfish, shrimp, crab, mussels, and oysters and stir. Add the peas, parsley, and cilantro and stir again.

5. Lay the phyllo pastry onto the top of the food in the skillet, brushing each sheet with the melted butter from the warmer and tucking the overhanging edges under and into the skillet. Bake until golden brown on top, about 25 minutes. Let rest for 5 minutes, then serve with the bread.

Mahimahi Pico de Gallo Wraps

This tortilla wrap is a real winner, always pleasing everyone and encouraging them to eat too much. The only thing that gets cooked in this wrap is the fish, which you do at the very last moment. It's easiest when you have all the ingredients prepared and ready to go, something you can do earlier in the day. Mahimahi works very well here, but you can use other firm-fleshed fish. One could also bread and fry the fish.

For the pico de gallo
1 large ripe tomato, chopped
1 avocado, cut in half, pitted, flesh scooped out and chopped
½ small red onion, chopped (about ¾ cup)
2 tablespoons finely chopped fresh cilantro (coriander leaf)
1 large fresh jalapeño chile, seeded and chopped
1 tablespoon fresh lime juice
Salt, to taste

For the sauce
½ cup mayonnaise
½ cup sour cream
1 chipotle chile en adobo, very finely chopped, with its sauce
Salt and freshly ground black pepper, to taste

For the assembly
Eight 12-inch flour tortillas
1 pound mahimahi fillet, cut into ½-inch slices
½ pound green cabbage, cored and thinly shredded

1. To prepare the pico de gallo, combine the tomato, avocado, onion, cilantro, chile, and lime juice in a bowl. Season with salt and set aside.

2. For the sauce, in another bowl, combine the mayonnaise, sour cream, and chipotle chile until well blended. Taste, season with salt and pepper, and set aside.

3. Preheat the oven on the warm setting. Wrap the tortillas in aluminum foil and place in the oven until needed.

4. Season the mahimahi with salt. Preheat a cast-iron skillet over medium-high heat, place the mahimahi in the skillet and sear it on both sides, turning once, until golden and crispy looking, about 3 minutes in all.

5. Arrange a tortilla in front of you and lay a portion of the cabbage on the lower portion of the tortilla. Drizzle on some of the sauce and then lay the fish and pico de gallo on top. Roll up lightly and set aside while you continue stuffing and rolling the remainder of the tortillas. Serve immediately.

Index